Health Attitude

UNRAVELING AND SOLVING THE COMPLEXITIES OF HEALTHCARE

John R. Patrick

Foreword by Dr. John M. Murphy

Attitude

ISBN: 069235736X
ISBN 13: 9780692357361
Library of Congress Control Number: 2015901208
Attitude LLC, Palm Coast, FL

Praise for Health Attitude

"When we look back ten years from now on the revolution that occurred in health-care, John Patrick's book *Health Attitude* will be viewed as one of the prologues of that revolution. We tend to overestimate technology in the short term and underestimate its role in the long term. Simply put, this book presents an optimistic future where innovation, technology, empathy and sound business principles collide into a "big-bang" of better healthcare!"

> Stephen K. Klasko, M.D., M.B.A., President and CEO, Thomas Jefferson University and Jefferson Health System

"It is quite encouraging to read John Patrick's crisp and accurate analysis of the most complex and pressing issues in the United States, it's healthcare system. While his focus is primarily on the U.S., most of his conclusions and proposed approaches to potential solutions are just as applicable for many European countries. This book is a must read for all who are concerned about healthcare cost and effectiveness in Europe."

> Hans Ulrich Maerki, former Chairman and CEO of IBM Europe Middle East Africa, Senior Fellow Advanced Leadership Initiative Harvard University, Board member of leading Orthopedic Clinic in Zürich, Switzerland

"John Patrick brings a fresh and insightful perspective to the healthcare debates in the U.S. His experience as technologist, entrepreneur and patient enables new thinking and innovative strategies that should drive policy, planning and delivery."

> James G. Neal, Columbia University Librarian Emeritus

"Reading *Health Attitude* helps all of us ask whether we as a nation are meeting our responsibilities to provide our citizens with healthcare in the 21st century."

> Dr. Eric Lutker, Psychologist

"If this was 1850 I would have died at age 40, and now I can expect to live to 79. The increase in health was due to prevention. *Health Attitude* can be the next paradigm to improve health with exciting prevention approaches including mHealth apps and devices. *Health Attitude* will revolutionize prevention and global health with cost effective solutions. It is the next wave forward for health -- I am not ready to die."

Ronald LaPorte, Professor Emeritus of Epidemiology, former Director WHO Collaborating Centre, University of Pittsburgh

"*Health Attitude* offers a valuable perspective for a layperson who makes healthcare decisions for his or her family and parents. It provides great hope for improved and more affordable healthcare ahead."

Peg Grimm, Pennsylvania Healthcare Consumer

"In *Health Attitude*, Dr. John Patrick opens our eyes wide to see the waste, excessive costs, absence of or poor medical care for those who cannot afford it, occurrence of iatrogenic injuries to patients, and diagnostic or therapeutic health care failures --- all of which need not occur. His background in engineering, computer technology, and health administration has prepared him well to describe how we as physicians may solve or diminish the above problems to create a better existence for mankind. His book provides much information, which if our attitudes change, will enable us to better fulfill the Hippocratic oath."

Richard J. Duma, M.D., Ph.D., Former Professor of Medicine, Pathology & Microbiology and Chairman of the Division of Infectious Diseases, Medical College of Virginia, Virginia Commonwealth University

"Many of the high costs and inefficiencies in our healthcare system can be addressed through automation and process streamlining with the aid of technology. John Patrick's *Health Attitude* clearly lays out a roadmap toward this end, which will result in an affordable and effective wellness based system in the future."

Robin Felder, Ph.D., Chair Medical Automation.org and Professor of Pathology, University of Virginia

"As one of the world's technology pioneers, John Patrick is a sought after innovator and strategic thinker. In *Health Attitude*, Patrick paints a grim portrait of America's healthcare system today, then unveils a canvas upon which we can create a better future using technology."

Skip Prichard, President & CEO, OCLC

Also by John R. Patrick

Net Attitude: What It Is, How to Get It, and Why Your Company Can't Survive Without It.

Dedication

I dedicate this book to my mother, Virginia Patrick. She was a loving wife to my father for 60 years and a proud mother of her three sons. She passed away from congestive heart failure in March 2009.

Preface

After 38 years at IBM, most recently as Vice President for Internet Technology, I finished my career at the company in 2001. I wrote my first book, *Net Attitude*, about the future of the Internet based on my technology experience. Then, I was invited to serve on a Community Hospital Board. My nine years of board service included chairing the Planning Committee and the Quality and Patient Safety Committee. I began to understand the complexity of the issues surrounding the provision of healthcare. I was surprised how slowly hospitals adopted new information technology. The sheer number of non automated, separate data gathering and record storage methods as well as the numerous, non compatible healthcare delivery processes appalled me. I began to think there must be a way technology and changes in healthcare attitudes could make a difference.

In 2010, I decided to pursue a Doctor of Health Administration degree which I completed in 2014. During my three and a half years of study, I learned about healthcare policy, technology and administration. I came to understand the clinical and cultural aspects of healthcare. I learned American healthcare costs much more than in other countries and our health outcomes and life expectancy do not compare favorably. I learned the United States is the only developed country without some form of universal healthcare. All of the citizens of our great country do not have healthcare insurance. I learned thousands of people die as a result.

I believe the provision of safe and affordable healthcare for all Americans is critical for our country's future. My goal in writing *Health Attitude* is to leverage my knowledge and decades of technology experience to explain and share solutions. It is my hope these solutions will lead to both improved patient care and healthcare for all citizens. I will attempt to unravel the complexities and cultural, attitudinal, and technological barriers keeping us from having a more affordable, accessible, and effective healthcare system. In *Health Attitude* I will suggest solutions to complex problems for providers and information for the layperson to help navigate the healthcare system. This book will help both groups to have a better understanding of the future of healthcare.

Health Attitude includes my experiences with the healthcare system. The book includes a number of personal stories with which readers will be able to identify. These include two major encounters I personally experienced with the continuum of care. The first occurred in 2009 when my mother died from congestive heart failure. This inspired me to pursue a doctoral research study about the effectiveness of home telemonitoring. I will describe the potential of this technology to improve the life of chronically ill patients. Although I am a healthy, 69 year old man who logs 5 miles of exercise per day, I have experienced treatment for cancer, surgery, and other medical treatments. My experiences with patient care, in the hospital, and extensive testing qualify me to speak personally about healthcare delivery issues.

A substantial part of the problem with our healthcare system is rooted in attitudes. The inability to share personal healthcare information between hospitals, specialists, and primary care doctors for more effective healthcare is not a technical problem. It is attitudinal. Offering expensive emergency room care to the uninsured instead of preventive care is not limited by healthcare capabilities, but by the attitude of healthcare policy makers. There is an attitude the fee for service model is a provider entitlement. I demonstrate in *Health Attitude* the effects of a new attitude centered on patients and utilizing accountability oriented, fee for value model. I believe we need a wellness attitude with incentives for healthy lifestyles and keeping people well. I do not believe in rewarding providers for visits, procedures, and tests we may not need. *Health Attitude* will help both providers and lay people to have a better understanding of the future of healthcare.

Foreword

By Dr. John M. Murphy

President and CEO, Western Connecticut Health Network

I t is hard to imagine a more pressing and complex challenge today than fixing our healthcare system. Our nation spends approximately $2.9 trillion a year on healthcare, a sum that exceeds the gross domestic product of all but four nations worldwide. It spends far more per person on healthcare than any other nation yet the quality of results is below average. For example, the infant mortality rate is 55th in the world, behind countries like Cuba, Estonia, Lithuania, and Slovakia. American life expectancy ranks 42nd in the world. It appears many other countries around the world have figured out how to deliver better healthcare outcomes at much lower costs and do so within systems that provide nearly universal access to care.

The problem of affordability presents a serious challenge to the federal and state governments, both of which are awash in red ink with healthcare expenses. Between 1975 through 2008, for example, Medicare spending grew 2.5 % faster than our nation's economy, consuming an increasingly larger share of our nation's economic resources. This affordability issue has also become a matter of great concern to businesses across the country. They cannot remain competitive in the face of double-digit annual increases in health insurance premiums. Warren Buffet, in fact, in 2013 on CNBC, said healthcare costs are "a tapeworm in the US economy." Many individuals struggle with their own share of healthcare expenses. A recent survey shows for the average Medicare household, 14% of household expenses are related to healthcare. More than one out of five Americans has medical debt they must pay down over time, sometimes with interest they can ill afford, or that forces them to avoid further care they may need.

For good reason, trying to fix healthcare is one of our nation's top priorities. The challenges of sorting out how to go about that fix are enormous. The financial incentives embedded in our system still center around providing services to our patients, rather than fostering accountability for health outcomes, patient satisfaction, and cost efficiency. The federal government eventually stepped in during 2010 and passed the Affordable Care Act. Despite the fact that the legislation was approved over four years ago, the majority of Americans, in a July 2014 Rasmussen survey, said they still have unfavorable views of the ACA. This underscores the polarizing nature of any solution that attempts to fundamentally alter an industry as large and complex as healthcare. Many other issues contribute to the immense challenges associated with reform including: the lack of true price transparency, prevalence of health disparities, fragmentation among providers along the continuum of care, difficulty sharing information across different electronic health records, and the emergence of increasingly expensive treatments. For example, a single drug recently approved for the treatment of HCV costs approximately $84,000 per course of therapy. If this drug were used to treat, and effectively cure, the 3.2 million Americans with HCV, it would result in an expense of approximately $250 billion, more than the money spent on all other pharmaceuticals combined.

My own career path has given me a broad view of healthcare and a deep understanding of its complexities. As a former president of our hospital's medical staff, as a member and then Chairman of its Board of Directors, I have had the opportunity to view the landscape from many different vantage points. From there I moved over to the administrative side and am now in my fifth year as CEO of a multi-hospital health system in New England. Even with the demands of this role, I continue to spend time seeing patients and cherish my 25 years at the bedside as clinician, teacher, and researcher. Because these opportunities give me a front row seat to the challenges we face in the healthcare industry, I am delighted that John Patrick is sharing his insights in *Health Attitude*. His book comes at a critical time and his perspective and background are particularly relevant as we engage in this national discussion.

John's successful career at IBM included a number of positions, among them Vice President for Internet Technology. He was involved in the early years of the World Wide Web and was part of the consortium at MIT that ignited the phenomenon that has redefined much of our world. He was part of the group that wrestled with the large, complex, and undefined issues of the early Internet in-cluding its infrastructure, quality of information, privacy, and governance, all of which are concerns relevant to today's healthcare. His degrees in engineering, management, and law, coupled with his varied corporate roles, provide him with remarkable insights to successful innovation. I sat beside him as a director on our health system board for eight years and, when I transitioned to the role of CEO, I frequently relied upon his sage advice on a host of topics. His background and expertise in IT is enormously relevant. Much of what we do in healthcare revolves around sharing information and our success depends, to a large extent, on how well and how quickly we distribute data and knowledge. John understands the power of information and the need to get it to the right people in the right place at the right time. He has spent a career delivering the promise that he brings to this book.

What I find particularly thought provoking about his analysis and approach to the healthcare puzzle is how he thinks differently than most of us in the field. While he holds a Doctorate in Health Administration and understands the op-erational challenges embedded in the healthcare system, he doesn't look at the industry as a series of problems or obstacles, as many of us in healthcare do. He inexorably draws attention to what we are capable of rather than what we lack. Combining that focus on solutions and opportunities with his talent for innova-tion and experience in healthcare governance offers a much needed prescription for success. And that prescription starts with a single word, **attitude**.

Every day, people across America look to the healthcare system for answers to some of life's most important questions. Those of us who work in the field are deeply committed to providing the right answers and to deliver results that make a difference. But our good intentions will only carry us so far. As John understands, and eloquently shares in this book, only when we confront the challenges of the healthcare system can we create meaningful change. And we can work together to create a healthier tomorrow where each of us has an equal opportunity to become healthier versions of ourselves. Enjoy the read.

Table of Contents

Introduction

I n 2012, healthcare represented 17.9% of the United States economy, a larger share than any country in the world.[1] For millions of people, healthcare is the most important aspect of their lives or the lives of their loved ones. However, the American healthcare system has significant problems preventing it from being effective and affordable. High cost is the first and foremost barrier. As a percentage of gross domestic product, a measure of the size of a country's economy, American healthcare cost is the highest among all developed countries in the world, and is unaffordable for many millions of people.

The complexity of obtaining and paying for healthcare, coordinating healthcare providers, and assuring the best possible health outcomes is mind-boggling. Healthcare advice comes from friends, families, pharmaceutical company TV advertising, and potentially misleading sites on the web. Good advice exists in the healthcare system, but it is buried in silos of providers who do not communicate effectively between themselves or with patients.

Despite the most expensive healthcare in the world, Americans do not always get better outcomes than persons in other developed countries. Quality of care is not nearly what it could be. For the average person, no one coordinates his or her healthcare, and many questions go unanswered. Patient safety is often compromised because of lack of effective information technology. Thousands of people die every year from medical errors. There is also the question of equity. Neither our political leaders nor experienced policymakers can agree on what universal healthcare means. There are many unresolved questions. Who should get it? Who should pay for it? Who should manage it? How should it be regulated?

Fortunately, there are solutions to all of these problems and they lie in three broad areas: (1) a shift in healthcare to make it patient-centered with providers who are compensated based on how healthy we are, (2) adoption and deployment of provider and consumer technology, and (3) development of enlightened and common sense policies from providers and government. *Health Attitude* describes a consumer-led movement in healthcare. It unravels the complexities of the American healthcare system. It paints a positive vision of the solutions which can be made a reality and lead to more affordable and effective healthcare for all.

As has happened with many dimensions of the Internet, healthcare is nearing a tipping point. Social scientist Malcolm Gladwell said, "The tipping point is that magic moment when an idea, trend, or social behavior crosses a threshold, tips and spreads like wildfire."[2] *Health Attitude* describes what it is we are tipping toward.

Health Attitude is divided into four parts. Part One describes the big picture and presents Big Pharma, the good and the bad. Part Two presents the problems of cost, quality, and equity. Part Three describes healthcare solutions for consumers and providers. It describes the essence of health attitude, how consumers and providers alike must change their ways. Part Four covers healthcare policy and management techniques which provide a path to improved healthcare.

The examples and commentary in *Health Attitude* refer to the United States unless stated otherwise. The views expressed are my own based on personal experience and study. The names of any individuals, except for my family and me, are fictional.

Part One

The Big Picture and Big Pharma

CHAPTER 1

Evaluation of Our Healthcare System

The performance, efficiency, and equity of healthcare will improve with health attitude solutions presented in this chapter. Healthcare is the largest industry and employs nearly 15 million people.[3] The industry has a highly developed infrastructure with advanced medical education and research capabilities. Medical device and pharmaceutical products, long-term care and rehabilitation service providers, community teaching hospitals, and academic medical centers support the healthcare of a quarter of a billion people. Despite the enormity of our healthcare system, more than 40 million people have limited access to these medical products and services.[4]

Current Performance

One way to assess the current performance of our government's provisioning of healthcare is to compare the efficiency, effectiveness, and equity to other developed industrialized countries. There are many positive attributes of American healthcare, and the government deserves credit for the encouragement and incentives it currently provides. The greatest strength of the country's healthcare system is the advanced state of medical technology and pharmaceutical innovation.

People older than 80 tend to live longer than in most other countries and premature babies have a better chance of survival.

Despite some great strengths, the weaknesses of our healthcare stand out. More than 40 million people have no health insurance. Healthcare expenditures as a percentage of a country's economy are significantly higher than in Canada and Germany, yet life expectancy is lower than in both countries and the infant mortality rate is higher than in both.[5] The following paragraphs include further evidence of the significant deficiencies in efficiency, effectiveness, and equity.

Efficiency

Given the cost to provide healthcare for tens of millions of uninsured, one could conclude the only way to add the uninsured to the healthcare system is to either raise taxes or ration care. However, research done by Sutherland, Fisher, & Skinner shows large savings can be achieved from what the government is spending in existing healthcare programs and thereby provide funding for reform.[6] The largest variation in the cost of care under Medicare is from regional differences. After adjusting for regional cost of living factors and the socioeconomic status of residents, the variance remains. The leading contributors to the cost difference are length of hospital stays, number of doctor visits, and number of imaging studies.

Part of the high cost in certain geographies is related to excess capacity. For example, *Modern Healthcare* reported in 2010, Miami-Dade and Broward counties in Florida had 41 acute-care hospitals with 14,500 beds serving a population of 4.3 million people.[7] That's 3.4 hospital beds per 1,000 people, compared with the national average of 2.6, according to figures from the Florida Hospital Association[8] and the American Hospital Association[9]. The variance is only partly explained by the fact that Florida has an older population than average.

Arnold Milstein, Medical Director of the Pacific Business Group on Health in San Francisco and Chief Physician at Mercer Health & Benefits, and Helen Darling, President of the National Business Group on Health in Washington, DC, described five broad categories of waste in American healthcare: (1) providing healthcare services that are not proven to improve health, (2) delivering healthcare using inefficient methods, (3) charging non-competitive prices for products and services,

(4) incurring excessive administrative costs in delivering healthcare and the processes used for payment of healthcare, and (5) missed opportunities to lower healthcare spending by focusing on prevention of injury and illness.[10]

Effectiveness

The effectiveness of healthcare is related to efficiency because spending money on ineffective care contributes to overall inefficiency. Two areas of ineffective outcomes are in chronic disease management and end of life care.[11] A disproportionate amount of healthcare spending occurs in the latter part of people's lives but does not always produce an improvement in quality of life. In "How to Achieve a High-Performance Health Care System in the United States", Casscells et al. suggested that chronic care could be more effective through the use of telemonitoring and appropriate reimbursement for remote management.[12] Telemonitoring is part of the larger subject of telehealth, which includes the use of telecommunications and the Internet for diagnosis, consultation, information exchange, supervision, and assessment of health. Telehealth can be as simple as two doctors having a conference call via telephone to discuss the diagnosis of a patient or as sophisticated as a surgical procedure performed where the surgeon is in a different location than the patient.

Defensive medicine is another area of ineffective healthcare. Some physicians' attorneys brief them to be sure to take all measures to avoid being sued. The slightest possibility of a particular diagnosis can prompt physicians to order expensive and unnecessary or duplicative tests and procedures. Researchers Avraham and Schanzenbach reviewed more than 25 years of damage caps, collateral source reforms, and joint and several liability reforms. They concluded tort reform could reduce expensive damage awards and reduce the perceived need to practice defensive medicine.[13] The legal system and the plaintiff's bar encourage lawsuits. Congressional attempts to reform the process have been unsuccessful.

Equity

The United States has made little progress during the past decade in addressing healthcare disparities.[14] Healthcare disparities related to race, ethnicity, socioeconomic status, and markers of social disadvantage arise from a complex set of factors emanating from clinicians, patients, and the infrastructure of healthcare support. In "Health Care Reform and Equity: Promise, Pitfalls, and Prescriptions", Fiscella said that making healthcare more equitable requires the elimination of bias and the creation of a patient-centered model of care that provides care and healing relationships.[15] The Institute of Medicine (IOM) has a more formal definition of patient-centered care, but for the purposes of *Health Attitude*, I consider it to mean care which supports and encourages active involvement of patients and their families in decision-making about options for treatment. Patient-centered healthcare is an essential attitude for providers.

The Patient Protection and Affordable Care Act (ACA) offers an opportunity to create a more equitable healthcare system. Some key areas which could improve equity include: access to care, stronger support for primary care, enhanced communications programs to increase awareness, and methods for the monitoring of healthcare disparity. One potential initiative which has the potential to improve equity is the patient-centered medical home (PCMH), where primary care physicians can reach across the continuum of care and champion healthcare responsive to the needs of all patients.

Another method to evaluate the healthcare system is to compare it to another large American system. Dr. George D. Lundberg, Past President of the American Society for Clinical Pathology and Professor and Chair of Pathology at the University of California, Davis, compared large American healthcare systems to the U.S. Post Office. In 1993, he developed an 11-factor grid to compare the effectiveness of large American healthcare systems. In 2014, he used the same factors to compare and evaluate the United States Healthcare System (USHC) as a whole and the United States Postal Service (USPS). Medscape published the results in April 2014.[16]

Dr. Lundberg examined each of 11 factors. A perfect score for each factor was 9; a perfect total was 99. For example, the first factor is how well healthcare providers and the postal system provide basic access to their service. The healthcare systems received a score of 5 and the Postal Service received a 9. The basis of the score is 40 million Americans remain uninsured while everyone can access the post office. The Scorecard includes the list of factors Dr. Lundberg examined.

Table 1: The Scorecard

	Factor	USHC	USPS
1	Provides access to basic care for all	5	9
2	Produces real cost control	3	7
3	Promotes continuing quality and safety	3	7
4	Reduces administrative hassle and cost	3	8
5	Enhances disease prevention	4	0
6	Encourages primary care	3	9
7	Considers long-term care	3	7
8	Provides necessary patient autonomy	4	9
9	Safeguards physician autonomy	4	0
10	Limits professional liability	3	9
11	Possesses staying power	3	9
	Total Score	38	74

The results were USHC 38, USPS 74.[17] Dr. Lundberg's analysis is subjective, but a number of the factors for which he gave low scores are factors I believe are key problems of the healthcare system.

Solutions

Solutions to the various problems in our healthcare system are what *Health Attitude* is about. This section is an overview of some key problems. I think the number one solution could be a broad based adoption of Electronic Health Records (EHRs), which can impact efficiency, effectiveness, and equity.[18] Efficiency can be improved by eliminating redundant tests. Effectiveness can be enhanced through more sharing of healthcare information among providers. Equity can be improved by eliminating bias and utilizing patient-centered medical homes.

EHRs can accelerate the process of automating patient registries, enabling epidemiologic population health, and potentially reducing decision-making bias, all of which can improve equity. For example, a Lyme Disease Registry in Connecticut, where Lyme disease is endemic, enables the regional hospital to look at the disease across the population it serves, not just at one patient at a time that may have the disease. Although there are significant problems and concerns with EHRs, the United States government should continue to provide incentives for the meaningful use of the technology. In the long run, EHRs can produce significant benefits for patients and providers.

In the legal arena, the government should apply prudent antitrust reviews and litigation to ensure competition to reduce the cost of medical devices. A second legal recommendation is for the government to support tort reform to help reduce costly defensive medicine. The government should establish requirements for the monitoring of healthcare disparity so that progress can be measured over time. A single-payer system is not needed, but standards for payer methods need to be enforced to help reduce the administrative cost of healthcare. The government should take a leadership role with industry to promulgate standards for use across all public and private payers.[19]

The role of the government should not be to issue mandates, but to show leadership through working with the information technology industry to develop EHR and payer standards. This can be accomplished by working with physician groups to establish standardized clinical performance measurements, and by providing incentives for improved quality, enhanced patient safety, and cost reductions. As a payer for more than half of the population, the government should pay for population based healthcare services which can reduce the cost of chronic care through the reimbursement for telemonitoring and other new technology based approaches to maintaining good health. Finally, the government should work with communities and support their communications efforts to increase awareness of healthy lifestyles.

Summary

Providing healthcare for a population three times larger than Germany and ten times larger than Canada is a major challenge. While the track record for efficiency, effectiveness, and equity is not great, progress is being made. The ACA has the potential for unprecedented reform of healthcare. Change is underway. Healthcare systems are rolling out patient-centered medical homes and building Accountable Care Organizations. Adoption of electronic prescribing and EHRs has increased dramatically. New incentives are causing hospitals to focus on readmissions and coordination across the continuum of care. Research studies have not yet validated the impact of these changes, but there are reasons to be optimistic costs will decline. Patient safety will improve, access and equity will improve, and technological innovations will continue to emanate from the United States.

CHAPTER 2

Big Pharma

Gretchen Gavett wrote about a tragedy for PBS's *Frontline*. According to her story, Kyle Willis, a single, unemployed father, was experiencing a toothache. A dentist told the 24 year old his wisdom tooth needed to be extracted, but the young man had no health or dental insurance and chose to ignore his discomfort.[20] When the pain increased and his face began to swell, Willis went to the emergency room (ER), and left with prescriptions for a pain medication and an antibiotic. Willis could not afford the antibiotic, and purchased only the pain medication. The infection spread. When it reached his brain, the organ became swollen, causing his death. The young father and aspiring paralegal left a six year old daughter behind. One might argue Mr. Willis should have taken more responsibility for his condition or the ER staff should have encouraged or even arranged a visit to a community dental clinic for treatment. The lack of insurance seemed to be the dominant factor in the tragedy.

Health Affairs published a study estimating by 2016 the number of Americans still without healthcare insurance will be 26-27 million.[21] Many of the uninsured cannot afford needed medications. For example, a North Carolina woman had a household income from her husband's disability checks of $15,700.[22] She had multiple comorbidities including emphysema and chronic obstructive pulmonary disease causing shortness of breath. Her medications cost more than $150 per month. The woman's doctor prescribed a new drug, called Spiriva, which could have helped her breathing, but it cost $500 per month. Combined with her other medications, her total expenditure would have been 50% of her income. The *Charlotte Observer* reported the woman quit taking the drug because she couldn't afford it.

Foregoing Needed Medications

Unfortunately, foregoing prescribed medications is not rare. The Consumer Reports National Research Center conducted an interview based survey in 2011 of 1,158 adults who were over 18 and currently taking a prescription drug.[23] The survey showed nearly half of adults take prescription drugs and 28 percent of them put their health at risk, because of affordability. They do not comply with what their doctor prescribed because the drugs cost too much. Sixteen percent did not fill a prescription, 12 percent took expired medications or skipped scheduled doses. Eight percent cut pills in half, and 4 percent reported sharing medications with a friend or family member. Health risk is not confined to non-compliance with prescribed medications. More than half of those in the Consumer Reports study declined a medical test, postponed a visit to the doctor, or skipped a medical procedure because they could not afford the tests and procedures. The problem is affordability.

Determining Fair Healthcare Costs

The world's top pharmaceutical companies are often referred to collectively as Big Pharma. *Forbes* ranked Big Pharma companies with a market capitalization of more than $50 billion. The magazine gave Gilead Sciences Inc. a rating of A- and ranked it fourth out of 16 companies.[24] As of February 1, 2015, the company's market capitalization was $158 billion.

Gilead has developed a breakthrough drug called Sovaldi which provides a cure for chronic liver disease associated with hepatitis C (HCV) patients. Sovaldi has a higher than 90% cure rate, and unlike many complex disease cures, it has few side effects. The bad news is the typical Sovaldi cost of $84,000 per treatment. UnitedHealth Group Inc., the largest U.S. healthcare insurance company, said it invested more than $100 million during the first three months after Sovaldi came to market.[25] The cost to treat one million HCV patients would be nearly $100 billion. Sovaldi has spurred a national debate about specialty medicines and practices of the pharmaceutical industry.

The first concern is the price tag. A study done by the Henry Ford Health System examined the healthcare costs for treatment of patients with chronic liver disease. The annual cost ranged from $17,277 to nearly $60,000, with an average of $24,176.[26] The researcher said most people infected with HCV remain without symptoms for years, and then develop a serious condition leading to years of costly medical care, and often the need for a liver transplant. One could argue on an economic basis $24,000 per year is less cost-effective than a one time treatment for $84,000. The problem is, out of necessity, healthcare payers like state Medicaid programs, focus on short-term costs.

A complicated question is about Gilead Sciences Inc.'s pricing strategy for Sovaldi. The World Health Organization estimates there are 130-150 million people globally who have chronic HCV infection.[27] Many of those people are in countries with large populations and low per capita income. Gilead has adopted a tiered-pricing strategy to make Sovaldi available in such countries at a significant discount. For example, patients in India, Egypt, and Brazil would pay $840 per treatment, 1% of the treatment's cost in the United States. The problem with this strategy is the black market. According to the World Anti-Doping Agency, about 25% of the world's pharmaceuticals are sold on the black market.[28] In effect, Sovaldi might be purchased in one of these countries at a deep discount and sold in a country where the price is much higher. Critics say the multi-tiered pricing strategy encourages such activity. Another point of view is the company's strategy provides a humanitarian benefit to impoverished third world countries.

Congressional leaders are asking questions too. Senator Ron Wyden, (D-Oregon) and Senator Chuck Grassley, (R-Iowa), have asked Gilead to explain why Sovaldi's $1,000 per pill price differs from other countries and from the price set by Pharmasset.[29] Pharmasset, the original developer of Sovaldi acquired by Gilead in 2012 for $11 billion, had originally set the price at less than half of the price set by Gilead. Perhaps Gilead had to expend a lot of effort and expense to get the drug approved after the acquisition from Pharmasset.

There are ethical issues in the treatment of HCV. It is caused by a virus that spreads when blood comes into contact with HCV infected blood. Although it is possible to get the virus as a result of blood transfusions, organ transplants, and other causes, the most common cause is the sharing of contaminated needles. Members of groups such as prisoners and those with psychiatric disorders have a higher prevalence of HCV infection than the general population.[30]

The ethical issues spawn policy issues which have no easy answers. Does discrimination against persons in stigmatized groups prevent patients from receiving new antiviral treatments? Should Medicaid and other payers allocate limited funds to pay for treatment of those who have followed unhealthful practices resulting in significant burdens on the healthcare system? Should pharmaceutical companies earn substantial profits from providing drugs which are extraordinarily expensive?

Gilead is already encountering competition, as the prospect HCV sales could be as much as $20 billion annually by the end of the decade. Sovaldi is confirming the potential. They reported sales of $5 billion in sales of Sovaldi during the first half of 2014. At least a half-dozen other pharmaceutical companies are going after the HCV market and the patent fights are underway.[31] A competitive market may be better than Congressional intervention as a way to arrive at the appropriate market price.

Pharmaceutical companies are developing amazing new cancer drugs, but some of them are so expensive and extend life so little, the issue of the value of one's life surfaces. For example, Provenge, a new drug from Dendreon extends the life of a man with incurable prostate cancer by an average of four months. The cost of a treatment is $93,000. Bob Svensson, an 80 year old retired corporate financial executive from Bedford, Massachusetts said that the benefit did not seem worth the cost. He only took the drug, "because his insurance paid for it". Otherwise, he said, "I would not spend that money."[32]

Government healthcare payers are beginning to take a hard look at drug pricing.[33] Basel, Switzerland based Roche Holding AG has developed a break-through drug called Kadcyla which was designed for women who have difficult to treat breast cancer. The drug is used in cases, often terminal, where the cancer has spread to other parts of the body and may no longer be operable. A particularly positive feature of Kadcyla is more accurate treatment than typical chemotherapy and much less distressing side effects. Hester Plumridge at the *Wall Street Journal* reported that the cost to treat a patient with Kadcyla is $151,000. The United Kingdom's National Institute for Health and Care Excellence has declared the drug too expensive and will not approve its use.[34] The drug, on average, adds an extra six months to the life of a patient, and the National Institute is implicitly saying the cost is not worth the benefit. As Big Pharma continues to seek breakthrough drugs, it is likely many governments will challenge the pricing.

Robust Profits

Some executives in the pharmaceutical industry espouse the idea robust profits are needed to ensure significant investment in research which yields important new drugs. Drug research, development, testing, and getting from laboratory to high quality manufacturing are costly. Increasingly complex clinical trials can take longer than a decade and cost more than a billion dollars to validate the intended benefits of a new drug. The FDA should accelerate efforts to automate the clinical trial process to lower the cost and timetable for bringing new drugs to the market.

As of September 30, 2014, ClinicalTrials.gov listed 175,684 studies with locations in all 50 states and in 187 countries. Sanofi, the $45 billion global healthcare giant based in Paris, France, has more than 100,000 employees, and as of Spring 2014 had more than 2,000 clinical studies underway. Not all of them will be successful. For the industry, 30 drug discoveries are needed to achieve one successful product launch. Sanofi developed an ovarian cancer drug called Iniparib, for which it had great hopes, but the drug failed to meet its primary goal of improving the overall patient survival rate compared to an existing drug. The company ceased development of Iniparib and took a write-off of $525 million. The risks are high, and the financial returns need to be high to sustain research efforts. The question is, how high?

First, let's look at the size and profitability of the healthcare industry and pharmaceutical companies to put them in perspective. The total value of all United States companies is approximately $23 trillion, and the Standard & Poor's 500 companies, which represent 80% of the total, are valued at $18 trillion. The healthcare sector, representing $2.4 trillion in market value or 13.2% of the total, is the third largest in the S&P 500 sector breakdown. While policymakers and taxpayers are concerned about the rapid growth of healthcare costs over recent years, that cost growth has meant revenue and profit growth for the industry. For 2014, analysts forecast that the healthcare sector will see an average revenue growth rate for 2014 and 2015 at 75% higher than that of the S&P 500. See Table 2 for the sector list and market capitalizations.[35]

*Table 2/*S&P 500 Sector List as of April 30, 2014		
S&P 500 Sector	Market Share	Market Cap (trillions)
Information Technology	18.6%	$3.3
Financial Services	16.0%	$2.8
Healthcare	13.2%	$2.4
Consumer Discretionary	11.9%	$2.1
Industrials	10.8%	$1.9
Energy	10.6%	$1.9
Consumer Staples	9.8%	$1.7
Materials	3.5%	$0.6
Utilities	3.1%	$0.6
Telecommunication Services	2.6%	$0.5
Total	100.0%	$17.8

Source. From INDICES, by McGraw Hill Financial - April 30, 2014

The Yahoo! Finance Industry Browser provides a breakdown of the health-care industry into 16 segments such as biotechnology, healthcare plans, hospitals, long-term care facilities, medical appliances and equipment, and the major drug manufacturers. Of the 16 segments, pharmaceutical companies account more than a trillion dollars, or nearly half of the total market cap. When you look at the profit margin, you can see what accounts for such a high valuation. The average healthcare segment has a profit margin of 5.4%, while the major drug manufacturers have a profit margin of almost 21%. I think we can conclude the major drug manufacturers are achieving robust profits. For that and reasons related to afford-ability, some policymakers and political leaders have called for lower prices for medications.

The Editorial Board at *USA Today* said that drug makers give the familiar argu-ment cutting prices will reduce research and development and thereby stunt the supply of new drugs.[36] Gagnon and Lexchin performed a study that concluded drug companies spend nearly twice as much on promotion of medicines than they do on basic research.[37] In 1997, the U.S. Food and Drug Administration (FDA) began to allow pharmaceutical companies to broadcast advertisements for prescription drugs. Over the ensuing years, the ad spending grew at 20% per year, peaking at more than $5 billion. By 1999, the average American was exposed to nine prescription drug TV advertisements every day. Even more money is spent promoting prescription drugs to physicians. TV advertising of drugs is not allowed in Canada or any European country. The American Medical Association is studying whether the drug ads lead to unnecessary prescriptions and higher healthcare costs.

International Drugs

A few years ago, a friend of mine told me his doctor prescribed Celebrex for his arthritis. He took the prescription to a local pharmacy, which rejected it saying Medicare would not approve without a prior authorization from the physician. The physician filled out a multi-page form describing why Celebrex was the right drug for his condition. Medicare did not agree. My friend asked what the price would be if he purchased without Medicare coverage. Answer: $166 for a 30-day supply. He then checked with a retail Canadian online drug website and found branded Celebrex, not a generic, with a physician prescription, was offered for $91 for a 60-day supply, $1.52 per pill compared to $5.53 in the United States. The same drug is made by the same company, but in a foreign country.

How could the same drug from the same company be more than three times as expensive as in Canada? No doubt, there is a multitude of reasons, including the cost of TV advertising, but two of the reasons have to do with politics. The Medicare Part D Prescription Drug Plan was enacted as part of the Medicare Modernization Act of 2003 and went into effect on January 1, 2006. Congress barred Medicare from negotiating with drug companies to get lower prices, allowing only private insurance companies to negotiate. Medicaid, on the other hand, was allowed to negotiate minimum discounts and other pricing enhancements. If Medicare were allowed to do what Medicaid does, the savings would be more than $100 billion over ten years.[38]

Help From Congress

Congress not only indirectly raised the cost of healthcare by not allow-ing Medicare to negotiate drug prices, but also in at least one case, it raised the cost of drugs through a pinpoint piece of legislation. *The New York Times* reported a provision buried in the "fiscal cliff" bill passed in January 2013 gave Amgen, the world's largest biotechnology firm, a two year pass on Medicare's plan to regulate the cost of Sensipar, a drug used by kidney dialysis patients.[39] The politicians behind the provision were Senators Max Baucus (D-Montana), and Orrin Hatch (R-Utah), both of whom have received contributions from Amgen.[40] The news about the provision's passing was so positive for Amgen the company communicated the coup to Wall Street analysts. The *Times* reported the provision is projected to cost Medicare up to $500 million over the two year period.

Despite issues raised in this chapter, pharmaceutical and biotechnology com-panies have a lot of merit. Drugs have played a large role in raising American life expectancy from 45 in 1900 to nearly 80 today. Americans are living healthier lives and living longer to enjoy them. Other developed countries have better healthcare outcomes on average than the United States, but those outcomes could not be achieved without the research and development of Big Pharma in America, in my opinion. Funding of R&D requires profitability, and arguably above average profit-ability to offset the risk of developing drugs that may never be approved or have to be withdrawn. However, a shift from protecting high industry profits to a focus on controlling healthcare spending is an essential element in achieving affordable healthcare.

Some members of Congress have proposed a fix to allow such savings, but they are opposed by a very strong pharmaceutical lobby. The pharmaceuticals and health products industry have more than 1,500 lobbyists and spent $236 million dollars on lobbying activities in 2012, far more than any other industry.[41] The phar-maceutical industry also sends a lot of money the way of healthcare providers. The Centers for Medicare & Medicaid Services (The Centers) says relationships with providers can include money for "research activities, gifts, speaking fees, meals, or travel."[42] The Social Security Act requires The Centers to be transparent about the payments, and they have placed all the details on the web. A federal program called Open Payments collects and reports the information. During the last five months of 2013, payments from drug and medical-device companies to physi-cians and teaching hospitals exceeded $3.5 billion.

The *Wall Street Journal* reported in "Doctors Net Billions from Drug Firms" a New York orthopedic surgeon received $4 million in non-research payments, mostly from Johnson & Johnson's DePuy Synthes unit for royalties.[43] If the surgeon invented and patented an orthopedic device or procedure for the company, then receiving a reasonable percentage of sales may be perfectly reasonable. However, in some cases, you have to wonder. Roche Holding AG 's Genentech unit paid $122.5 million to City of Hope Medical Center in Duarte, California as royalties on the sale of several blockbuster cancer treatments including Herceptin and Avastin.[44] The Medical Center said payments were distributed between inventors and for further research. Once again, it sounds reasonable, assuming there is no conflict of interest which would motivate the hospital to prescribe expensive non-essential drug treatments which are not essential or when a less expensive treatment option may exist. A look at the income statement of the City of Hope reveals the significance of royalty income. For fiscal 2013, the hospital had approximately $750 million of revenue from patient services and $250 million of royalty income. Without the royalty income, the hospital would have been at roughly a breakeven for the year.

Countries in Europe negotiate with the pharmaceutical companies, and as a result, the price they pay for drugs is less than half of what Medicare pays. The drug companies presumably accept the lower prices in Europe, in part because they can charge higher prices in the United States. In effect, Americans are subsidizing the cost of drugs for some of the wealthiest countries in the world, including Germany and Switzerland.

In 2004, Portland, Maine established a new prescription drug plan for its 1,400 city employees.[45] Under the plan, employees gained the option to get drugs by mail from licensed pharmacies in Australia, New Zealand, Canada, or the United Kingdom. There was no copay. One employee was able to get a three-month supply of Advair, an asthma drug needed by his daughter, for $150 including postage from Australia compared to $600 at a local pharmacy. The town was able to save $300,000 per year. Two years later, the largest employer in one of Maine's poorest counties implemented the same plan as Portland. The company, Hardwood Products, which makes Popsicle sticks, reported savings of $400,000 per year.[46] As enthusiasm for the mail order plan gained momentum, and both houses of the state legislature passed a bill with bipartisan support to legalize the mail-order drug plan, the pharmacy and pharmaceutical lobbyists ramped up efforts to block the plan adoption. In addition to the argument lost revenue to the industry would mean less research and fewer new drugs in the world, the lobbyists raised patient safety issues.

While the state of Maine argues it has provisions in the plan to protect its citizens, the industry lobby is arguing public health is being threatened. The pharmaceutical industry and its affiliates have filed a Federal lawsuit to strike down the law. The state court kicked the drug companies out of the pending lawsuit for lack of standing, and the pharmacy groups and pharmacists are left as plaintiffs. The case remains with the Federal court as of January 2015.

Safety does need to be assured, but Maine believes there are ways to do this regardless of the source of the drugs. The implication is "foreign" drugs are not safe. However, one of the largest patient safety issues with regard to drugs occurred in September 2012 when the Centers for Disease Control and Prevention (CDC), in collaboration with state and local health departments and the FDA, began investigating a multi-state outbreak of fungal meningitis and other infections in patients who received contaminated steroid injections from the New England Compounding Center in Framingham, Massachusetts.[47] The CDC reported 751 cases in 20 states and 64 deaths.

Summary

Health expenditure per capita is nearly double France and Germany. Although the Affordable Care Act is making strides to expand availability of insurance and implement reforms to reduce costs, healthcare is still not affordable. There are numerous reasons for the high cost of American healthcare. One of them is the cost of drugs.

Big Pharma issues represent a number of cost reduction opportunities, but there is a long list of others. Many solutions to reducing healthcare cost are clear, but Congress has a poor track record in addressing them. The problem is not unique to Medicare and Medicaid. For example, the United States Postal Service leadership knows what they need to do to reverse the multi-billion dollar losses - stop Saturday deliveries, close unprofitable post offices, partner with lower cost retail outlets, and implement affordable benefit plans. Any such changes must be approved by Congress, which refuses to follow a common sense business approach.

In my opinion, we need a common sense approach to confront the issue of high healthcare costs. We need political leaders who are tough negotiators with hospitals, pharmaceutical companies, device manufacturers, and health-care insurance companies. I believe asking the taxpayers to subsidize the cost of drugs for other countries is wrong. Our political leaders should provide tax policies which are globally competitive, and not pick favorites, nor tie the hands of the largest purchaser of drugs. Policymakers should read the research reports about the effect of direct to consumer advertising for prescription drugs.

Part Two

Cost, Quality, and Equity of Healthcare

CHAPTER 3

Cost

T his chapter provides statistics about the cost of healthcare. There are many self-proclaimed healthcare experts on cost including government agencies and study groups, political leaders, insurance companies, hospitals, physician groups, and various advocacy groups. Milliman is a Seattle, WA company that provides actuarial services about healthcare. It studies the numbers from many sources and has a consistent, six-decade track record. In May 2014, the firm estimated the healthcare cost for a typical family of four at $23,215, an amount that has more than doubled since 2004.[48] The good news is the growth rate from 2013 to 2014 fell to 5.4%, the lowest annual change since Milliman created the index more than a decade ago.

Comparing the United States with Developed Countries

There are multiple ways to measure the cost of healthcare: per person, per type of service, or by healthcare provided by private insurance versus provided by government. The Organization for Economic Cooperation and Development (OECD), a 34 country member organization with headquarters in Paris, France, promotes policies that will improve the economic and social well being for people around the world. The OECD takes a broad look at the cost of healthcare. The cost per capita for healthcare for 2011 (or nearest year available) was $8,508 in the United States compared to $5,643 in Switzerland, $4,522 in Canada, $4,495 in Germany, $4,118 in France, and $3,213 in Japan.[49] The differences are dramatic. For example, France is known to have excellent healthcare and yet spends approximately half of what we spend per capita in the United States.

Almost every book or article about healthcare cost highlights large differences among developed countries. The fact our healthcare expenditures are greater than other countries is a given. The question is why are our costs higher? Do we demand more services than people in other countries, or are the prices for the services we demand higher? I believe the answer to both questions is yes.

Healthcare Appetite and Rationing

Some countries ration the availability of healthcare services. For example, the target wait time for an MRI in Canada is 28 days. The actual wait time during 2012 was 308 days. Twenty-eight days does not seem like an unreasonable waiting time, but in the United States, it would be considered unacceptable. Canada has 8.5 MRI scanners per million people. The U.S. has 31.5 per million.[50] There is controversy about wait time in Canada. With 10 provinces and 3 territories, there is a lot of variability, and the measurement of wait time is not precise. Another variable is how effectively and efficiently the scanners are used. In some parts of Canada, scanners are run 24 hours per day. All things considered, Canada is a bit conservative in making MRI scans available and the United States is a bit liberal at making them available.

A hospital CEO told me that the biggest driver of the cost of American healthcare is what he called excessive "healthcare appetite". I was having some knee trouble a few years ago, with an injury from too many marathons. I saw an orthopedic surgeon for relief. Although I had an MRI in the previous year, he wanted a radiologist to take a closer look at a particular area of my knee joint. I had the MRI two days later and received the results the following day. This is the level of expectation in many parts of America that would be unheard of elsewhere.

There are at least three imaging centers within 10 miles of my home. These were not the result of independent hospital decisions in an "arms race" versus competitors. The installation of a new scanner requires a certificate of need. A detailed clinical and business analysis must be presented to the Department of Health for the state for approval. In theory, the imposition of the certificate prevents excessive capacity from being implemented, but some studies have shown it has no effect on the cost of healthcare.[51] MRIs do add quality to the decision making and surgical procedures conducted by surgeons. But, could I have waited a month for the MRI? Could I have driven 25 miles instead of five? Canadian friends tell me if a person is in serious need of an MRI due to significant pain and lack of mobility, he or she can get the MRI expeditiously. If it means an inconvenience that can be tolerated, the wait is considered reasonable.

Payers are beginning to require pre-authorization and often challenge the need for an MRI and other services as a way to control the demand. Another factor that may have an increasing effect on demand is the high deductibles of healthcare insurance plans, which means that the patient has to pay for the MRI out of pocket.

Healthcare Pricing

There is a second question concerning healthcare pricing. Is the U.S. cost higher than elsewhere? Researchers Koechlin, Lorenzoni, and Schreyer published a study in 2010 about their results from comparing the price of seven common hospital services across seven countries. The countries in their study were Austria, Canada, Germany, Finland, France, Sweden, and the United States.[52] The cost of services in the United States ranged from 1.3 to 2.1 times more expensive than the average. In some cases, the cost differences were much more significant. For example, the cost of a hip replacement in Germany was $8,899 compared to twice that, or $17,406, in the United States. A coronary angioplasty was more than four times as expensive than in Germany. The cost of a normal child delivery was slightly less than three times as expensive as in Finland. The high differential in the cost of surgical procedures will cause nearly a million Americans to travel to foreign countries for medical care.[53]

Table 3: Average Cost Of Certain Hospital Procedures, In U.S. Dollars, For U.S. And Selected OECD Countries, 2007.

Procedure	AUS	CAN	GER	FIN
Appendectomy	$5,044	$5,004	$2,943	$3,739
Normal delivery	$2,984	$2,800	$1,789	$1,521
Caesarean section	$7,092	$4,820	$3,732	$4,808
Coronary angioplasty	$7,131	$9,277	$3,347	$5,574
Coronary bypass	$21,698	$22,694	$14,067	$23,468
Hip replacement	$15,918	$11,983	$8,899	$10,834
Knee replacement	$14,608	$9,910	$10,011	$9,931

Procedure	FRA	SWE	U.S.	Average
Appendectomy	$4,558	$4,961	$7,962	$4,375
Normal delivery	$2,894	$2,591	$4,451	$2,430
Caesarean section	$5,820	$6,375	$7,449	$5,441
Coronary angioplasty	$7,027	$9,296	$14,378	$6,942
Coronary bypass	$23,126	$21,218	$34,358	$21,045
Hip replacement	$11,162	$11,568	$17,406	$11,727
Knee replacement	$12,424	$10,348	$14,946	$11,205

Source: Koechlin et al. (2010).

Another source of high cost can be from assistant surgeons who participate unnecessarily in patient surgery. *The New York Times* reporter Elisabeth Rosenthal wrote an article "After Surgery, Surprise $117,000 Medical Bill From Doctor He Didn't Know" which illustrates this. Peter Drier, a 37 year old patient in New York, had a three-hour neck surgery for herniated disks at Lenox Hill Hospital in New York City in December 2013. Drier had carefully researched his health insurance coverage with Anthem Blue Cross and was prepared for the bills he would receive, or so he thought.

Lenox Hill Hospital charged Mr. Dreier $56,000, the anesthesiologist charged $4,300, and the orthopedist $133,000 charged. Mr. Dreier knew the orthopedist would accept a fraction of his charge. The big surprise was a bill for $117,000 from an assistant surgeon, another New York neurosurgeon who Mr. Drier never had met. There was no negotiated lower rate like there was for the primary surgeon. The assistant surgeon's practice was out of network, meaning it did not accept Mr. Drier's insurance. Under Medicare, an assistant surgeon can only charge 16% of what the primary surgeon charged. In this case, both surgeons charged the same amount for each step of the surgery. Complicated surgeries, such as Mr. Dreier's, often require a second set of hands. Those can often be provided by a resident, a neurosurgical nurse, or a physician assistant employed by the hospital. Often, there would be no additional charge for these personnel. Apparently, in this case, none was available. Even though the assistant surgeon was out-of-network and Mr. Drier attempted to negotiate a splitting of the fees, his insurance company agreed to pay the full amount.

During a required pre-operative examination, the hospital sent Mr. Drier's blood to an out-of-network lab and required him to have an echocardiogram. He had no history of cardiac issues. The American Society of Echocardiography discourages cardiac testing for patients with no known heart problems. Mr. Drier encountered other out-of-network charges he could not avoid. At the last minute, Mr. Drier was asked by a consulting company to sign a financial consent form that would provide electronic monitoring of his nerves during the surgery. This is not an unusual service, but it was also out-of-network. Although not as large as the as-sistant surgeon charges, the practice of significant use of out-of-network services add to America's nearly $3 trillion in annual health costs.

Another reason for the higher cost is pharmaceutical prices are higher than in other OECD countries. Prescription drug costs in wealthy European countries are subsidized by the United States. Researchers Kanavos and Vandoros published a study in 2011 showing the top 50 prescription drugs were at least 60% more expensive than in five large European countries.[54]

Dr. Eric Topol, noted healthcare author, discussed the topic of using gene sequencing to help reduce the cost of drugs in a recent interview on NPR. He believes increased use of gene sequencing would reduce the necessary required size of test groups and make testing more targeted. Both of these improvements would bring down the costs of drug research.[55]

It is difficult to say whether there are too many or too few treatments in the United States. Compared to other countries, the U.S. does not have more doctors or consultations per person, and hospital stays for American patients are shorter than other countries. However, the U.S. healthcare system has a penchant for new medical technology and it has many more MRI and CT scanners than other coun-tries. It also has more elective surgery, the necessity for which is not always certain.

The data strongly suggests it is the prices for healthcare goods and services that are significantly higher than elsewhere. The studies further suggest it is the higher price, not the higher level of services provided, that leads to higher health spending in the United States. What factors contribute to the higher prices?

Increased Hospital Pricing Power

Reduced payer reimbursements to hospitals have resulted in increased financial pressure. One response has been for hospitals to merge and thereby get the opportunity to eliminate duplicate overhead functions. A by-product of hospital consolidations is they gain negotiating power in the markets they serve. Hospital merger activity has been growing at double digit rates since 2009. When mergers occurred in concentrated markets, double-digit price increases often followed.[56] The American Hospital Association reports that only 10% of community hospitals have been involved in a merger in the past five years, but there are numerous benefits to the community when mergers do occur. Scholarly studies have not yet proven the benefits, but one thing is clear. Hospitals are under increased scrutiny over their market power and what are perceived to be high prices.

Researchers studied the charges for ten common blood tests performed at all non-federal hospitals in California for 2011. The variations in charges were hard to comprehend. One common blood test called a lipid panel is used to measure cholesterol and triglyceride levels. The hospital charges for the test ranged from $10 to $10,169, a thousand-fold difference.[57] Researchers have described the prices hospitals charge for various services as irrational. The average consumer would call the prices mind-boggling. A person might ask, are these prices for real? Who pays the high price and who pays the low price? At the center of these questions is the chargemaster.

Chargemaster

The chargemaster is a database in the information technology system of all American hospitals. It is their master price list including thousands of procedures, tests, supplies, medications, and other healthcare related products and services. In a seminal article in *Time* called "Bitter Pill: Why Medical Bills Are Killing Us", Steven Brill describes the prices in chargemasters. He says they are "devoid of any calculation related to cost".[58] Prior to 1982, The Centers reimbursed hospitals based on charges they submitted. Those charges came from the chargemaster. Today, hospitals are reimbursed fixed amounts based on the services they perform. However, the chargemaster still lives on as a master price list used to negotiate rates with health insurance companies. The prices in the chargemaster are artificially inflated to insure they are above what any payer would pay – and with nothing left on the table.

For those who are insured either by government or private insurance companies, they would never pay the price in the chargemaster. Wealthy consumers, in the U.S. or from outside the U.S., who have no insurance pay the high prices. Unfortunately, for tens of millions of Americans who have no health insurance, they too are asked to pay the high prices. Even those with insurance, but with an inexpensive policy offered by an insurer which has little bargaining power with the hospital, may pay a much higher price than those with Medicare or an expensive health insurance plan.

Transparency

A key issue in healthcare pricing is a lack of transparency. In "The Healing of America: A Global Quest for Better, Cheaper, and Fairer Health Care", T. R. Reid describes his visits to France, Germany, Switzerland, Canada, and Japan to learn about all aspects of their healthcare system. In a visit to a French physician, he saw a poster on the wall in the waiting room showing the prices for the various services the physician provided. That is transparency of pricing. California is making strides to put chargemaster pricing on the Internet, but generally speaking, we have no visibility to healthcare services pricing in America. When the government or insurance company is paying the bill, consumers have no incentive to understand the pricing of services. The same is true for providers. During the past six months, I asked two department heads at a hospital what the price was for one of their common procedures. They didn't know.

Contrast healthcare pricing transparency to other industries. Consider Mucinex DM Expectorant & Cough Suppressant, an over-the-counter cold remedy. If you do a web search for the medication, you will see thousands of relevant pages, including websites showing price comparisons, including the cost of shipping. The price range I found was $7.95 to $19.98. Some consumers may choose a particular retailer or e-tailer based on their past experience or preference. They know exactly what they will pay. Because of the transparency of the pricing, the pricing is not likely to vary widely like was the case with the California blood tests.

Another price issue is perception. If a Dr. Smith charges $10,000 for delivery of a baby and a Dr. Jones charges $4,000, some people might think Dr. Smith is a better doctor. Who wants to have their child delivered by the lowest price doctor? Patients often select providers based on hearsay and perception without regard to the quality and outcomes a particular provider actually may deliver. Consumers are becoming more aware of patient safety, outcomes, and quality metrics, all of which are gradually becoming more available from the web.

American healthcare providers often charge high prices because they can. The situation will change as consumers and regulators demand transparency of pricing. As more people gain health insurance, often with high deductibles, they will ask about prices and evaluate competitive alternatives.

Medical Technology

Breakthrough technology is routine in healthcare, and it introduces treatment options not previously available. Hospitals invest in new technology to attract new patients. While the new technology sometimes brings better outcomes, it often increases the cost of healthcare by replacing older lower-cost options. It is not unusual for new technology to be introduced into clinical practice with neither the supporting clinical studies to prove the effectiveness of the technology nor the rigorous economic analysis to prove the benefits exceed the cost.

There are many cancer treatment options including surgery, chemotherapy, and radiation. A relatively new technology that often achieves a 90% cure rate is intensity-modulated radiation treatment. The equipment bombards the targeted area with photons without harming the nearby tissues thereby minimizing side effects. A newer technology is proton beam therapy. The Hospital at the University of Pennsylvania is one of a handful of hospitals to own the highly sophisticated proton beam equipment. The cost was $144 million. David Whelan and Robert Langreth wrote in *Forbes* about "The $150 Million Zapper". They said the equipment is "the length of a football field and contains some of the most complex and expensive medical machinery ever built".[59] The value proposition of using protons instead of photons is there is greater precision and hence less risk of damaging healthy organs or tissues. A team of researchers at the Department of Radiation Oncology at the Fox Chase Cancer Center in Philadelphia performed a study using extensive amounts of data and simulations. Their conclusion was proton beam therapy is not cost effective for most patients with prostate cancer.[60] The mortality was slightly better, but the cost, which Medicare reimburses, was nearly double.

When hospitals cannot make the business case to acquire leading edge and unproven new technology, they often rely on philanthropy. In the University of Pennsylvania case, the Roberts family of the Comcast Corporation fortune donated $15 million.[61] Other funding came from nearby hospitals expecting to benefit and from government grants. An ethical question is whether the $144 million for an unproven technology was a good use of healthcare dollars compared to the impact those funds could have had elsewhere. For example, in making care available to those with no health insurance or to develop clinics to address the high incidence of chronic diseases.

Productivity

Another contributor to higher healthcare prices is poor productivity. If it takes more labor or materials to produce something, the price is higher to recover the added cost. Dr. Robert Kochner and Nikhill R. Sahni studied the cost of healthcare labor and wrote a widely cited article, "Rethinking Health Care Labor", published in The *New England Journal of Medicine* in 2011. The article reported 16.4 million healthcare employees constitute 12 percent of the labor force as of 2010, and collectively experienced no gains in productivity in the past 20 years.[62] Any other industry would find this unacceptable. The lack of productivity gains is not a reflection on the healthcare employees. Duplicative work, manual procedures, excessive paper forms, and a lack of electronic documentation contribute to the lack of productivity gains. Healthcare remains the last bastion of paper based industries. Hospitals are beginning to focus on integrated systems to address the poor productivity record.

Many factors affect productivity, but those with the largest effect are duplicative tests, procedures, and administrative processes. Patients find it unproductive to have to fill out the clipboard every time they visit a new provider, but providers themselves also have redundant procedures. Providers order new tests because they can't access the tests that may have been done recently by a different provider. The estimates vary, but redundant tests cost hundreds of billions of dollars per year.

The fee for service model does not encourage the most cost effective use of healthcare skills. As a result, the least costly level of provider is not always used to provide care. Using a higher level of skill than required results in higher cost. For example, if a primary care physician (PCP) provides treatment for a common cold a nurse practitioner could have provided, or an orthopedic surgeon provides a consultation for someone with a sore knee a PCP could provide, significant cost is added to the healthcare delivery.

Specialists

Specialists create tremendous value and extend the lives of millions through their highly specialized knowledge, experience, and treatment capabilities. However, the over-use of specialists can cause unintended side effects, including the frustrations of the "merry-go-round" phenomenon experienced by patients shuffled back and forth between PCPs and multiple specialists. The PCPs are under pressure from healthcare administrators to see more patients per hour. One way to increase PCP productivity is to quickly diagnose a condition as needing a specialist, create a referral, and move on to see the next patient. This practice increases the cost of healthcare because of the higher reimbursement rates received by specialists.

A New York based healthcare start up, RubiconMD, has focused on the consequences of using more costly skills than required.[63] The company discovered one out of five referrals to a specialist results in duplicate or unnecessary imaging or other tests.[64] The company believes more than 40% of referrals are poorly timed, incomplete, or could be managed within the primary care setting with the availability of appropriate specialist input.[65]

Tort Reform and Defensive Medicine

One in every 33 babies (about 3%) is born with a birth defect.[66] Defects or perceived imperfections lead to lawsuits. Litigation expenses and settlements contribute to the healthcare cost problem in America. Many believe the unnecessary tests, medications, and procedures ordered by physicians to protect themselves from being sued represent even larger costs. Physicians and policy experts hold widely different views on the topic.

All physicians I know, and possibly most in America, believe defensive medicine exists because of the malpractice system. I believe such practices are a major reason for the high cost of American healthcare. Many healthcare policy analysts, on the other hand, believe the malpractice insurance and settlement costs represent a miniscule share of total healthcare costs They also believe reform would not lead to significant cost savings. Dr. Howard Brody and attorney Laura Hermer at the University of Texas Medical Branch reviewed numerous studies on the topic of tort reform, malpractice costs, and defensive medicine.[67] They concluded both the physician and the policy analyst points of view are partly but not completely valid.

Hermer and Brody reported in their study the total cost of all insurance premiums, payouts and settlements, court costs, and the entire malpractice liability system amounts to approximately one-and-a-half percent of total healthcare spending.[68] The cost of defensive medicine is much harder to determine. Studies have shown it be as much as 10% of healthcare cost, but Hermer and Brody found the study less than inconclusive. They found wide variations in the definition of defensive medicine used in the studies. One definition includes those tests and procedures performed compared to what would have been performed if the malpractice system was reformed. Although the definition of defensive medicine is highly subjective at best, David Studdert, a leading expert in the fields of health law and empirical legal research, found a survey of physicians showed more than 90% practiced it.[69] The more important question is what is the motivation behind practicing defensive medicine?

Dr. Atul Gawande, in "The Cost Conundrum: What a Texas Town Can Teach Us About Health Care", suggested there are a number of reasons for why so called defensive medicine is practiced.[70] He said that one is because ordering more tests and procedures can lead to higher incomes for physicians who share in the profits of organizations providing the tests and procedures. In some cases, he said that physicians have a bias to use the latest technology available when other less expensive and equally effective techniques may be available. Another factor he described is as physicians practice in a certain way, such care can become the standard of care in a particular region. Gawande noted all of these factors were present in an area of Texas he studied, despite the fact Texas has had significant malpractice reform.

The topic of tort reform and defensive medicine is complex. There are no clear answers, I believe, except for one. Tort and malpractice reform are necessary but not sufficient to have a significant impact on the cost of healthcare. Reform is necessary because even just 1% of the total cost of healthcare for 2014 would be $40 billion. Reform is not sufficient because it barely gets at the overall manner in which healthcare is delivered.

Waste and Fraud

The New England Health Institute defined waste as spending that can be eliminated without reducing the quality of care. The Institute of Medicine defined it as activities or resources that do not add value.[71] Healthcare waste falls into six categories: unwarranted use (40% of the total), fraud and abuse (19%), administrative inefficiencies (17%), provider inefficiency and errors (12%), lack of coordination of care (6%), preventable conditions, and avoidable care (6%).[72] Waste can be further broken down in the following types: (1) unnecessary hospitalization and rehospitalization, (2) paying for more care that is not necessarily better care, (3) treatments that are not evidence based and have no record of efficacy, (4) unnecessary or redundant tests, (5) end of life care providing no cure or comfort to the patient nor comfort to loved ones, (6) medical errors, (7) hospital acquired infections or injuries, (8) fraud and abuse, and (9) inefficiency in the delivery of healthcare services. It is a long list that could be expanded further, but it takes a long list to accumulate a trillion dollars in waste.

The White House Office of Management and Budget, consulting firm PricewaterhouseCoopers LLP, research firm Rand Corporation, and numerous academic institutions have conducted studies about wasteful healthcare spending. The estimates vary but all believe the waste is more than $500 billion per year and some believe it is more than $1 trillion, or nearly 40% of all healthcare spending in 2009. If the percentage of waste continues at the same level, the waste would be more than one-and-a-half trillion dollars in 2014.

To put the level of waste in perspective, consider how many people could receive healthcare with the amount of spending that was wasted. Using the 2012 per capita healthcare cost of $8,915, divided into $1.5 trillion yields 170,499,159 people. That is 54% of the population as of August 2014. If waste could be eliminated, the cost of American healthcare would be competitive with that in other developed countries. A policy alternative could be to allocate a portion of the savings from eliminating the waste to providing preventive medicine for those with no health insurance. In any case, eliminating waste offers multiple positive opportunities.

David A. Pratt, Professor at Albany Law School, wrote "Focus On Waste in the Health Care System" in the *Journal of Pension Benefits*.[73] Healthcare waste may not seem at first to be related to pensions, until you consider the economics for seniors who are on relatively fixed pensions. For those receiving health benefits from a former employer, the retiree contribution toward the cost of healthcare gets deducted from their pension. For those on social security, there is likewise a deduction for the cost of Medicare. Waste that leads to higher costs of healthcare directly reduces the value of both public and private pensions.

In 2012, total healthcare spending grew 3.7% to $2.8 trillion. Medicare spending grew 4.8% to $572.5 billion and accounted for 20% of total spending. Fraud-enforcement officials estimate 10% of Medicare's yearly spending, more than $57 billion in 2013, was in bogus payments to healthcare providers, and the U.S. government recovered just $2.86 billion in Medicare funds that year.[74] Congress recently mandated Medicare claims must be paid within 30 days of receipt, so the focus of fraud detection is shifting so billings can be frozen before they are paid.

Healthcare fraud is rampant and has been very difficult to stop, but The Centers for Medicare & Medicaid Services are making some progress. In the Los Angeles area, one of the highest fraud locations, strike force offices have been established. The two year old program aims to, among other things, identify bad actors before they get paid. In 2013, The Centers developed leads for 469 new investigations through a new Fraud Prevention System.[75] The program identified or prevented $211 million in fraudulent payments. This was nearly double the prior year, but the amount recovered is miniscule compared with the tens of billions lost.

The fraud program is a good start, but it has a long way to go. Fraud is easy to understand when you see the details of a specific case, but discovering the cases is complex. The perpetrators include a range of providers including physicians, pharmacies, nursing homes, home healthcare services, medical device manufacturers, and even Medicare beneficiaries themselves. The common fraud schemes used by the providers include: (1) billing for "phantom patients", medical goods or services not provided, or more hours than there are in a day, (2) billing separately for procedures normally covered by a single fee, (3) charging more than once for the same service, (4) charging for a more complex service than was performed, (5) concealing ownership in a related company, and (6) using false credentials.

The solution to such a complex problem lies in big data and analytics. Big data refers to the enormous amount of data created every second of every day – tweets, emails, Facebook postings, photos, Fitbit activity, GPS tracking information, home telemonitoring of chronically ill patients, and, of course, healthcare claims from providers. The $500 plus billion that Medicare spends per year consists of nearly 5 million claims that pour into their systems every day. Big data is complex. It is not just the amount of data that makes it challenging; it is the complexity of the data.

In the past, working with claims data was simple. Each claim included basic information such as date of service, claim #, procedure or treatment number, patient number, and a dollar amount. Medicare would add up the amounts and make the payments. However, when you combine millions of claims per day and introduce fraud to the mix, the challenge is to gain deeper insight about the data, not just adding up the amounts and making payments.

Analytics is the process of discovering the details of big data and developing an understanding of meaningful patterns in the data. For example, a data scientist may discover in the Miami area there are 30% more prescriptions for electric wheelchairs than in any other metropolitan area. Digging deeper he or she might discover that 60% of those prescriptions come from one physician practice. Digging deeper still, it may turn out a physician owner of the practice is also an investor in a company making electric wheelchairs. In other fraud cases, providers have been found to submit numerous claims on a regular basis for multiple patients with exactly the same diagnoses and treatments.

The Fraud Prevention System uses dozens of models and predictive algorithms to uncover fraud, waste, and abuse. Engineers and economists look at known cases of fraud. Then they develop models and algorithms to root out suspiciously similar claims having a high probability of being fraudulent. Armed with the data, The Centers and the Justice Department executed raids in early 2014 in six cities. They busted 90 Medicare providers, including 16 doctors. The total false Medicare billings represented by the providers were $260 million.[76]

There is a lot of fraud inflating the cost of healthcare, but big data and analytics is coming to the rescue. The data is vast and complicated, but as data scientists, engineers, and healthcare experts work together to enhance the algorithms and models, they will become more accurate and timely. It will take time, but the bad guys should not expect The Centers to be asleep at the switch. Fraud is a significant element of the healthcare cost problem, but progress is being made and the trend is in the right direction.

Costly Unhealthy Lifestyles

Smoking, obesity, hypertension, drug and alcohol abuse, and lack of adherence to medical advice and prescriptions represent billions of dollars of healthcare expenditure that are avoidable. The expenditures could go toward making healthcare more affordable or to expand care for those not receiving it. Is it waste to treat people who lead unhealthy lifestyles? No, it is not a waste, but I believe if education and healthcare clinics got proper focus and funding, much of the cost of treatment could be saved.

I strongly believe making healthy lifestyle choices could reduce healthcare costs significantly. Following are my personal comments about smoking, hypertension, and obesity.

As more cities, hospitals, bars, restaurants, work places, and entire states prohibit smoking, it continues to be an issue in the military. It as been argued the stressful conditions soldiers encounter create a need to smoke. However, soldiers who smoke, like all smokers, have increased risk of cardiovascular disease, lung cancer, and other illnesses. The Department of Defense estimates it spends more than $1.6 billion per year as a direct result of smoking by military personnel. The editors of *BloombergView* reported in "Why Can't the Pentagon Stop Smoking?" the Veterans Administration spends billions more to care for veterans with lung disease.[77] In 2009, the Institute of Medicine made a recommendation the military should be tobacco-free. The Pentagon agrees and has been working toward that end for years. Unfortunately, a California congressman inserted a provision in the defense authorization bill requiring military commissaries sell discounted cigarettes to military members and their families.[78]

Hypertension means high blood pressure, and it has multiple causes. For most adults, there is no specific identifiable cause of high blood pressure. Called essential hypertension, this type of high blood pressure, develops gradually over time. However, for many Americans, hypertension can be caused by diabetes, chronic kidney disease, pregnancy, or medications. For millions of others, it can be a direct consequence of lifestyle choices such as self-imposed anxiety or stress, too much alcohol, smoking, or a high salt diet.[79] The prevalence and consequences of hypertension are significant. It afflicts 67 million American adults, approximately 75% of people with heart attack or stroke have high blood pressure, nearly 350,000 deaths in 2009 included high blood pressure as a primary or contributing cause. The cost of treatment is nearly $50 billion per year.[80] A combination of medications, if necessary, and healthy lifestyle choices can lead to a positive prognosis for anyone with hypertension.

Obesity is a chronic condition that has become a pandemic[81]. In 2013 at the annual meeting of the American Medical Association, physicians voted overwhelmingly to categorize obesity as "a disease that requires a range of interventions to advance treatment and prevention".[82] The simplest definition of what it means to be obese is a person has too much body fat. It is not the same as being overweight, which means weighing too much. Some persons, including athletes, can be overweight from extra muscle or bone. An indicator for obesity is the body mass index (BMI), which is defined as a person's weight divided by the square of their height. According to the National Heart, Lung, and Blood Institute online calculator, a person who is five feet 11 inches tall and weighs 175 pounds has a BMI of 24.4, and that is considered normal.[83] Between 25 and 30 is considered overweight, and above 30 is considered obese. In the United States, 34.9% of adults are obese. A BMI above 35 with obesity-related health conditions or a BMI above 40 are considered morbidly obese. A rule of thumb is morbid obesity is a condition of weighing double or more a person's ideal weight. It is called morbidly obese because it correlates with numerous serious and life-threatening conditions.

Obesity has a large economic effect in the United States. Three percent of the population are considered morbidly obese, but the treatment of the condition and related healthcare costs represent 21% of healthcare spending.[84] Obesity is a serious problem beyond the condition itself. Comorbidity is two or more coexisting medical conditions. Serious comorbidities, impaired quality of life, higher mortality, and inability to be productive in the labor force are significant inhibitors to the country's positive growth and development.

Eating more than the body needs is a simple explanation of the cause of obesity but such an explanation is incomplete. There are additional related causes for obesity.[85] In some cases obesity is genetic. A biological basis can exist from a strong will to survive. Eating can start as a necessity and later become an addiction. A socioeconomic condition of poverty correlates to the development of obesity. Other related factors include inability to understand nutrition labeling and general lack of education.

Obesity encompasses many undesirable components. Obesity causes serious comorbidities including diabetes, cancer, sleep apnea, osteoarthritis, and cardiovascular disease, including myocardial infarction. The quality of life for an obese person is reduced significantly.[86] Unfortunately, there is no simple procedure or medication to eliminate the negative conditions from obesity.[87]

There are three main approaches to managing obesity; lifestyle modification, pharmacological treatment, and bariatric surgery. Each has significant economic and ethical implications. The most effective treatment for obesity is a combination of behavior modification and bariatric surgery.[88] Pharmacological treatments have limited benefits in most cases and are not effective unless taken in conjunction with a lifestyle change program. Bariatric surgery is not without risks, but it often results in an improvement in the quality of life for the patient.[89] Advancement in surgical techniques such as minimally invasive laparoscopic surgery have reduced the risks and shortened the recovery time. However, if the obesity of a patient was caused by a habitual lifestyle of overeating, the surgery alone cannot provide long-term benefits to the patient. Most surgeons require a successful behavior modification before they will perform the surgery and the hospital often facilitates support groups and follow up nursing care.[90]

According to criteria developed by the National Institutes of Health, the number of Americans who medically qualify for bariatric surgery exceeds 20 million.[91] Healthcare providers perform 225,000 bariatric surgeries per year, demonstrating a significant imbalance between supply and demand. Unless there is a medical or behavioral breakthrough, the imbalance of supply and demand will result in continuing escalation of healthcare costs.[92]

Many healthcare programs exclude bariatric surgery from coverage because the economics of the surgery do not present a positive case when considering only the obesity condition of the patient. However, when considering the reduction in the comorbidities of diabetes, myocardial infarction, and stroke, there is significant benefit.[93] The quantification of the value of saved lives and improvement in the quality of lives provides additional economic benefit. The time value of the economic benefits should also be considered. The cost for treatment of obese patients is high and immediate. The benefits of reducing the number of people who are obese are spread over time. Some payers are facing pressure from stakeholders to improve profits or reduce expenditures and may not consider the net present value of the future economic benefits.

Healthcare providers cannot change socioeconomic factors such as household income, median earned income, employment, poverty status, and welfare participation[94]. These factors influence lifestyle changes through clinics, counseling, and home healthcare. A bariatric surgeon told me the surgery is just one small encounter with a lifelong obese patient. She said that patients understand they have to change their lifestyle or surgery won't solve the problem, but often they do not make the required changes. She went on to tell me that bariatric surgery could help people achieve an improved level of health

Qualitative considerations for doctors working with patients who are obese include: the ethics of encouraging bariatric surgery, bias and stereotyping of patients, and horizontal and vertical equity. Moral issues are prominent and must be considered. It is easy to become committed to one particular point of view about obesity and not be sensitive to the many human and social considerations.[95]

This section on obesity is more prescriptive than other parts of *Health Attitude* because I strongly believe the growing impact of the disease is extraordinary. There are numerous actions healthcare providers can take to have a positive impact on obesity.

1. Develop an obesity care program including bariatric surgery plus dietary, lifestyle, exercise, and behavior counseling.
2. Promote social media on the web such as patientslikeme.com and encourage consumer-to-consumer exchanges. This can neutralize any potential bias from providers.
3. Offer free community seminars where consumers can learn about the full range of available treatments for obesity, before and after surgery.
4. Establish criteria for the prioritization of bariatric surgery candidates based on medical need.
5. Direct the Ethics Committee at your hospital to evaluate bariatric surgery cases to ensure ethics and equity are fully considered.
6. Initiate a study under the guidance of the Chief Financial Officer and the Chief Medical Officer to examine the cost of care of obese patients over an extended period. Include the costs and reimbursements for all comorbidities.
7. Develop an economic analysis using discounted cash flow to determine the net present value of the costs and benefits and present the results to payers as encouragement to provide fair reimbursements for comprehensive treatments, not just for surgery.
8. Promote healthy life style choices and positive health attitudes for both patients and their care givers to reduce the number of people becoming obese.

Chronic Disease

Life expectancy reached 78.8 years in 2012, up significantly from 62.9 years in 1940.[96] The increase in life expectancy introduces a demographic shift leading to a dramatic increase in the number of older Americans. The older population (65+) numbered 43.1 million in 2012, an increase of 8.1 million or 22% since 2000. It is projected to increase to 55 million in 2020, a 36% increase for the decade. Currently, more than one in eight, or 13.8%, of the population is an older American. Persons reaching age 65 have an average life expectancy of an additional 19.1 years, and the 85+ age group is projected to grow from 4.7 million in 2003 to 9.6 million in 2030. This is good news for seniors.

The bad news is chronic illness, which is more common among older adults, has reached epidemic proportions. One out of two Americans has a chronic illness. One out of four has two or more chronic illnesses. Chronic illness accounts for half of all deaths, and represents 75% of American healthcare cost.[97]

Even if efforts to reduce healthcare cost per capita are successful, the large increase in the number of people needing care will continue to grow. Unfortunately, many of them will have costly chronic illnesses. Researchers predict a 42 percent increase in chronic disease cases by 2023, adding $4.2 trillion in treatment costs and lost economic output. Much of this cost is preventable, since many chronic conditions are linked to unhealthy lifestyles.

Effects of Taxes and Fees

The ACA aims to bring 25 million uninsured Americans under healthcare coverage by 2019. Some will receive subsidies and others will fall under expanded state Medicaid programs. The Federal government will provide funding for the premium subsidies and the majority of the cost of the Medicaid expansion. According to the Congressional Budget Office, the expansion of health insurance will cost $1.2 trillion.[98]

Where will the $1.2 trillion come from? The ACA intends to offset slightly less than half of the increased cost through spending reductions and a little more than half through 13 new taxes and fees totaling $775 billion.[99] Who pays the taxes and fees? There is something from everyone: health insurers, employers, medical device manufacturers, and individuals.

It is rational to think when a medical device manufacturer has to pay the new 2.3% tax on a knee implant, they will pass that cost on to hospitals who in turn will pass it on to payers. Economists are divided on what will happen in the future. Past history demonstrates spending reductions will not occur but new taxes and fees will be proposed instead.

Aetna, the fifth largest health insurance company, estimates the combination of two of the thirteen new taxes and fees found in the new Health Insurer Fee and

Reinsurance Contribution, will add approximately 3.5 to 4.5 percent to the cost of health insurance coverage. These taxes and fees will increase the cost of health coverage by nearly $5,000 per family over the next decade.[100]

Summary

Our healthcare system consumes a larger share of the economy than in any other country. On a per capita basis we spend two to three times more than other developed countries. There are many reasons for the high cost of healthcare. In part it is because of our appetite for care. The prices we pay are higher than other countries. A lack of transparency limits comparison shopping. Other factors behind high cost include: technology investments, low productivity, poor health attitudes, fraud, waste, unhealthy lifestyles, and chronic illness. A subtler source of our high cost comes from the practice of medicine.

CHAPTER 4

The Practice Of Medicine

For centuries, physicians have been practicing according to the Hippocratic Oath. Patients continually have placed their trust and confidence in their physicians.[101] Those relationships are important and enduring. However, the current way in which medicine is practiced doesn't reflect the realities and necessities of cost control, quality, and safety. The fee for service model by which hospitals and physicians are compensated based on each visit, test, or procedure is no longer affordable.

I believe the unaffordable situation we find ourselves in does not exist because providers unilaterally decided to make it that way. Numerous legal, regulatory, and governmental forces have transformed the practice of medicine from the way it was 50 years ago to the way it is today. Regardless of the history or explanation of how we got here, the practice of medicine must change.

Merry-Go-Round

Clayton M. Christensen is the Robert and Jane Cizik Professor of Business Administration at the Harvard Business School. Jason Hwang, M.D., is an internal medicine physician and Senior Strategist for the Healthcare Practice at Innosight LLC. In *The Innovator's Prescription: A Disruptive Solution for Health Care* they said that one-fourth of Medicare beneficiaries have at least five chronic illnesses, see an average of 13 physicians, and receive 50 drug prescriptions per year.[102] Some obvious questions arise from these statistics. Is there someone who coordinates the care for the patients? Do they really need that many physicians? Are all the physicians aware of what medications their patients are taking? Does each physician have access to the physician notes made during visits to other physicians? Unfortunately, I think we know the answers to all of these questions are no.

I can explain more clearly the problem areas of current practice of medicine by sharing what I learned in helping my mother through the decade prior to her passing in 2009. Mom was healthy for more than three-quarters of her life. She had a mastectomy when she was 75 and a knee surgery when she was 80. Otherwise, she had minimal encounters with the healthcare system until she was diagnosed with congestive heart failure (CHF) in her early eighties.

CHF is a chronic disease. It causes a disproportionately high cost of healthcare for the elderly. CHF afflicts more than 5 million people in the United States.[103] Due to an aging population, more than 400,000 new cases are diagnosed each year.[104] CHF accounts for the largest share of hospital admissions, and 10% to 50% of the discharged patients are readmitted within six months of their initial hospitalization.[105] The International Journal of Environmental Research and Public Health said that CHF has become an emerging epidemic.[106]

Once Mom was designated as a CHF patient, the merry-go-round of doctor visits, specialist visits, and tests began. Her primary care physician referred Mom to a cardiologist. Like many specialists, Mom's specialist wanted a fresh set of blood tests. The tests the PCP had ordered were deemed either not current enough or they did not include certain specific tests the specialist wanted. Although Mom was under the care of a cardiologist, the PCP would periodically tell the assisted living home Mom was due for a follow-up visit.

A number of Mom's friends at the assisted living home were seeing multiple specialists. For people who are 80 to 100, doctor visits can be an ordeal for them and their caregivers. Folding and unfolding walkers and wheelchairs, helping people into the building, parking the car, and spending time in the waiting area add a lot of time and effort to the ten-minute visit with the doctor. Then, the cumbersome, time-consuming process is repeated to return to the residence. Again, the entire process is repeated for the next appointment.

One of Mom's follow-up visits with the PCP resulted in the usual set of blood tests and periodically a test for fecal occult blood, blood not visibly apparent but which can be detected from a stool sample. The blood finding resulted in a referral to see a gastroenterologist, who immediately recommended a colonoscopy. At this point, Mom was 87.

Scientific American reported on a study performed in Texas showing nearly 25% of colonoscopies performed on patients older than 75 were inappropriate.[107] The U.S. Preventive Services Task Force is an independent panel of non-Federal experts in prevention and evidence based medicine.[108] They conduct reviews of scientific evidence about a broad range of clinical preventive healthcare services such as screening, counseling, and preventive medications. They develop and publish recommendations for primary care clinicians and health systems. The Task Force recommends people who do not have specific risks for colon cancer should begin regular screening at age 50 and cease screening after age 75. I knew the head of the gastroenterology practice had a mother about the same age as mine. I asked him if he would recommend she have a colonoscopy under the circumstances. He said that he had to recommend it for legal reasons. Another example of defensive medicine.

A healthy 87 year old person in good health potentially could benefit from removal of a bleeding polyp. However, CHF patients, such as my mother, are typically taking a blood thinner to prevent stroke. Stopping the medication can be risky, and the preparation for a colonoscopy for a frail 87 year old lady would be difficult, risky and uncomfortable. She would have called it torture! I declined the test for Mom. Now, let's check in on her merry-go-round treatment ride.

Going between PCP and specialist to PCP with tests at every visit is not easy for an 87 year old person. When CHF causes an acute condition, things get worse. A typical scenario is an elderly person with CHF experiences dizziness or shortness of breath. Their caregiver calls the emergency medical service. An ambulance takes the CHF patient to the ER. The ER performs a complete diagnostic evaluation and stabilizes the patient's condition. The hospital's cardiac care unit admits the patient for further care. After several days of monitoring, adjusting medications, and stabilizing the patient's condition, the patient is typically discharged and returns to his or her place of residence. At least 20% of patients in this scenario return to the hospital with the same conditions within 30 days, and 50% are readmitted with six months.[109]

Mom endured the hospital merry-go-round several times. The readmission cycle is stressful for the patient and for the family. Until recent changes The Centers made to the reimbursement model for hospitals, the more CHF readmissions the hospital received, the more revenue the hospital earned. Each admission generated multiple diagnostic tests, including daily blood tests. For frail and elderly patients with paper-thin skin, the blood tests nearly unbearable.

Another frustration for patients who make multiple visits to the hospital is medication reconciliation. When a patient goes to the hospital, they are not allowed to bring any medications with them. A new set of prescriptions, based on physician orders, must be compliant with the hospital formulary, which is a list of medications the hospital has on hand and for which it has a contract to acquire at negotiated prices. At the time of discharge, the medication list for the patient may look nothing like the medications he or she was taking at the time of admission. Some patients are admitted with more than 15 prescriptions. Mom did not know the name or purpose of some of her prescriptions, but she knew the sizes, shapes, and colors. The medications she would take home from the hospital showed no resemblance to what she had before.

In a typical case, the hospital sends a fax to the assisted living home or nursing home listing the patient's prescribed medications. It is unlikely to be the same list as what he or she was taking before admission. This adds to the confusion for both patient and family. Who reconciles the before and after medication list? This task is generally left to the PCP, but it is not always easy to decipher the fax, adjust prescriptions where needed, and, most importantly, explain the new list to the patient and family. Also another important confusing situation concerns who makes the appointment with the PCP and how soon does the visit happen after discharge from the hospital? This task usually falls to the family or the assisted living or nursing home. Sometimes, making the appointment went through the cracks. Sometimes, no appointment was made with the PCP. The missing ingredient in the merry-go-round process is coordination. There often is little or none.

The merry-go-round of hospital visits, doctor visits, and tests continues until the end. Some hospital visits result in infection, either acquired in the hospital or brought from the assisted living or nursing home into the hospital. Infection increases the cost and complexity of care and places additional burdens on the patient and the family. Each visit requires a sterile gown and gloves. The patient often gets confused. The blood draws and tests continue. Some hospital visits require staying in the intensive care unit (ICU) where the cost and complexity rockets even higher. Nearly one-third of Medicare beneficiaries are admitted to an ICU during the last 90 days of their lives.[110] Doctors do not always provide candid assessments and families often do not want to discuss end of life. The merry-go-round continues and the pain and suffering continues for patient and family – until the end. I will describe an alternative end in Chapter 9.

Anecdotal Medicine

Another problem is anecdotal medicine. The patient sees the doctor with certain symptoms and the doctor recalls a similar patient with similar symptoms and prescribes what he or she recalls worked previously. That method has worked pretty well for the last hundred years, but in a world of big data and analytics, following anecdotal evidence for diagnosis and treatment is no longer adequate.

One of the many examples of anecdotal medicine occurred in the field of urology. In 1970, Dr. Richard J. Ablin discovered a prostate-specific antigen (PSA) while looking for a way to detect and predict prostate cancer. Dr. Ablin discovered PSA in both malignant prostates and benign prostates. Although Dr. Ablin believed an elevated PSA level could be useful for predicting a recurrence of prostate cancer in men who were thought to be in remission, he never believed it was a good tool for diagnosing prostate cancer. Despite his concerns, the FDA approved the PSA test in 1986.

In an interview with Dr. Eric Topol, Dr. Ablin said that he believes the approval and the use are financially motivated. He said the healthcare system spends $3 billion per year on PSA screening that not only cannot do what people purport it to do, but it is a test with a 78% false-positive rate. Dr. Ablin said in the interview that the use of the PSA as a diagnostic test continues because of "Fear and money, because other than melanoma, prostate cancer is the most prominent cancer in men. It went on because of the continual proselytizing of fear and the money that was being generated by the screenings." [111]

In his 2014 book, "*The Great Prostate Hoax: How Big Medicine Hijacked the PSA Test and Caused A Public Health Disaster*", Dr. Ablin reveals how fear based and inaccurate testing is resulting in unnecessary high risk surgeries, arguing that the PSA test was never intended for prostate cancer screening. Topol summed it up in his interview with Dr. Ablin by saying, "Patients and doctors believe that lives have been saved by the PSA test. This is offset by all of the men who have developed urinary incontinence or who have lost sexual function -- all of the travesties that have occurred".[112] The Preventive Services Task Force suggested a reduction in the PSA test for men in 2012, citing a similar concern about risks versus benefits[113], but both the controversy and PSA tests continue. The anecdotal belief is PSA testing is the right thing to do.

Unnecessary Office Visits

There is little debate over the value of the colonoscopy as a tool to lower the risk of colon cancer. The American Cancer Society has a detailed set of recommendations on how often to have a colonoscopy based on age, risk factors, and results from the prior exam. Many years ago when I had my first colonoscopy, the gastroenterologist recommended the procedure and suggested I speak with the scheduling assistant to set the date. The assistant said I would need to schedule an office visit one or two weeks prior to the colonoscopy. When I arrived for the pre-procedure visit, I was led to an office where I was asked to watch a video about the procedure. I don't recall if the gastroenterologist examined me while I was there or not. If so, could that examination not have been done during my original visit? Obviously, it could have. I could have watched the video on the Internet at home. What was the real purpose of the extra visit? I am sure my health insurance company paid for the visit.

Recently, my wife called her doctor's office and asked for a renewal of a medication. The office assistant said that the prescription could only be renewed if my wife came in for an office visit. The doctor acknowledged my wife is in near perfect health, but it is the doctor's policy to have an office before renewing the medication, another unnecessary office visit.

Physician Entitlement

When the U.S. Preventive Services Task Force recommended routine mammographic screening of average-risk women should begin at age 50, instead of age 40, and routine screening should end at age 74, there was an uproar. Some women's and political groups were outraged and called it a healthcare reform designed to discriminate against women. Many women were upset and felt the change was based on reducing health care costs rather than on sound medical research.

Although the cost benefit analysis followed research rigor, when an independent panel of experts suggests reducing tests, they are prescribing a reduction in revenue for hospitals, physicians, and laboratories. In my opinion, some providers previously lived in a world of an entitlement oriented, fee for service model where they were reimbursed for any and all services they provide, whether those services were medically necessary or not. That was then. Now we are transitioning to an accountability oriented, fee for value model.

Office is Closed

If you call your doctor's office between noon and one o'clock, there's a good chance you will get a message announcing the office is closed until one or possibly two. Since healthcare is approaching 20% of the U.S. economy, it is obviously a business. Patients are the customers. I cannot think of any other business closing during the time when potential customers may want to engage in some way. Carrying this point a bit further, what consumer businesses are closed on weekends and evenings? Working parents may not be able to get time off from work to take a child for a visit? Customer oriented businesses are open evenings and weekends.

These limited hours have opened an opportunity for a new class of providers. Walk in clinics are offering 24-hour coverage, often located in grocery stores and banks. Consumers view this positively because of the convenience. Many of the "little clinics" now take insurance and don't require cash payments for services.

Central Planning

The entitlement oriented, fee for service model drives up healthcare costs. The Centers use panels of experts to set reimbursement rates for the many different tests and procedures physicians and hospitals provide. Hospitals have gotten very good at analyzing the profit margins on the services they provide, and not surprisingly, pursue the most profitable procedures like coronary bypass surgery. Service areas such as psychiatric or neonatal intensive care get lower reimbursements and often get deemphasized or even discontinued. Primary care and preventive care can be at risk for the same reason, even though they both can save costs in the long run. In effect, The Centers drive behavior through the rates they set.

The entitlement oriented, fee for service model can drive behavior that may not be best for the long-term health of the population. The fee based model can also discourage innovation. If a physician has a unique idea that could benefit a patient, he or she may not use the idea if it is not associated with a fee. Many physicians and hospital administrators intuitively know getting paid for wellness instead of sickness would be better for the health of the population, but the fee for service model discourages such an approach. The Centers are beginning to change the reimbursement model with a shift to an accountability oriented, fee for value model.

The Internet

The Internet has the potential to provide an integration of consumer devices and cloud computing to improve outcomes, reduce cost, and empower consumers to actively participate in their healthcare. Consumers have learned to communicate effectively through email and various social media, and they would like to do so with their doctors. Kaiser Permanente, a healthcare giant in California with 9.5 million members, 174,415 employees, 17,425 physicians, 48,285 nurses, 38 hospitals, and more than $50 billion in operating revenues, has been a pioneer in leveraging the Internet for patient communications. Some providers resist the concept of electronic mail exchanges between doctor and patient. This method of communication would be a big shift for many physicians. Kaiser Permanente has found it quite effective and is making it work. Kaiser Permanente members send nearly one million emails to providers each month and member satisfaction is high.[114]

In 2001, when I wrote *Net Attitude*, I described how many companies resisted the idea of customers sending them emails. Their argument was they did not have the staff to answer "all those emails". I argued if there was a large amount of incoming email, it might mean customers or potential customers had questions or valuable feedback or they might want to buy something.[115] It is safe to say most companies now embrace customer email, but not so for many healthcare providers. Although office staffs often use email, physicians who like to get email from patients and interact with them electronically are the exception.

Secure portals are now available to comply with the Health Insurance Portability and Accountability Act (HIPAA), so the security and privacy excuse is no longer valid, but many physicians are still uncomfortable with email. Their logic is partly related to what I saw a dozen years ago, but partly a discomfort in having an electronic dialog instead of the standard form of personal communication. Recently, I made an inquiry to a specialist. He had his office manager send a message to me on the patient portal saying that he advised an office visit, not additional eMessages, if your symptoms persist.

Although provider reluctance to change is a barrier to using the Internet for telemedicine, an equally big barrier comes from our political leaders. Gupta and Saot wrote in "The Constitutionality Of Current Legal Barriers To Telemedicine In The United States: Analysis And Future Directions Of Its Relationship To National And International Health Care Reform", that regulation constitutes a major barrier to the effective use of telemedicine. The authors described the barriers as falling into five key areas: (1) licensing requirements, (2) medical malpractice coverage, (3) legal liability, (4) privacy of information, and (5) payment of services.[116] The problem in each of these areas is overlapping, inconsistent, and inadequate regulations slowing down the growth of telemedicine. If the goals of the Affordable Care Act are to be achieved, our political leaders must act to align the legal framework with the emerging technological framework.

Concierge Healthcare Service

Many consumers are not happy with the cost and complexity of healthcare. Payers, public and private, are not happy with the cost of healthcare. Policymakers are not happy with the access and equity of the healthcare system. That leaves physicians, and they are not happy either. Sandeep Jauhar, from The *Wall Street Journal*, wrote in "Why Doctors Are Sick of Their Profession", "A majority of doctors express diminished enthusiasm for medicine and say they would discourage a friend or family member from entering the profession."[117] Jauhar cited a 2008 survey of 12,000 physicians showing only 6% of physicians described their morale as positive. Eighty-four percent were not happy about their flat or declining incomes. A majority of the survey respondents complained they don't have enough time to spend with patients because of paperwork. With the adoption of electronic health records, physicians have become frustrated – as have patients – with the lack of eye contact since many physicians using EHRs have their eyes on their laptop. Some physicians complain their job has deteriorated into the role of data entry clerk. Nearly half of the respondents said they planned to "reduce the number of patients they would see in the next three years or stop practicing altogether."[118]

One way to see fewer patients is to become a concierge physician. The concept is simple and appealing to both patient and physician. Instead of providing care to one thousand patients and get reimbursed less than $100 per patient, a concierge physician may have 100 patients and get paid $3,500 per year by the patients directly. Not having to deal with payers is great for the physician, and having unlimited access to the physician is great for the patients who can afford a concierge service. Making such a transition, however, is accompanied by a number of issues.

Debra Cascardo, an expert in setting up concierge practices for physicians and physician groups, wrote in *The Journal Of Medical Practice Management* that a concierge practice could offer significant benefits for both patients and physicians.[119] For the physician a concierge practice can mean predictable hours and predictable income. Cascardo said that the average concierge physician earns an income equivalent to a specialist such as a radiologist, cardiologist, or gastroenterologist. The concierge physician can feel he or she is not rushed and is providing high quality care. Perhaps the biggest benefit is the ability to shed the time spent with insurance-related paperwork.

From a patient perspective, there is much greater predictability of healthcare cost outlays. For a fixed fee ranging from $1,800 to as much as $15,000 per year, the patient gets unlimited access, often including the doctor meeting at the ER or on late nights or weekends. Patients would not feel rushed and there is time for the doctor to review questions in more detail and schedule discussions without a concern about reimbursement.

What are the problems providing and using concierge medicine? The move to concierge medicine is not without issues. Seeing fewer patients requires a physician to segregate those patients willing to pay the fixed fee from those who are not. Some patients may feel they are dumped. Others may be receiving regular consultations for the management of a chronic illness. The physician will have to find an alternative physician to pick up the patient. If the ACA is successful, there will be tens of millions of additional insured patients seeking care. For each physician leaving a primary care practice to become a concierge physician, the result is a decrease in the number of physicians to see a larger number of patients.

If a large number of physicians move to concierge practice, a two-tiered system would emerge separating those who can afford unlimited care and those who cannot. A two-tiered system is not the aim of the ACA and I believe the government may challenge concierge medicine on an ethical basis. Despite the challenges, Cascardo says, "As the economic pressures on physicians intensify, more of these practices are likely to surface around the country."[120]

Summary

The practice of medicine currently follows a culture of fee for service encouraging multiple visits to multiple providers. Some of those visits are not needed. Duplicative tests also add to the high cost of healthcare. The adoption of electronic health records and patient/provider email has lagged other industries. Many providers have not adopted a customer attitude and have not always put the patient at the center of care. Physicians spend an increasing percentage of their time on paperwork. Some seek ways to reduce the number of hours they practice. One of the frustrations of patients and providers is the complexity of the system.

CHAPTER 5

Complexity

C omplex processes and the lack of standards make information sharing difficult while adding unnecessary cost. Critics suggest healthcare delivery should be as safe as the best airline, have quality as good as the best automobile, and offer the consistency and low cost of a fast food chain. These are laudable goals but difficult to achieve because of one major difference between the industries, complexity. Weeks and Wadsworth in "Addressing Healthcare Complexity" suggested a comparison to the fast food industry.[121] The authors explain that if a consumer decides to have a hamburger served to her, she has many places to choose from for the service. At each point of service she can easily determine exactly what she will pay and what she will get for it. The consumer would be the payer for the hamburger. None of these statements are true for the acquisition of healthcare. The following paragraphs describe some examples of the complexity faced by patients and providers.

OneExchange

From 1967 to 2001, I was a full-time employee of IBM Corporation. I never gave a lot of thought to health insurance. My wife, four children and I received excellent healthcare during those years, and during most of those years the cost was paid entirely by IBM. When I retired in 2001, I began to pay more attention to the cost. IBM had frozen its contribution to retiree healthcare at $7,500 per year in 1999. Combined with the decision for employees and retirees to contribute toward their health insurance, the cost became noticeable and significant.

Like other large companies, IBM decided in 2013 to turn to private health insurance exchanges as a way to simplify the access to healthcare insurance for IBM retirees. Administering healthcare plans for more than 100,000 retirees became a huge burden. The company turned to OneExchange, a Towers Watson company to provide an online exchange for IBM retirees. The site provided details about insurance plans and prices for coverage in four areas: Medigap or Medicare Advantage, prescription drug plans, dental plans, and vision plans.

In the Fall of 2013, my wife and I enrolled on the site and provided our personal details. The next step was to have a conference call with an expert at OneExchange. The call took place on Friday and lasted three hours and 40 minutes. It was the most painful administrative process I have encountered in my life. The prices and plans the expert described were different than what appeared on the website. OneExchange said a government shutdown prevented certain data from Medicare becoming available. For each of the four areas of coverage, my wife and I had to repeat all of our personal details already recorded at the website. We then had to listen to audio recordings of legal details concerning what is included and excluded in the various plans and then record our own voice providing our consent.

The complexity of the various choices was mind numbing. For basic Medicare supplemental insurance, 35 choices were provided. Each had different terms and conditions. Even the OneExchange consultant could not explain all of the options. To say the choices were complicated would be an understatement. A government study found more than 20% of adult Americans were not "able to locate information in text", could not "make low-level inferences using printed materials", and were unable to "integrate easily identifiable pieces of information."[122] How are those challenged with literacy going to understand health insurance choices? Legislation was proposed to simplify the number of choices, but lawmakers voted against simplification under pressure from insurance companies fearful they would loose business.

Who is to blame for the complexity? Is it IBM? No. IBM is providing a fixed amount of money toward healthcare cost for each retiree, but is not involved in creating the health insurance choices. IBM has turned to OneExchange as a way of administering the program in the best possible way. Even though it was painful, it likely is the best possible approach. Is OneExchange the culprit? No. They have created a business to help IBM and other companies cope and provide a service to the retirees. Is it Medicare? No. They are trying to reduce healthcare cost while increasing quality and patient safety.

I blame Congress for allowing thousands of lobbyists to convince them to insert exceptions in thousands of pages of legislation that become tens of thousands of pages of regulations. Unfortunately, many of our political leaders are focused primarily on remaining in office. They do so by insuring pharmaceutical companies, medical device manufacturers, and health insurers get what they want, not what is best for consumers and patients.

Healthcare.gov

A lot of knowledgeable experts have expressed their points of view about went wrong with the launch of healthcare.gov. I am not going to pile on, but hope to offer a perspective that may be of interest. A project as massive and complex as healthcare.gov can have many possible points of failure. When I first heard about the upcoming October 1, 2013 launch, it reminded me of the website my team at IBM built for the Atlanta Olympics of 1996. In 1995, there were not many people who knew a lot about how to build really large websites. The Olympic website was the largest in the world back then and we learned a lot in building it. We were humble about our expectations. We didn't know how many people would come to the site, when they could come, or what they might do when they got there. We learned many lessons, but I can summarize it in a simple mantra that I continue to espouse: Think big, act bold, start simple, iterate fast. Another way to say it is to take a lot of baby steps.

It appears the direction for healthcare.gov was think big, act in hiding, start big, fail big. Clay Shirky, author of Here *Comes Everybody: The Power of Organizing Without Organizations*, posted a thoughtful analysis of what went wrong in his blog.[123] Shirky offered a non-political description of the planning behind the site, the management system influencing it, and the interactions of various constituents. One of the principals he revealed was the testing plan. Every significant website development I have seen over the past two decades followed the principle of get an early version of the site out there, declare it a "beta", let people poke at it, and respond quickly with fixes and take a lot of baby steps. Shirky, in his blog post "Healthcare.gov and the Gulf Between Planning and Reality", said that the management behind healthcare.gov purposely did not want to get the site out there early for fear of political criticism of bugs.[124] In my opinion, this approach turned out to be a set of self-inflicted wounds.

With respect to complexity, the topic of this chapter, consider the status of healthcare.gov one year later (October 2014). Under the revised system, 70% of the people who had not yet purchased coverage through healthcare.gov will be directed to an identity-verification portal. After that, they must go to a different site to complete a 16 page application. A 16 page application is hard for me to imagine, but the prior year application was 76 pages. This is the problem. The management of healthcare.gov apparently thought it was ok to launch a brand new website with a 76 page application. A superior plan would have been to include early and open testing with millions of people and then provide a longer window of time to complete the purchase.

Medicare Plan D

A good example of how political compromises create complexity is the Medicare Part D prescription drug plan, also called the Medicare prescription drug benefit. This is a federal program to subsidize the cost of prescription drugs and prescription drug insurance premiums for Medicare beneficiaries. The plan was enacted as part of the Medicare Modernization Act of 2003 which went into effect on January 1, 2006. The delay in the implementation was to allow Medicare, pharmacy, and insurance companies to get their information technology systems ready to handle the complexity. The projected cost of Plan D almost prevented the legislation from passing. A compromise was reached after the introduction of the donut hole, a pricing scheme that lowered the cost but introduced significant complexity.

We all know how complicated the Federal Tax Code is, but many of us may not have encountered the complexity of Part D. My mother was 87 at the time the program was introduced. She received a mailing which overwhelmed her. Mom was a very smart lady, and could do *The New York Times* crossword puzzle every day, but Part D stumped her. She handed me the mailing and said, "Here John, explain this to me." I read the materials and found myself stumped. I had not started my doctoral journey to learn about the details of healthcare at that point, so I turned it over to my brother, who did a lot of research and eventually deciphered it.

Researchers have found my mother and I were not alone in finding Part D challenging. Regrettably, one large study found elderly people did not make the best prescription drug plan choices they could have made because of the complexity. This is an example of legislators having good intent but then making compromises followed by complicated regulations describing the implementation. The result is the intended beneficiaries do not always get the intended benefits.

Medicare Donut Hole

The most complicated part of Part D is the drug plan's coverage gap, known as the donut hole. It means you are covered up to a certain point, and then you are not covered for further spending until you get to a certain accumulated amount, and then you are covered again. The following is an abbreviated version of how Medicare explains the donut hole.

Most Medicare Prescription Drug Plans have a coverage gap (also called the "donut hole"). This means there's a temporary limit on what the drug plan will cover for drugs.

Not everyone will enter the coverage gap. The coverage gap begins after you and your drug plan have spent a certain amount for covered drugs. In 2014, once you and your plan have spent $2,850 on covered drugs (the combined amount plus your deductible), you're in the coverage gap. This amount may change each year—for 2015, you're in the coverage gap once you and your plan have spent $2,960 on covered drugs. Also, people with Medicare who get extra help paying Part D costs won't enter the coverage gap.

Once you reach the coverage gap in 2014, you'll pay 47.5% of the plan's cost for covered brand-name prescription drugs (you'll pay 45% in 2015). You get these savings if you buy your prescriptions at a pharmacy or order them through the mail. The discount will come off of the price that your plans have set with the pharmacy for that specific drug.

Although you'll only pay 47.5% of the price for the brand-name drug in 2014, 97.5% of the price—what you pay plus the 50% manufacturer discount payment—will count as out-of-pocket costs, which will help you get out of the coverage gap. What the drug plan pays toward the drug cost and toward the dispensing fee isn't counted toward your out-of-pocket spending.

In 2014, Medicare will pay 28% of the price for generic drugs during the coverage gap. You'll pay the remaining 72% of the price. What you pay for generic drugs during the coverage gap will decrease each year until it reaches 25% in 2020—in 2015, you'll pay 65% of the price for generic drugs during the coverage gap. The coverage for generic drugs works differently from the discount for brand-name drugs. For generic drugs, only the amount you pay will count toward getting you out of the coverage gap.

If you have a Medicare drug plan that already includes coverage in the gap, you may get a discount after your plan's coverage has been applied to the price of the drug. The discount for brand-name drugs will apply to the remaining amount that you owe. [125]

Government guidelines suggest medical-related explanations should be written at a seventh grade level. The six paragraphs above do not sound like seventh grade level to me. The Agency for Healthcare Research and Quality developed a survey technique to measure a patient's ability to read and pronounce common medical words. In a study of more than 400 patients, the survey results showed that 75% of the patients were at less than a ninth-grade level and 50% were below seventh-grade. This would suggest a major challenge ahead as complex healthcare provisions such as the donut hole are developed which are too complex to be understood.

Explanation of Benefits

An Explanation of Benefits (EOB) is a document your health insurance company sends to you after a healthcare provider has billed them for services provided to you. The EOB purports to explain what was paid and not paid by the insurance company. The EOB sometimes arrives several months after your visit to the provider. I saw a large number of EOBs during the last years of my mother and father's lives. I have received many for me recently. I would not be alone in saying that the EOBs are complicated. However, the EOB usually point out "THIS IS NOT A BILL", and therefore most people probably do not spend a lot of time trying to understand it. There is no motivation to analyze and scrutinize a bill someone else, Medicare and or your private health insurance payer, has paid or is going to pay. This casual attitude is a major problem in healthcare. If a consumer knows someone else is going to pay the bill, there is no incentive to understand or challenge the bill.

After the EOB is received, a bill comes from the provider requesting you to pay the amount your health insurance didn't pay. The following is an extract from the bill I received from my PCP practice after my annual physical examination in June 2014.

DATE	CPT/CODE	DESCRIPTION OF SERVICE	CHARGES	CREDITS	BALANCE
6/23/2014	99397	Preventive, Est. 65 & o	$91.00		
6/23/2014	G0438	Annualwellness visit i	$203.00		
6/23/2014	99214	Office/Outpatient Visit	$171.00		
7/14/2014	891059142	Insurance Payment		$269.50	
7/14/2014	891059142	Insurance Adjustment		$75.84	
7/14/2014	891059142	Insurance Adjustment		$5.50	
7/14/2014	891059142	Insurance Payment		$0.00	
7/14/2014	891059142	Insurance Transfer			
8/11/2014	1155437952	Insurance Payment		$3.16	
8/11/2014	1155437952	Insurance Payment		$0.00	
8/11/2014	1155437952	Insurance Transfer			$111.00

!!!This was a non-covered service per your insurance company. Please remit payment.

The first three lines describe three charges made by the physician. The description of the three items is hardly clear. Recall the hamburger where you knew exactly what you were getting and what it cost. The next items on the bill were insurance adjustments, payments, and transfers. Clear as mud. The last line on the bill showed "This was a non-covered service per your insurance company. Please remit payment." The requested amount was $111.

I called the billing office and asked them what the "this" was that was not covered. She explained that Medicare does not cover the $91 for the preventive health aspect of my physical, plus there is a $20 co-pay. When I asked how I could have been able to get that understanding from the bill, she apologized and said she gets calls all day every day asking for explanations of the bills.

The more I looked into this bill, the more confused I got, but I did learn two things. Medicare does not cover the $91 for preventive care. I visited the Medicare website and found that Medicare does cover the following preventive services and screenings, subject to certain eligibility and other limitations:

➤ Abdominal Aortic Aneurysm Screening
➤ Adult Immunizations

➢ Annual Wellness Visit
➢ Bone Mass Measurements
➢ Cancer Screenings
➢ Cardiovascular Screening
➢ Diabetes Screening
➢ Diabetes Self-Management Training
➢ Diabetes Supplies
➢ Glaucoma Screening
➢ HIV Screening
➢ Initial Preventive Physical Exam
➢ Intensive Behavioral Therapy for Cardiovascular Disease
➢ Intensive Behavioral Therapy for Obesity
➢ Medical Nutrition Therapy
➢ Screening and Behavioral Counseling Interventions
➢ Primary Care to Reduce Alcohol Misuse
➢ Screening for Depression in Adults
➢ Screening for Sexually Transmitted Infections
➢ Tobacco-Use Cessation Counseling Services

The initial preventive physical exam is covered only within 12 months of enrolling in Medicare. The other 19 exams and screenings are covered, but the physical exam, where the doctor examines your body to look for something abnormal, is not covered after the first year. Blood work is not covered either unless it is tied to a specific diagnosis. There may be a rationale for these limitations, but I could not find it, nor could the doctor explain it. The annual wellness visit is covered. The wellness exam includes the basics of blood pressure and weight. There is also a survey the patient completes during the annual visit. Medicare reimburses the physician $203 for a couple of pages of paper the patient fills out about his or her health.

A final source of complexity in the EOBs and bills is IT-related. The first line of the bill contained the following: "Preventive, Est, 65& o". It means preventive care, established patient, 65 and over. The second line contained "Annual wellness visit I". It means Annual Wellness Visit, including personalized prevention plan services. Why are these lines unintelligible? If you count the number of characters in the two lines, you will see they both have exactly 22. Chances are that the software application was based on decades-old technology when data storage was very expensive, and consequently, some of the information fields had to be truncated to conserve space. Storage today is very inexpensive, but someone has to make the decision to upgrade the information along with the technology.

For the provider and the payer, there is only one field of information on the bill which is important, the Current Procedural Terminology (CPT). The CPT code is a medical code set maintained by the American Medical Association through the CPT Editorial Panel. The CPT is how the provider bills and gets paid. Making EOBs and bills readable by consumers is obviously not a priority. The lack of clarity adds to the complexity.

Contrast this complexity with Amazon's simplicity. You can go to My Orders at Amazon and review everything you have bought all the way back to 1995. Not only are the words clear, you can click and get all the detail you want about the transaction. When Medicare or a private payer is covering the bill, the complexity doesn't matter except for the curious. As consumers begin to pay from a health savings account (HSA) or have a large deductible, as more and more people do, the consumer will care about the complexity. Consumers will expect EOBs and bills that are understandable.

Electronic Health Records

Electronic Health Records (EHRs) are part of the healthcare solution set, but also are part of the problem. The problems are discussed in this chapter and the solutions are described later. For consumers, two key problems with EHRs are access and understanding. Providers of EHRs have not done a good job of explaining EHRs. There are multiple similar but unique kinds of EHR including: the EHR, electronic medical record, personal health record, and universal health record. Each has a different purpose and use depending on who is describing them. I use the abbreviation EHR throughout the remainder of the book.

Although EHRs are an important tool, it is not clear whether you should get the tool from your doctor, your hospital, pharmaceutical company, pharmacy, employer, or from an independent source. Any of them can create an EHR for you. A lot of education will be necessary to understand the relative benefits. Access to an EHR for most people will be through patient portals created by hospitals or physician practices.

The New York Times published a story in January 2013 "In Second Look, Few Savings From Digital Health Records".[126] The article said that companies providing

EHR software and services funded a prestigious study in 2005, which forecasted significant savings from EHRs thereby suggesting a conflict of interest. Eight years later, the same prestigious study group said savings have not been realized.

Both the Obama and the Bush administrations believed electronic medical records could provide many benefits for patients and healthcare providers. Policymakers developing the healthcare reform legislation recognized EHR benefits would materialize only if the EHRs were used in a meaningful way. The policymakers developed a set of standards, defined by The Centers, called meaningful use. Significant financial incentives were offered to healthcare providers who met the meaningful use criteria. Even a small hospital could earn millions of dollars if they met the meaningful use targets by a certain date.

Responsible healthcare executives made achieving meaningful use standards a top priority. If the team developed the comprehensive planning needed to ensure optimum implementation and maximum savings but missed the target date specified for meaningful use incentives to be earned, they would be leaving a lot of money on the table. The government incentives resulted in the desired acceleration of EHR implementations but not necessarily the cost savings expected. Some implementations were technically achieved on time but were not thoroughly tested. Clinicians and patients were not ready either. Although projected savings were missed and implementations were not as smooth as they should have been, the foundations were put in place to leverage the value of EHRs in the future.

Recently a physician friend and I discussed a broad range of healthcare issues, including the status of EHRs. We had both seen the *USA Today* article written by Dr. Kevin Pho, who presented a negative view of using EHRs.[127] Dr. Pho's main point was filling out electronic forms takes time away from the patient. I have experienced this from the patient perspective. It is frustrating to sit next to a doctor who never looks at you because he is too busy entering data. The time consuming data entry task certainly detracts from the positive potential of EHRs, but it should not deter patients or doctors from embracing them.

The time consuming nature of data entry is real for physicians. Medscape reported a survey from the American College of Physicians revealed, "As more and more physicians adopt EHR systems, they like them less and less."[128] Physicians not only find the data entry task demeaning, but also they have not been convinced of the benefits.

Most doctors do not find the EHR software intuitive or easy to use. The focus of the software design taken by the EHR vendors was to assure compliance with the meaningful use criteria set out by the government, not necessarily to make it easy to use. Using the EHR software can be tedious. It is especially laborious and time consuming during the transition from paper records to electronic records.

One of the solutions to the physician data entry problem is the use of scribes. A scribe is a low-level administrative assistant who is present with the doctor, and enters the data spoken by the doctor. This may make sense in an ER setting, but in the privacy of a physician examining room, it is a different story. Patients may not be comfortable fully describing symptoms or concerns with a stranger, the scribe, in the room. Technology can offer a much better solution than scribes. In particular, voice recognition and dictation systems will make it possible for doctors to talk to the EHR instead of typing or using a scribe.

Patient Portals

The federal government incentives for meaningful use continue to drive rapid, but not necessarily effective, implementations of EHR systems. July 1, 2014 was a cutoff date to receive certain incentives. There was a rush to get the new systems up and running – ready or not! My primary care physician is part of a large family medicine practice. It adopted a patient portal provided by Allscripts, one of the leading healthcare software vendors. The portal is called FollowMyHealth. I found it easy to enroll. All information entered by the physician appears in the portal, including test results. The patient can enter her or his own information, such as a lab report from another provider, a history of prior surgeries, or anything he or she chooses. The tagline under FollowMyHealth is Universal Health Record, but they don't explain what it means. It is presumed to mean information entered by your physician and yourself. Another assumption is you can choose to share the information with other providers or not. However, it is not straightforward, as I will explain.

A month after joining the portal provided by my PCP, I was in the hospital for some surgery. When I was discharged, I was invited to join the hospital portal. The hospital had rushed to meet the Federal deadline, and the portal was not quite ready for prime time. I found it difficult to enroll and once I had, the portal was empty! A few weeks later, I found the hospital and my PCP used the same Allscripts portal software. There was some overlap between the two systems. Once the confusion was straightened out, I found logging into the FollowMyHealth portal, I could access doctor and hospital provided information and link to other physician practices which used Allscripts software. That is the good news.

The bad news is some physician providers use portal software provided by vendors other than Allscripts. I next joined a portal provided by a specialist practice using software from eClinicalWorks. The eClinicalWorks portal refers to their EHR as a personal health record. While my primary care physician and the hospital upload all lab results to their portals, the specialist practice decided not to upload lab results to their portal. They feel doing so would result in a lot of phone calls from patients. In effect they said test results are theirs, not yours. They will tell you what you need to know. This despite the fact it is the patient's body or blood imaged or tested. It was the patient or payer who paid for the imaging or laboratory work. Ownership of health data will emerge as a major issue in the future of healthcare.

The complexity continues. I had a test ordered by the specialist practice, and I wanted to read it. I completely trust the specialist and I know they will review the results for me, but I still wanted a copy for myself. The specialist does not upload the results to the portal, but they do provide a copy to the PCP. Before I got a chance to ask the specialist to send me a copy of the test results, I got a call from my PCP. He explained his interpretation of the results and told me he had uploaded the report to the FollowMyHealth portal, and I could read it there. That is what he thought, but it turned out not to be true. The way the PCP portal is set up allows patient access only to those reports ordered by the PCP. Since the specialist had ordered the test, I could not access it. I subsequently got a copy faxed from the specialist.

The patient portal complexity I have described so far is based on my three portals: PCP, hospital, and specialist. Medicare beneficiaries see an average of 13 physicians. If a patient is lucky, some of the providers will be sharing the same type of portal as my PCP and the hospital, but surely all of them will not. Each type of portal has its own EHR moniker, different functionality, and different terminology throughout the portal. Some portals allow the patient to reply to a message sent by a provider and some do not. Some upload all test results and some do not. Some allow prescription refill and appointment requests and some do not. If a patient should get a relevant medical report from someone outside the normal provider network, and they want to share it with the local team, to which portal do they upload it?

Another factor adding to the complexity of using the EHR further is travel away from home. Increasingly, older adults take extended vacations, spend time in a second home, or travel out of the country. If a New York resident is in Florida for the winter and becomes ill, will their physician in Florida have access to their EHR in New York? At present, the answer is probably not. The solution for now is phone calls and faxes. Software interchanges linking incompatible portals through health information exchanges have been around for more than a decade but none have been highly successful.

Summary

The complexity of signing up for health insurance, deciphering prescription drug plans, understanding healthcare bills, and using EHRs and patient portals not only adds cost to the system, but also creates a lack of confidence in our healthcare system. Physicians and patients are frustrated. There has to be a better way, and there is. After discussing quality and patient safety in the next chapter, I will describe attitudes and technology that can be part of the solutions.

CHAPTER 6

Quality and Patient Safety

Q uality and patient safety are the most important elements of healthcare. Hospitals can be dangerous places to visit. Thousands of people die each year as a result of medical errors. Patients can get infections or receive other forms of harm inside the place they went for treatment. Unfortunately, our complex and costly system of healthcare does not produce better outcomes for Americans compared to those in other developed countries. I will review how we stack up globally and then take a closer look at some of the most significant quality and patient safety issues in hospitals.

Comparison of Quality

According to the *World Fact Book*, the United States ranks 42nd out of 223 countries with an average life expectancy of 79.6. Countries with longer life expectancy include Japan (84.5), Singapore (84.4), Hong Kong (82.8), Switzerland (82.4), Australia (82.1), Italy (82.0), Sweden (81.9), Canada (81.7), France (81.7), Norway (81.6), Spain (81.5), Germany (80.4), the United Kingdom (80.4), and South Korea (79.8).[129]

According to the World Health Education Initiative, Americans are not enjoying good health compared to people in other industrialized nations.[130] The U.S. was ranked the 12th lowest out of 13 countries based on 16 health indicators including life expectancy and infant mortality. The mortality rate in the U.S. is high. Studies have shown American deaths, ranging up to 225,000, were caused by unnecessary surgery, medication errors in hospitals, hospital-acquired infections, and the negative effects of drugs. Barbara Starfield, a pediatrician at Johns Hopkins University, was an advocate for better healthcare worldwide. She concluded that America's healthcare system is the third leading cause of death in the United States, after heart disease and cancer.[131]

Patient Safety

The Institute of Medicine (IOM) published *To Err is Human: Building a Safer Health System* in 1999. The book's finding from two major studies was between 44,000 and 98,000 people die each in hospitals from preventable medical errors.[132] The report made major headlines, dropped a bomb on the medical community, and set off congressional and public debates about what to do.

Patient safety and quality initiatives were put in place following the recommendations of the IOM report, but five years later, Robert Wachter at the University of California in San Francisco authored "The End Of The Beginning: Patient Safety Five Years After 'To Err Is Human'", which was published in *Health Affairs*.[133] Wachter said that since 1999 there was some progress, but it was insufficient. Stronger regulation, improvements in information technology, and workforce training had helped, but error-reporting systems had little impact, and unfortunately, there was no progress in improving accountability. Wachter's pessimistic study caused him to describe the patient safety and quality status as "the end of the beginning."[134]

Preventable medical errors take a significant toll in addition to the cost in human lives. Not only do errors cost tens of billions of dollars, but also they shake trust and confidence in the healthcare system. In cases where errors cause a long hospital stay or disability, patients pay with physical and psychological discomfort. Health professionals pay too, with negative morale and frustration at not having provided the best care possible and a positive outcome. Society as a whole incurs lost productivity and a lower level of population health.

Medication and Surgical Errors

The IOM highlighted errors in many different areas in healthcare treatment. There were errors or delays in diagnosis. Providers skipped some prescribed tests.

Outmoded tests or therapies were used, and there was a failure to act on results of monitoring or testing. Errors were made in the performance of an operation, procedure, or test, and there were errors in the dose or method of using a drug. Avoidable delays occurred in treatment or in responding to an abnormal test. Finally, there were many failures of communication.

More than ten years later, in 2010, the Office of Inspector General for the Department of Health and Human Services said that 180,000 Medicare patients died in a given year as a result of inept hospital care.[135] Unfortunately, the story gets worse, not better. Using significantly more current data from numerous studies, the *Journal of Patient Safety* reported the true number of premature deaths associated with preventable harm to patients was more than 400,000 per year, and serious harm is 10 to 20 times more common than lethal harm.[136] Although there was some disbelief in the IOM number of 98,000 published a decade earlier, Marshall Allen wrote in "How Many Die from Medical Mistakes in U.S. Hospitals?" a spokesman for the American Hospital Association has more confidence in the 98,000 estimate.[137] ProPublica, an independent, non-profit newsroom that produces investigative journalism in the public interest, asked three prominent patient safety researchers to review the *Journal of Patient Safety* study, and all three said that the study findings were credible.

In all of the studies, researchers used samples of medical records and then applied statistical techniques to extrapolate what was found in the samples to the entire population of hospital patients. There is room for debate about what the right number is. But, there is no debate, even if the smaller numbers are correct, thousands of deaths due to unintentional medical errors is unacceptable.

For example, a 50 year old woman was hospitalized after taking Flomax, used to treat men with symptoms of an enlarged prostate, instead of Volmax, used to relieve bronchospasm. A 19 year old man showed signs of potentially fatal complications after he was given clozapine instead of olanzapine, two drugs used to treat schizophrenia. Unfortunately, there are many drugs that have similar sounding names, and may have not only different purposes, but also orders of magnitude differences in dosage. At least one and one-half million preventable adverse drug events occur in our healthcare system every year, resulting in hundreds of thousands of injuries and deaths.[138]

Although e-prescribing is gaining rapidly due to government incentives, millions of prescriptions are still scribbled on a piece of paper. Patients take the script to a pharmacy where different situations can arise. One scenario is the prescription is unreadable so the pharmacist calls the physician's office for clarification. A deadlier scenario is the prescription is unreadable and the pharmacist guesses what he thinks was intended. Sometimes, the guess is wrong, resulting in the untimely death of a patient.

Physicians perform more than 48 million inpatient surgical procedures and more than 53 million ambulatory procedures annually in the United States.[139] The majority are safe and improve the quality of life for patients. However, errors and adverse events occur in multiple areas including performance of the wrong procedure, malfunction of equipment, administration of an antibiotic despite a noted allergy, nerve damage related to positioning, implantation of non-sterile devices, post-operative deep vein thrombus, retained devices or sponges, and wrong site surgery.[140]

It is hard to imagine how a surgery could result in the amputation of the wrong limb or the wrong hip is opened for a replacement, but such adverse events occur 2,700 times per year.[141] When I had my right knee joint replaced in 2009, I was not only asked to confirm multiple times which knee I was having replaced, but handed a magic marker and asked to place an X on the target knee. Imagine how a 90 year old patient with Alzheimer's disease and no caregiver to provide assistance can answer those questions. A surgeon may consult an image and depend on an R or L on the bottom of the image which was reversed during the imaging process. By the time a patient is in the operating room, it becomes a hectic place. A lot of information is exchanged among multiple participants and the possibility of significant distractions can occur at any time.

Medical Devices

The United States is the largest medical device producer in the world with a market size of approximately $110 billion, and it is expected to reach $133 billion by 2016.[142] Medical devices perform previously impossible tasks for patients, but they are not always perfect. If you use a computer or a smartphone, you know electronic devices can make errors. The same thing is true for medical devices. For example, a ventilator might shut off without warning and without sounding an alarm due to a flaw in the underlying software. A nurse may hear an alarm but assume it is the alarm for the warming blanket and may delay checking to see if there is a problem. The ventilator alarm sounds exactly like the alarm on the warming blanket. The consequences can be fatal.[143]

Of the thousands of medical devices in use, most are beneficial to consumers, but where pre-market evaluations and post-market surveillance were inadequate, significant harm can be done. Medtronic, a Minneapolis device maker, introduced the Sprint Fidelis implantable cardioverter-defibrillator lead. The FDA approved the device in 2004, and more than 268,000 of them were implanted in patients around the world.[144] Three years after the device's approval, independent cardiologists discovered the device had a propensity to fracture. Several deaths were attributed to the device failure, and Medtronic recalled it.[145] The consumers who had the implant were left with two very unpleasant choices: pursue a risky surgical removal of the device, or live with the uncertainty of death if the device should fail. The Sprint Fidelis tragedy highlights the need for thorough testing before approval and a transparent reporting system for devices in current use.

Hospital Acquired Conditions

A hospital-acquired condition (HAC) is one that could have been prevented and occurs after a patient is admitted to the hospital. The most common example of an HAC is a hospital-acquired infection, an infection the patient contracted in the hospital. Consumers generally are not aware of HACs, but researchers are extremely interested. Upon searching ProQuest, a database of six billion digital pages from the world's most important scholarly journals, dissertations, and periodicals; for hospital-acquired conditions, I found nearly 40,000 relevant peer-reviewed journal articles. This is an indication of how important researchers think HACs are to the cost of care and the outcomes for patients.

The Centers defined two-dozen HACs including retention of foreign objects such as sponges or instruments inside a patient after surgery, air embolisms caused from injections, use of incompatible blood, pressure ulcers from being in a bed in the same position for too long, falls, burns, hypoglycemic coma from not managing glucose level properly, catheter-associated urinary tract infections, infections from surgery, deep vein thrombosis, and a number of other more complicated conditions.[146] These conditions are serious and can lead to pain, suffering, and even death. The common link of these serious HACs is they can occur after being admitted to the hospital. It is reasonable for people to expect they can go to the hospital to become cured of some acute condition, while in fact many go for routine treatment and end up getting an HAC that is worse than what brought them to the hospital.

The Centers, conforming to a mandate from Congress, implemented financial penalties by refusing to pay a hospital for the additional treatment needed because of an HAC. However, a study of 398 hospitals published in *The New England Journal of Medicine* found that the penalties had no effect on the occurrence of HACs.[147]

The magnitude of HACs is staggering. Just the five most common infections patients get after being admitted to the hospital cost the U.S. healthcare system almost $10 billion a year. Five percent of patients admitted to the hospital become a victim to a serious infection. Researchers have estimated half of the infections were preventable.[148]

Need for Transparency

More transparency about HACs is needed to ensure the public and regulators know how many serious incidents occur. Consider the aviation industry. Even the slightest incident, like a wing hitting a hangar door or a non-essential electronic component in the cockpit failing, must be reported to the FAA. Consumers can see the safety record of every airline in the world on various websites, and the National Transportation Safety Bureau has a publicly available database of every civil aviation accident since 1962.[149]

Summary

The United States has some of the greatest healthcare providers in the world, significant pharmaceutical innovation, outstanding medical education programs, and contributions of globally recognized clinical research. Nevertheless, healthcare outcomes could be better and safer. Fortunately, reform is underway to create more transparency of patient safety data, better coordination across the continuum of care, a focus on quality, and a shift from entitlement oriented, fee for service to accountability oriented, fee for value. Technology is emerging to provide more engagement for consumers and better tools for providers.

Part Three

Solutions for Consumers and Providers

CHAPTER 7

Consumer Initiated Health Attitude

C onsumer attitudes about their healthcare are beginning to shift. I will discuss the rapid adoption of mobile health apps and devices and the role of cloud computing in healthcare. I will discuss the advent of self diagnosis, its risks and rewards.

The only healthcare products or services my 89 year old mother used were the ones her doctor told her she needed. Her attitude was seeking healthcare products or services was not her responsibility. It was the doctor's responsibility. Among her generation, doctors were revered and never were challenged or even questioned. Mom would see the doctor, the doctor would prescribe healthcare products or services, the healthcare providers would deliver the products and services, and someone either public or private would pay for them. That was how it was. As pointed out in Chapter 3, the model is unaffordable. An affordable healthcare model will require a health attitude change on the part of consumers, providers, and payers.

Consumers

The generations following Mom see their health responsibility quite differently and with a proactive attitude. They not only don't wait for providers to tell them what to do, but also tell healthcare providers what they want. Jeff Munn wrote in "Looking Beyond Health Reform: The Future of Consumer-Focused Health Care" a consumer-driven model for healthcare products is here to stay and will increase dramatically in the years ahead.[150] Consumer expectations for healthcare are changing.

The types of services demanded by patients follow a pattern similar to Maslow's hierarchy of needs. These include following a progression including physiological, safety, love and belonging, esteem, and self-actualization.[151] Similarly, there is a range of needs in healthcare. If there is an emergency, then consumers expect the ER to have the necessary services. If a surgical procedure is recommended, then consumers expect high quality service with a good outcome. In the future, consumers will expect genetic analysis including a projection of disease that is likely to develop and what to do to prevent it.

Many hospitals already do an excellent job of providing high quality emergency and surgical services and meeting the needs of consumers. The providers may receive high ratings for what they deliver, but consumers will expect more. Genetic research is being done by major hospitals in search of certain cancer cures. Consumers will expect genetic analysis as a routine part of their care, not just for research. President Obama's 2015 call for 1 million volunteers to have their genes sequenced is just the beginning.

The Joint Center for Cancer Precision Medicine, a collaborative initiative among Dana-Farber Cancer Institute, Brigham and Women's Hospital, Boston Children's Hospital, and the Broad Institute of MIT and Harvard are developing a new way of practicing cancer medicine. Rather than treating all patients with a particular type of cancer in the same way, the scientists at the new center study the DNA, RNA, and protein from individual biopsy samples to determine how cancers will respond to typical cancer drugs physicians prescribed.[152] Some patients may respond very well to a certain cancer drug while others may respond poorly. By knowing which response a patient may have, the pain and suffering of side effects can be avoided when the genetic analysis suggests the drug would provide no benefit to the patient.

The Joint Center is deploying state-of-the-art capabilities including "DNA sequencing and other tumor molecular profiling technologies, pathology, radiology, surgery, computational interpretation, and new tumor model systems, which are not available at most hospitals."[153] The genetic analysis performed at the center is utilizing the skills of biologists, bioinformaticians, and software engineers to develop new algorithms for processing and interpreting the gene sequencing data with the goal of directly applying the results to individual patients. While what Dana-Farber is doing may sound more like research than patient care, it will not be long before patients will expect such interventions. Providers will develop such capabilities as a competitive differentiator in their market.[154]

Healthcare Information

People's attitudes on healthcare are shifting and they are accepting more responsibility for their health. People also are collecting data related to their health. A study about migraine headaches published in *Neurology* more than a dozen years ago established the principle that keeping notes on one's health is a good tool for improving it.[155] Tracking one's health today is becoming a part of our daily lives.

The Pew Research Center's Internet & American Life Project performs surveys to study the evolution of the Internet, how Americans use the Internet, and how their online activities affect their lives.[156] In a January 2013 report, "Tracking for Health", Pew Research said that 69% of adults keep track of at least one health indicator. The survey of 3,014 adults indicated 60% tracked weight, diet, or exercise. Thirty-three percent tracked blood pressure, sleep patterns, headaches, or other healthcare indicators. Twelve percent tracked a health indicator for a loved one.

Exercise Tracking

One of the easiest health related measurements to track is the number of steps taken while walking or miles run. For athletes tracking may be essential for training, but exercise is important for everyone. Mechanical pedometers have been around for many years. The advent of electronic accelerometers silently and accurately counting each step we take and each stair we climb can be embedded in very small devices. Fitbit and Jawbone devices have made tracking really simple. A device in your pocket, clipped to your clothing, or worn on your wrist can count each step and report the results to your smartphone. The smartphone then updates the results in your fitness database in the cloud. Users can set goals, join groups, share their results, and receive email awards and motivational messages.

Apple has taken exercise tracking to another level by incorporating a motion coprocessor chip in its iPhone 6 and iPhone 6 Plus. The new M8 chip continuously measures motion data using its accelerometer, compass, gyroscope, and barometer.

The sensors automatically measure your steps, distance, and changes in elevation. Apple iPhones include a built-in Health app. An app is the abbreviated name for a computer software application. The Health app is a built-in companion to the calendar, messages, reminders, mail, address book, and other apps that are part of the operating system of iPhones and iPads. Third-party apps can build upon the basic measurement of steps and distance. For example, the MapMyWalk fitness app draws a map of where you walk or run. The app saves the route so you can take the same route in the future or share the route with friends. The log in MapMyWalk shows a cross-section of the elevation you encountered during the exercise. At each mile, a voice announces your distance, cumulative pace, and your split pace.

In "Exercise: Seven Benefits of Regular Physical Activity", Mayo Clinic suggests exercise is better for you than you think. It says, "From boosting your mood to improving your sex life, exercise can improve your life."[157] Mayo Clinic outlines specific benefits saying that exercise controls weight, combats health conditions and diseases, improves mood, boosts energy, promotes better sleep, puts the spark back into your sex life, and can be fun.

Mobile Health

Although exercise is irrefutably important in our lives, mHealth can provide assistance in many more ways. As important as recording steps and miles are, they represent the tip of the iceberg of healthcare data consumers will be collecting. An explosion of healthcare related devices connected to smartphones is enabling a consumer-led revolution in healthcare. The National Institute for Health (NIH) has defined the burgeoning area as mHealth, the use of mobile and wireless devices to improve health outcomes, healthcare services, and health research.

According to the Healthcare Information and Management Systems Society, health, fitness, and technology companies are marketing more than 40,000 health-related apps. Many of these apps will work in conjunction with HealthKit, Apple's foray into the healthcare space announced as part of its newest line of iPhones. The concept behind HealthKit is to provide a repository for the storage of not only steps and miles, but sixty different types of data such as respiration rate, cholesterol, blood glucose, body temperature, weight, body mass index (BMI), oxygen saturation, sleep analysis, and nutrition. Apple has given technical details about HealthKit to app developers so they can create apps that store data in the Apple repository. For example, an app might connect a body temperature sensor via

Bluetooth to the iPhone and transfer the date, time, and temperature into the HealthKit repository. A consumer may have dozens of apps that are collecting data and placing it in the iPhone or iPad Health app.

Apple's vision does not stop there. Using rigorous security techniques, the Health app can allow data to be shared with friends, family, physicians, and research databases. The consumer will have complete control over who can see what and whether it is a one-time look or continual access. When a physician orders a lab test or imaging study, the results will be returned directly to an app on the consumer's iPhone. Consumers will be able to see statistical analysis and graphs of their health data. Apple is negotiating with major healthcare providers such as Athenahealth, Cerner, Kaiser Permanente, Mayo Clinic, and EHR providers such as Epic and Allscripts to help them use HealthKit to integrate their systems with the Health app. In effect, Apple is putting itself in the position of a conduit through which vast amounts of health data will flow between consumers, physicians, hospitals, medical device manufacturers, laboratories, and healthcare software providers.

The risk to Apple's brand is significant if security is not ironclad, but if Apple is successful, it could give them a significant advantage as the mobile device maker of choice. For consumers, it has the potential to empower them to manage their health and use the healthcare system more effectively.

Personal Supercomputers

In 1976, Seymour Cray introduced the first supercomputer, the Cray-1. The term supercomputer meant it was the most powerful computer at the time. As for the Cray-1, it was super in many respects. It cost $5-$10 million, weighed more than 5 tons, and used as much electricity as ten homes. Super as it was, the Cray-1 had no app store, could not play a song, or even make a phone call. Scientists and researchers embraced the Cray-1 because it enabled them to perform scientific simulations and explore data at a speed not previously possible. In total, the Cray-1 sold less than 100 supercomputers.

Fast-forward 39 years from the introduction of the Cray-1 to Apple's iPhone 5S and iPhone 6 Plus. These devices are more than 100 times more powerful than the Cray-1 in every respect, and hundreds of millions of people around the world carry them in their pocket or purse. The iPhone 6 may make the S in 5S stand for slowpoke. The iPhone 5S has a processing chip called the A7 that set a new level of performance. The iPhone 6 has a new chip called the A8 that includes more than two billion transistors and even is faster. In addition to the Apple A7 supercomputer chip, the iPhone 5S includes a second chip called the M7, and the iPhone 6 and 6 Plus have an M8. The M stands for motion and the chip is able to determine if you are moving, how fast you are moving, your latitude and longitude, direction of travel, your pace, and the barometric pressure to determine your altitude. The iPhones and iPads we take for granted are truly supercomputers. I call them personal supercomputers and will take the liberty to label them as PSCs.

Apple is not the only manufacturer of PSCs, but the company focus on healthcare and the introduction of the HealthKit are particularly relevant to *Health Attitude*. We will see an amazing growth of apps to take advantage of the iPhone's features and performance. IBM and Apple have announced a strategic partnership to focus on healthcare and other important industry segments. Analysts expect IBM will develop over 100 apps focused on healthcare.

PSC Apps and Devices

The availability of mHealth apps can help consumers to proactively manage their health and wellness. The mHealth apps can promote healthy living, and gain access to a plethora of useful information whenever they want and on whatever device they want to use to retrieve it. Innovators are developing new mHealth apps and devices at a frenetic pace. Consumers have a healthy attitude about adopting them. According to industry estimates cited by the FDA, 500 million smartphone users worldwide will be using a healthcare application in 2015, and by 2018, 50% of the more than 3.4 billion smartphone and tablet users including healthcare professionals, consumers, and patients, will have downloaded mobile health applications.[158] As consumers adopt mHealth devices, they will be performing tests at a much lower cost than traditional laboratories.

The term regulation is anathema to many technology innovators who fear the bureaucrats will inhibit getting new ideas to market. When it comes to healthcare, regulation is a different story. The FDA sees the widespread adoption and use of mobile technologies as creating new ways to improve health and the delivery of healthcare services. The key to determining if a smartphone app or attachment should be subject to regulation is based on whether or not they are classified as devices. The FDA defines a medical device as one used as an accessory to a regulated medical device, or that transforms a mobile platform into a regulated medical device. Through 2013, the FDA has approved more than 100 such devices, and as of the middle of September 2014, the agency approved 23 additional devices.[159] The paragraphs that follow describe some mHealth apps and devices, some of which are not approved by the FDA.

AliveCor. The AliveCor is an FDA approved heart monitor which attaches to the back of an iPhone. The consumer simply holds two fingers from each hand on the back of the iPhone, and in 30 seconds, the AliveCor device takes the equivalent of a single-lead electrocardiogram (ECG). The device saves the ECG data in the iPhone and the app allows the consumer to annotate, store, display, and share the ECG data with a doctor. AliveCor claims clinical studies demonstrated the AliveCor Heart Monitor's accuracy to be comparable to readings from Lead 1 of standard ECG machines, but at a fraction of the cost.[160] The ease of use and lack of potentially irritating sensors attached to the skin will be appealing to consumers. AliveCor received FDA approval in September 2014 to extend the basic ECG to detect atrial fibrillation, a condition presenting a major risk for stroke.

Dr. Eric Topol, author of *The Creative Destruction of Medicine: How The Digital Revolution Will Create Better Health Care*, said that 75% of monitoring performed in the doctor's office or hospital could be eliminated with smartphone devices such as the AliveCor Heart Monitor.[161] Steven G. Burrill said that the rapid growth of such devices might bend the healthcare cost curve favorably.[162]

The CellScope Oto. My four children and six grandchildren's ear infections required many hours in the doctor's offices. Ear infection, or otitis media, is the most common diagnosis in preschoolers and affects 75% of children by age six. In the United States, the disease results in 30 million physician visits per year.[163] The doctor visit and follow-up care add billions of dollars to the cost of healthcare.

Enter the CellScope Oto, a new consumer device turning an iPhone into an ear-inspecting otoscope.[164] A simple clip-on attachment puts a scope over the iPhone's camera lens and enables it to take pictures of a child's ear canal. The accompanying app magnifies the image and sends it to a pediatrician who can study it remotely. Taking pictures daily could allow the physician to monitor progress and potentially avoid unnecessary antibiotics, which could help reduce cost and the risk of antibiotic resistance. With the power of the PSC, the analysis of the photo will ultimately be done in the smartphone with the diagnosis merely corroborated with the doctor. Parents will save many trips to the doctor's office.

Cholesterol Application for Rapid Diagnostics. Some apps can take photos to a new level and leverage the power of the mobile PSC. A team of engineers at Cornell University has developed the smartphone Cholesterol Application for Rapid Diagnostics (SmartCARD).[165] A consumer can extract a single drop of blood and place it onto a small paper strip whey they then insert the strip into a slot in the SmartCARD attachment to the iPhone. The camera takes a photo of the strip and the PSC performs a colorimetric analysis displaying your cholesterol level in a matter of seconds. Not only could such an mHealth device and app save millions of dollars of laboratory blood tests, but they also could enable a consumer to better manage their cholesterol level and determine the effectiveness of dietary changes. A more frequent test, rather than as part of an annual medical examination, could enable better cholesterol management by the consumer. The new app is not yet commercially available but, when it is, it will probably include the differentiation between "good" and "bad" lipids, just like the labs do.

Propeller. More than 50 million people are affected by either asthma or chronic obstructive pulmonary disease. Many of those affected use inhalers when they experience symptoms resulting in swollen airways making it difficult to breathe. The propeller device is a sensor, which connects to a smart inhaler. The inhaler reports the latitude and longitude at the time of an inhalation.[166] The FDA approved the Propeller inhaler in September 2014 for both diseases.

Propeller Health worked with data scientists from IBM to collect data from consumers with asthma. The data was supplemented with data about weather and air quality. This allowed researchers and IBM to develop maps of where the conditions are most hazardous for asthma patients so they can avoid such locations.

Lumoback. I met Dr. Charles Wang, a young physician with an MBA who has a great vision for using mobile technology to address back pain at the Demo conference in San Jose. Dr. Wang developed a concept to use a stick-on sensor similar to a Band-Aid you place on your back. The sensor can tell when you are following good posture or when you are slouching. The sensor sends data to your mobile phone and an app alerts you to your bad posture and keeps track of your habits. The theory is looking at the data with your app will lead you to more healthy habits and less back pain. The FDA approved device lists for $149.

Cue. Since the iPhone has the power of a supercomputer, it is going to be the host for a wide range of healthcare related consumer devices and related apps. One of the latest comes from a San Diego startup named Cue. The company has developed a compact, consumer-oriented device which can detect five biological conditions at a molecular level. This is not a fitness tracker. To the contrary, the compact and simplistic looking device is a mini-laboratory that has been years in the making. With a simple nasal swab and insertion into the Cue device, the biological data is transferred to your iPhone and then compared with data from the Cue cloud to determine recommended dietary or other actions.[167]

When Cue launches in summer 2015, it will have five tests available:

1. Inflammation: The cue can detect the level of C-reactive protein, a commonly used marker of inflammation. Based on the level of the marker, a consumer may get suggestions on how to optimize workouts, speed up recovery, and maintain a healthy heart.

2. Vitamin D: Vitamin D, often called the "sunshine vitamin", is a hormone produced by the body when the skin absorbs sunlight. Cue suggestions might include spending more or less time in the sun to achieve well-balanced health.

3. Fertility: Cue says that tracking the detected level of Luteinizing Hormone is the best tool to determine the ideal time to conceive a child. The device helps women track the hormone level as an indicator of fertility trends, and Cue can recommend food choices that are claimed to support fertility. Cue will provide alerts when the hormone level is at an optimum time for conception.

4. Influenza: Cue detection of flu can find an early warning that can enable you to see a doctor early and get an appropriate treatment alert.

5. Testosterone: Testosterone is an essential hormone for health and well-being as well as the prevention of osteoporosis.[168] Cue claims its recommendations can help you plan exercise, training, and diet that can boost your natural testosterone levels.

In 2015, the Cue device is expected to retail for $199. It is considered a "consumer health product" at this stage, but the company is hoping for an FDA approval so that it can join the growing list of consumer medical devices.

World's Smartest Thermometer. Kinsa has received FDA approval for an innovative thermometer they call the world's smartest. The thin and flexible device plugs into the audio jack of an iPhone or Android smartphone. The senor end of the thermometer can be used orally, under the arm, or rectally. The engaging screen from the app may make it easier to take the temperature of a fidgety and sick child. Like other mHealth apps, the device information is recorded in the smartphone, and in the case of the iPhone, in the Health app. When you are at the pediatrician's office, you can tell him or her exactly when and how your child's symptoms began by pulling out your phone. The app accommodates individual profiles for each family member and tracks illness history. The Kinsa thermometer became available in 2014 for $29.99.

HomeLink. Alere Connect, formerly known as MedApps, received FDA approval for its HomeLink, a hub that connects to blood pressure monitors, pulse oximeters, glucose meters, and weight scales via USB or Bluetooth. Both connection methods are available on nearly all personal computers. The HomeLink hub transmits the data collected from the consumer by the individual devices to an alarm center or healthcare provider using a cellular radio link.[169] The advantage of this approach is it simplifies data transmission for consumers that may not have broadband Internet service or do not have the skills to connect the hub to a local area network in the house.

QardioArm. QardioArm is an FDA approved smart blood pressure monitor which measures your systolic/diastolic blood pressure and heart rate. The wireless monitor design makes it light, compact, and portable. In addition to blood pressure and heart rate, the device can detect an irregular heartbeat. QardioArm claims to have a proprietary relaxation function and multi-measurement averaging feature allowing greater accuracy.[170] The device turns on when you unwrap it and it connects to your smartphone with Bluetooth. After you put the device around your arm and press the start button, all readings are automatically recorded and uploaded to Qardio's secure cloud. You then can share your data as you see fit with your family, friends, or doctor. I anticipate Qardio will use HealthKit to develop the interface to Apple's Health app.

Otoharmonics. Otoharmonics, a startup supported by Cedars-Sinai Medical Center, received FDA clearance for an iPad and iPod Touch app which treats a medical condition called tinnitus.[171] Tinnitus is a condition with which I can identify because I have had it since 1985. I still remember the pleasant day in November when I was blowing leaves from my property. Ear protection was not commonplace back then. I was using a backpack-style leaf blower for more than two hours until the blower ran out of gas. At that moment I heard loud ringing in my ears like what one experiences when hearing a loud noise such as a gunshot. The ringing in both of my ears has continued 24x7 since then.

Subjective tinnitus is the perception of a sound within the ear that cannot be heard by others. Although tinnitus is usually described as 'ringing in the ears', the variety of sounds and combinations people perceive are as widespread as the condition. Some people get tinnitus from too much loud music, some from war-zone military service, and some from excessive noise in the workplace. Regardless of how it begins and what it sounds like, tinnitus can range from mildly bothersome to debilitation. There is no cure for tinnitus, but Otoharmonics has developed an mHealth app called the Levo System that may provide relief. Using an iPad app, a hearing practitioner works with you to determine the pattern of sound you experience. He or she then prepares a proprietary set of sound patterns and puts them on an iPod Touch outfitted with custom made ear buds. You take the iPod home and sleep with the sound patterns. Feedback to the practitioner allows for incremental changes and improvements over time.

Gmate Smart Glucometer. A glucose meter, glucometer, is a medical device for determining the approximate concentration of glucose in the blood.[172] The glucometer is a key element of home blood glucose monitoring for people with diabetes mellitus or hypoglycemia. The consumer places a drop of blood, obtained by pricking the skin with a lancet, on a disposable test strip the meter reads, calculates the blood glucose level, and displays the result.

New York City based medical device maker Philosys has received FDA approval for its Gmate Smart glucometer, which consumers plug into the audio jack of an iPhone and launch the Gmate Smart app. One of the advantages over the traditional glucometer is with each use of the app, the consumer can add supplementary notes to the reading such as nutrition or fitness data, or medication information. The app has a log of prior readings and can display averages over 1, 7, 14, 30, and 60-day periods. The Apple Health app will accommodate glucometer data, and it is likely Philosys will update their app with HealthKit.

Eko Devices. Connor Landsgraf, CEO of a San Francisco startup Eko Devices, believes it is time to upgrade the stethoscope, which he pointed out has not changed since the 1880s.[173] He claims many physicians do not get adequate training on how to interpret the sounds they hear with a classic stethoscope. He says the result is "rampant misdiagnosis".[174] Eko is developing a computerized insert for stethoscopes which is not approved by the FDA. The insert will provide data from the stethoscope to a PSC, which can then analyze the data and compare it with cloud based sound patterns representing various conditions. The goal is to help physicians make data-driven decisions resulting in improved patient outcomes.

iDoc24. mHealth apps can provide standalone monitoring or testing, or experts can supplement data the apps collect. Another San Francisco startup, iDoc24, offers a dermatology app that allows patients and caregivers to send images of skin conditions to its staff of dermatologists who, for $25, will diagnose your condition and prescribe medications. Pictures of skin conditions can be submitted anonymously and iDoc24 dermatologists will respond within 24 hours.

Illumina DNA Chip. Illumina, Inc. is a global life sciences company with a goal to apply sequencing and array technologies to the analysis of genetic variation and function. The sequencing will make previously unimaginable studies possible. Their ultimate goal is to make personalized medicine commonplace resulting in a transformation of healthcare.

Beginning in 1990, more than 200 scientists collaborated on a $3 billion project to sequence the roughly 3 billion bases of human DNA. Between 2002 and 2008 the cost to perform the sequencing gradually declined from $100 million to $10 million. The introduction of next generation sequencing technology in 2008 led to a plummeting of the cost over the six years until now, bringing the cost down to a few thousand dollars.[175] In March 2014, Illumina claimed it had brought the cost of sequencing a human genome to $1,000, a much anticipated target predicted some years ago and now fulfilled. President Obama in 2015 funded an initiative to sequence the genes of one million people. This is a large step toward individual gene sequencing.

Now, Illumina, Inc. has laid out a vision for a consumer product. The company believes it can build a DNA chip to plug into a smartphone, bringing genetic medicine into the world of consumer mHealth. Rick Merritt at *EE Times* has been following the development closely as reported in "DNA Chip Will Plug into Handsets."[176] In a recent technology forum, Mostafa Ronaghi, Illumina's Chief Technology Officer, said that Illumina's technology would make the smartphone "a molecular stethoscope".[177] Ronaghi predicted that we would no longer need a primary care physician in the future because consumers will make genetic tests at home or in a clinic, and go directly to a specialist. He said this would happen in six to seven years.[178]

Illumina scientists and engineers are making progress toward development of an mHealth DNA chip, but considerable challenges remain. One of the biggest challenges is finding biocompatible interfaces between "wet and dry science".[179] The app may require as much as a half of a shot glass of blood to perform the required analysis. The app may also require more data than today's smartphones can process. At this stage, it appears that FDA approval is not imminent or that PCPs need to fear being replaced by smartphones, but the future may surprise us.

Cognoa. Some mHealth apps, such as the Kinsa thermometer, deliver results directly to the consumer. In other apps, such as the Levo iPod Touch solution for tinnitus, the results require the app plus a practitioner. A new development is the use of mHealth in combination with artificial intelligence (AI). AI is intelligence exhibited by machines or software, not by humans. Cognoa, a Palo Alto, California startup, uses AI to analyze children's behavior from a video and questionnaire provided by the parents. The company analyzes the information using algorithms that can produce a risk score for autism and other developmental issues. The diagnoses take just three days. The company says many children get diagnosed too late and miss a window of opportunity where the children could receive the greatest benefit.

Wearable Technology. The realm of technology integration into our daily lives will extend far beyond smartphones and devices. A new category of consumer technology has opened up new opportunities for wearable items including watches, glasses, and clothing. Ralph Lauren is taking the lead with a new Polo Tech t-shirt. The shirts are interwoven with a set of sensors with close proximity to the body. The sensors can track heart rate, breathing rate, breathing depth, activity intensity, steps walked, calories burned, and heart rate variability. The data are transmitted from the shirts' sensors to a small transmitter device wearers can clip to shirt. The transmitter connects to an iPhone using a Bluetooth signal and relays the data to a Ralph Lauren iPhone app and probably to the Apple Health app.

A sub-category of wearable technology includes Band-Aid looking devices. Researchers from Northwestern University in Evanston, IL, and the University of Illinois at Urbana-Champaign have developed a wearable, wireless, skin-like device the researchers say can monitor cardiovascular and skin health 24 hours a day. The 2 inch long device is made with more than 3,500 tiny crystals organized on a thin, soft, and flexible strip consumers can attach directly to their skin. The device is nearly invisible and it stretches, twists, and compresses just like skin itself. The device monitors blood flow, temperature, and skin hydration level.

FDA Data Collection.

The FDA is encouraging the use of apps for data collection. During the H1N1 swine flu epidemic in 2009, some experimental drugs were used, but there was no efficient method of collecting data about adverse effects from taking the drugs. The FDA developed a smartphone app to provide reporting direct from the patient.[180] Collecting data directly from the public may turn out to be a boon for public health agencies and epidemiologists. As the accountable care model rolls out, health providers are going to become very interested in learning as much as possible about the population for which they will be providing care. Gathering data from the community could help healthcare planners design appropriate clinics.

Self Diagnosis

Home monitoring of blood glucose or blood pressure is not new. Gathering such data on a regular basis can help consumers with chronic illness to manage their condition. A more recent trend is gathering data such as cholesterol or C-reactive protein, a marker for detecting inflammation, for the purpose of self diagnosing conditions such as cardiovascular disease. Another example is UMSkinCheck, a free mHealth app from the University of Michigan letting consumers perform a skin cancer self-exam. The app provides surveillance allowing users to complete and store a full body photographic library, track detected moles or lesions, download informational videos and literature, and locate a nearby skin cancer specialist.[181]

Healthcare apps and devices can provide useful information for managing chronic illness or detecting a medical condition needing attention. Some physicians I know are very concerned about a trend toward self diagnosis. They are worried consumers will self diagnose and then self medicate with an ever expanding array of over the counter drugs. Some are concerned about lost revenue from profitable tests consumers can now perform on their own. The ultimate concern is a person could self treat with a fatal result. The concern is legitimate, but the trend is likely to continue as self diagnostic technology becomes more affordable and ubiquitous. TV advertising of medical conditions and related drugs may lead consumers to unnecessarily self diagnose. Healthcare resources on the web need to put up the red flag of caution and urge consumers to take the data they gather to their doctor before making conclusions about what treatment may be needed.

Self Diagnosis with Isabel

Very few physicians would say their diagnoses are right 100% of the time. One physician told me he would feel good if he were right 75% of the time. Unfortunately, sometimes a diagnosis is seriously wrong and leads to a bad outcome. In 1999, Jason and Charlotte Maude took their 3 year old daughter, Isabel, to the local hospital where she was misdiagnosed and had nearly fatal consequences. Isabel had chicken pox, and a new set of symptoms prompted her hospital visit. A physician told Jason and Charlotte Isabel's symptoms were typical of the chicken pox from which she was suffering. Isabel was later diagnosed with serious complications of chicken pox: Toxic Shock Syndrome and Necrotizing Fasciitis. Isabel spent two months in the hospital, including a month in the pediatric ICU after experiencing multiple organ failures and cardiac arrests.[182] Isabel was brought back from the brink and is now a healthy and beautiful young woman.

Rather than suing the hospital for the diagnostic error, Jason and Charlotte formed a company, Isabel Healthcare, to develop a better way to perform diagnoses. Their initial idea was the failure in Isabel's diagnosis was the physician failed to ask the simple question of what else could this be. Isabel Healthcare's first product, Isabel, was a web based Diagnosis Checklist System designed to assist clinicians in forming a diagnosis in which they can feel confident. Isabel enhances the process of determining a diagnosis by supplementing the expertise of the clinician.[183]

Isabel Healthcare believes the most effective way for clinicians to improve the quality and speed of diagnosis is for them to develop a comprehensive list of diagnostic possibilities for a patient. The Isabel Healthcare software can be integrated with the EHR workflow of a hospital or during a consultation with the patient. The company says clinicians who 'Isabel' their patients at an early stage are able to substantially reduce clinical risk by ensuring important possible diagnoses have not been missed.

"Patients are experts on their symptoms and doctors are experts in working out their probable causes. Patients and doctors need to work together to formulate a list of possible diagnoses." said Jason Maude, Chief Executive of Isabel Healthcare.[184] Some physicians cringe at the thought of self diagnosis, but others see the potential to enhance their productivity by having the patient, with Isabel Healthcare's assistance, develop a first pass at a possible illness or disease. By collaborating, a synergy can develop whereby patients and their medical providers can embark on a safe and effective treatment program. A study by Graber and

PART THREE SOLUTIONS FOR CONSUMERS AND PROVIDERS

Mathew published in the *Journal of General Internal Medicine* found Isabel software suggested the correct diagnosis in 48 of 50 (96%) complex cases.[185]

Isabel Healthcare software is now available as an mHealth app. Like the web based tool, the app uses a technology called differential diagnostics. After entering your age, gender, and the region of the world where you live, you enter all the symptoms you are experiencing. The Isabel app instantly returns a list of possible diagnoses from a database of more than 6,000 diseases. Self diagnosis and research by patients can be helpful. No physician can possibly read every journal article and know about every medication. As of December 31, 2013, the FDA has approved 1,453 drugs.[186]

There is a broader set of issues with regard to diagnosis in general. For almost every set of symptoms there will be a long list of potential diagnoses. A balance needs to be reached between identifying all possible diagnoses and diagnoses that should be explored. As in the case of Isabel Maude, a patient may have a rare condition that can only be diagnosed with expensive or potentially dangerous testing. Dr. Dempsey Springfield, an Orthopedic Surgeon in Boston, MA said, "The physician must weigh the relative risks and benefits of ruling a particular diagnosis in or out. The most experienced physicians select those diagnoses with the most likelihood of being accurate plus those if missed would have the most severe consequence, and pursue them first." As the practice of medicine has become more sophisticated, patients have increased their expectations. Physicians feel the pressure to determine the right diagnosis quickly and therefore broaden the list of diagnoses to exclude. Dr. Springfield added, " Thirty years ago a physician could be very thorough and still not do excessive testing. Today, the amount of testing and number of diagnoses to be excluded, if one is to be completely thorough, has expanded dramatically." If a patient comes to a physician with their own list of potential diagnoses and the odds of their likelihood, the patient and physician will have to decide how many to investigate. Physicians carry a large responsibility amidst complex situations and high expectations. Dr. Springfield said, "One of the reasons it is called the practice of medicine is the physician is always learning and improving their diagnostic skills."

A *Wall Street Journal* article, "A Better Online Diagnosis Before the Doctor Visit", cited a survey by Philips North America of more than 1,000 people about their use of online diagnostic tools. More than 40% said they were comfortable using websites to check their own symptoms. One fourth said they used self diagnostic tools as often as they visit their doctor. About the same number said they used online tools instead of visiting their doctor.[187] I believe self diagnosis is here to stay.

Sequencing the Baby's Genome

The ultimate self diagnosis may come from our genes. The dramatic reduction in the cost of gene sequencing is similar to Gordon Moore's iconic observation computing power tends to double and its price falls in half every 2 years.[188] This has held true for nearly 50 years with only minor revision.[189] Does this mean all of us will be sequencing our genomes? Yes, that is likely, and some will push the envelope even further. Razib Khan decided to sequence the genome of his unborn son, who was later born in early June 2014 in California. In "How a Geneticist Sequenced His Unborn Son's Genome, Using Do-It-Yourself Biology Tools", Khan said that he believes our genetic data and that of our unborn children belong to us.[190] Physicians and policymakers will not necessarily agree, and many debates will be ignited in the months and years ahead.

Khan said that his son turned out to be a "normal kid".[191] He used publicly available analytics tools to study the 43 gigabytes about his unborn son's genome. Fortunately, he found nothing alarming or even unusual. But, what if he had found some disturbing news such as his son would be born with some disability or with a likelihood of some future fatal disease? What actions would he and his wife decide to take and what ethical issues would arise? I don't think we know even a small fraction of the issues ahead. However, some things are certain. The price of sequencing will continue to decline and the availability of big data about our children and us will be commonplace.

On January 30, 2015, President Obama announced a precision medicine initiative to greatly expand the potential of sequencing the human genome.[192] Precision medicine, also known as personalized or individualized medicine, may lead to identifying defects earlier in our lives and provide solutions to correct them before they become life threatening. The government initiative plans to include collecting genetic information from one million people and use big data and analytics to develop cures. Nancy A. Brown, Chief Executive Officer of the American Heart Association, said that patients with heart disease, like those with cancer, could benefit from precision medicine. *The New York Times* reported that her organization is building a database that can help develop treatments for heart failure and drugs to lower high blood pressure.[193] Her organization is compiling a database of genetic information. She said the data could help doctors tailor treatments for heart failure or abnormal heart rhythms, or find the right combination of drugs to lower high blood pressure.

Summary

The Internet and the web have empowered consumers for more than 20 years. mHealth has provided even more empowerment to patients in a short time through the powers of the PSC, which I described as personal supercomputers. The number of devices and apps are exploding onto the healthcare scene. The FDA has approved more than 150 apps and devices through September of 2014. The pace will likely accelerate. Self-monitoring and self diagnosis are here to stay. Although some providers are not comfortable with consumer technology for self diagnosis, the new technologies surely will lead to a new model for collaboration between patient and physician. A key element of collaboration in healthcare is the electronic health record.

CHAPTER 8

Electronic Health Records

E lectronic health records (EHRs) are on the way, and not any too soon. In this chapter I present my view on the necessity of EHRs along with a discussion of the many issues and opportunities. The chapter describes the role of health information exchanges (HIEs), coordination and collaboration, security, privacy, standards, and ease of use.

The government is offering large incentives to healthcare providers to start using EHRs in a meaningful way, and for those who skip the incentive, there will be penalties to follow. Despite numerous issues, concerns, and problems, EHRs are a technological imperative which will reduce costs, enhance healthcare quality, and improve patient safety. Beyond the benefits for patients and providers, widespread use of EHRs could contribute to improving the health of the entire population of the United States.

Manila Folders

The predecessor to the EHR is the paper medical chart, still used by thousands of doctors. The chart resides in a manila folder with a patient's name on the tab. Inside the folder are physician notes from every visit, laboratory results, pathology reports, imaging studies, and faxes from other providers. Many folders are an inch or more thick. Physicians flip through the pages looking for historical information including important data for a current diagnosis. The only ways to transfer information from the folder to another physician or other provider are to mail it, fax it, or copy and hand carry it. Doctors are buried in faxes – as many as 1,000 per month.[194] Sometimes faxes don't go through, or get dropped and have to be repeated, or just get lost. Dr. P. J. Parmar, a family doctor, said, "Fax is a technology that should have disappeared along with beepers. Oh wait", he said, "Medicine is the only field that still uses beepers."[195] If a doctor shares a faxed record with another doctor, it may not be easy or efficient to do, but it does facilitate collaboration and sharing of data. However, manila folders are not an efficient way to collaborate across multiple providers.

Non-electronic records are not necessarily secure and private. Manila envelopes can be secure if they are locked in a safe, but the security of the millions of folders in grey metal racks in doctors' offices is uncertain. Any employee of the medical practice can access healthcare records of patients. When a folder is sent to a specialist, there is no control over who can open the envelope and read the contents. If multiple referrals are involved, medical records have to be copied and the process opens up another opportunity for a compromise of the privacy of healthcare data.

Not Having an EHR

Three years ago, a reader of my blog sent me an account of an EHR related incident he and his family experienced. With his permission, I am sharing their story, because I think it is one of millions of examples that justify the adoption of EHRs.

Frank, and his 15 year old son Alex, are from California. These are fictional names to protect their identity. Alex was scheduled for non-emergency pulmonary valve replacement surgery on Friday afternoon. He was born with a number of congenital heart defects. He had open-heart surgery when he was just 30 days old. A recent MRI showed his pulmonary valve to be leaking extensively. His cardiologist recommended it be replaced with a new adult-sized pig valve. Before leaving for the hospital on Friday morning, Frank received a phone call saying Alex had been bumped from the schedule due to a critical newborn with heart problems.

Although Frank understood the rescheduling, Alex took it extremely hard. As the day wore on, he got more and more upset and stressed out. Around 9 PM he mentioned he was having shortness of breath and pains around his heart. Since he had a full pre-op examination earlier that week, Frank's immediate thought was this was a combination of extreme stress and possibly indigestion. He decided to take Alex to the local hospital ER. Once there, clinicians checked Alex's vital signs and ran an EKG. The ER doctor did a quick echocardiogram. After reviewing the test results, the ER doctor asked if Frank had any of Alex's previous EKGs so a comparison could be made to Alex's abnormal EKG.

Around 11 PM Frank signed the paperwork to authorize a search for the previous EKG reports. The nursing staff started calling hospitals where Alex had been a patient to see if the doctor could obtain EKG data. They hit a brick wall. The large hospital where Alex had the pre-op wanted to help but had no access to data. Frank was unable to reach the cardiologist. As he reflected on the data void, he realized he could download an obscure piece of music from multiple sources on the web, but in spite of valiant efforts, he could not get a copy of Alex's EKG. He questioned why he could not get the information. He mused, "isn't an EKG a file of digital data just like music or pictures or anything else on the web?" Alex began to feel better after some rest and was able to go back to school after the weekend.

On Saturday morning Frank did an extensive web search, and found MedicAlert Foundation, a non-profit company in Turlock, California, maintains a database of members' medical information. They provide it to caregivers in an emergency if a physician had previously provided MedicAlert with the data. Frank thought this is a great service, but wondered why it wouldn't be an automatic byproduct of healthcare of any provider for an electronic copy of the data to be available online. From Frank's perspective, having access to someone's past EKG could either save a life, prevent misdiagnosis, or save time and money. For Frank, the EHR is a basic tool for anyone with a sick child, or for any family member with a potentially serious disease. Frank's perception is EKGs for the most part are still paper driven, and providers are not thinking about getting them on the web as a standard practice.

Alex received a new surgery date. The surgery was successful and he was able to finish his soccer season. He was an MVP in two sports and went on to college where he is studying exercise health.

It is time for healthcare to catch up to electronic banking, e-commerce, digital music, and the ease of use of YouTube, and social networking. What could be more important than the health of our families? Privacy is a valid and important concern, but it can and is being addressed as part of the rollout of EHR systems. Alex's privacy was intact – his EKG results were in a manila folder somewhere – private, secure, but unavailable when needed.

Using Electronic Health Records

It is 11PM. Do you know where your medical records are? Most likely they are scattered across multiple doctors' offices in the manila folders. Most of our healthcare information is stored with insurance companies, which pay for care if we are lucky enough to have the coverage. Most of the insurance information is about medical codes and money rather than about the actual healthcare we experience. Pharmacies have tons of information on what we were prescribed but not why it was prescribed. Specialists have notes about our visits. Meanwhile, thousands of people per year die from information related errors.

Government incentives are accelerating the move to make EHRs available via mHealth or patient portals. EHRs are emerging from insurance companies, pharmacies, community doctors, hospitals, regional health information organizations, employers, and software companies. It is not yet clear which EHR or combination will prevail. Personally, I will be glad when all my medical information is encrypted and stored in the cloud where I will know at last it will be safe and under my control.

Policymakers agree EHRs are a key element in the overall reform of our healthcare system. There are many potential benefits to using EHRs including not having to fill out a clipboard of paperwork every time you go to a healthcare provider and not having to get repeat blood work or imaging because the doctor can't get access to the data from tests you recently had. EHRs also have the potential to increase collaboration among doctors and other providers, resulting in better outcomes. Longer term, the electronic medical records can lead to evidence based medicine. This has the potential to base prescriptive care on the specifics of each patient, leveraging a large database of what worked and did not work for millions of people who have the same condition. Ultimately, we will have medications based on a sequencing of our genome stored in our EHR. There is great promise for improvement of care in an electronic world.

Electronic Financial Records Model

Millions of consumers download their financial transactions on a regular basis using Intuit's Quicken software. I think of Quicken as my financial health record. At any point in time, a Quicken user knows where every penny is: what came in and from where, what went out and for what, what assets and liabilities exist, and how his or her investments are performing. All of this data is available on the web or on a mobile device. Quicken users are on top of their financial health.

Contrast this with our mental and physical health records. Most consumers have paper records. Get a blood test and the data goes from your arm to a computer for digital analysis and then to a faxed piece of paper that may be hard to retrieve. Many doctors actually believe the data about your blood for which you or your insurance company paid does not belong to you. It is his or hers as the physician, not yours. Likewise for imaging studies, other tests, and the notes physicians take when you have a consultation.

Collaboration and Coordination

If an EHR was created for the sole use of the physician, we may as well return to the old way of making notes in a paper chart. The justification for EHRs comes through synergy. If a patient goes to his or her PCP for an annual physical examination, and the PCP updates the EHR, a large amount of extremely valuable information will have been recorded. If the patient is referred to a specialist, and the specialist has a different EHR system incompatible with the PCP's system, then, I believe, there is a breach of care. However, a health information exchange (HIE) can eliminate this breach by providing compatibility between various incompatible systems. The value proposition is simple. It is to enable any provider using the HIE to be able to get access to patient records; including lab results, imaging studies, and medications from any other provider.

The HIE can provide a seamless interoperability and integration between disparate systems. Even fax machines can participate in an HIE. A New England physician pointed out to me the main benefit from EHRs is realized when each physician seeing a patient takes an extra few minutes to carefully enter their notes so all physicians who may see the patient in the future benefit from the information. Five extra minutes spent by one doctor may save another doctor ten minutes. The primary beneficiary, of course, is the patient.

The EHR is much more than an electronic version of the paper chart in the doctor's office. It is a digital record of comprehensive health information about patients that can be shared among all healthcare providers and organizations which have been or will be involved with a patient's care. This includes laboratories, specialists, medical imaging facilities, pharmacies, emergency facilities, and school and workplace clinics.

The combination of the electronic data and advanced analytics software can add a new dimension to the coordination of care. ActiveHealth, a New York based health management company provides services to enable coordination among teams of physicians, nurses, nurse practitioners, aides, therapists, and pharmacists. Their advanced analytics can help physicians, or entire healthcare organizations, measure their performance against national or hospital quality standards.[196] ActiveHealth can also show trends in how patients are responding to treatment for a chronic disease, or adhering to drug regimens, and automatically alert doctors to conflicting or missed prescriptions. Dr. John Jenrette, CEO for Sharp Community Medical Group said, "This is going to revolutionize how we practice medicine. Instead of digging into volumes of paper to coordinate services, we're going to have information available at our fingertips. It's going to make us all more efficient."[197]

Healthcare Information Exchanges

The full effect of EHRs has yet to be seen. By themselves, EHRs do not do much, but when combined with networking and other users, the leverage takes effect. Software for healthcare has traditionally been focused on individual silos of automation; e.g. laboratory, imaging, and the emergency department, but the future promises a merger between the various systems. The impact of the software integration will grow as systems become more interconnected. Although HIEs have not achieved wide deployment, they are the key to the sharing of data between providers, and providers will be motivated to make them work.

The University of Pennsylvania Health System, otherwise known as Penn Medicine, has been participating in a regional HIE sponsored by the Delaware Valley Health Council. This collaborative group includes hospitals throughout southeast Pennsylvania, as well as several payer organizations. The Council is slowly making progress in sharing data between institutions.[198] Penn Medicine participates in a second HIE, called CareEverywhere that is provided by Epic, the software vendor which provides Penn Medicine's EHR software. The CareEverywhere HIE operates very smoothly because it works among providers only using Epic. Unfortunately, there are more than 200 EHR software vendors. The government has a role here and could greatly expand HIE use if there was a national standard for the sharing of data among HIEs.

Shared Benefits

There are numerous technical and financial challenges inhibiting the rollout of EHR and HIE systems. The biggest challenge is while the benefits are shared among the patient, provider, and payer, none can justify the cost individually. If the costs are shared, everyone can win.

The EHR challenge reminds me of the Universal Product Code (UPC) challenge of the 1970's. Despite large benefits from knowing what was sold and when, the grocery stores were hesitant to invest in UPC scanners because there were no products that had UPC symbols on them. The first product to have a code was a packet of Wrigley's Gum in 1974. As a result, the stores found it difficult to justify the cost even though there would be labor savings from scanning versus "ringing up".

The packaged goods manufacturers also were skeptical of using the UPC codes despite the codes providing the ability for manufacturers to know exactly how their products were doing at retail on a timely basis. I visited the M&M Mars candy factory in Hackettstown, NJ in the early 1970's and discussed UPC scanning with the Director of Product Packaging. She said that there were not enough benefits to offset giving up the "real estate" on the candy bag to place a symbol for which there was few scanners to read the codes. The first UPC scanner was installed at a Marsh's supermarket in Troy, Ohio in 1974. It took strong leadership, competition among retailers, and perseverance to get to the ubiquitous scanning we enjoy today.

EHRs and HIEs face a similar challenge. The benefits are huge: (1) increased accuracy of information leading to better outcomes, (2) reduction in duplicative procedures, and (3) more effective collaboration among providers. Physicians will spend less time ordering procedures and medications, and liability costs should go down due to fewer errors. Increased collaboration will improve caregiving, and patients will be able to relocate and take their healthcare data with them. Finally, patients will be able to take a more proactive role in their own health and selection of providers.

The ultimate benefits will accrue at two ends of the spectrum. On one end, the individual consumer will benefit from the data in their EHR specific to them alone. At the other end of the spectrum, entire populations will benefit from the accumulation of a large amount of data from many individuals in the population. All it takes is strong leadership by providers and payers and government assistance in setting the right standards. I am confident in the next five years we will see more progress with EHRs and HIEs than we have seen in the last twenty.

Electronic Prescribing

One of the features available to physicians who use EHRs is e-prescribing. The adoption of e-prescribing over the past ten years has increased dramatically, boosted by government incentives during the past five years. The benefits are clear and compelling. E-prescribing allows clear communications with providers and pharmacies about patient eligibility and benefits, their medication history, hospital drug formulary requirements, fill and refill status, and the actual prescriptions. E-prescribing systems also use clinical decision-support tools that provide automated screening for potential conflicts between a prescribed medication and other medications the patient is taking. The system also checks for any known drug allergies and validates the dose being prescribed.[199] The result is improved patient safety, reduced administrative costs related to follow-up, and reduced callbacks from pharmacists to clarify the intention or details of a prescription.[200]

In 2004, 4% of office based physicians e-prescribed. Surescripts, a health information network technology company connecting pharmacies, care providers, and benefit managers reported as of the end of 2013, the number had risen to 73%.[201] Surescripts implemented an electronic prior authorization system, which previously had been a tedious telephone-tag-prone process. E- prescribing is now legal in all 50 states and is accepted at 95% of pharmacies. The Surescripts network routed more than one billion e-prescriptions in 2013, representing 58% of all eligible prescriptions. The growth is impressive, but more than 40% of prescriptions are still done the old way.

I believe using IT more effectively in healthcare should not be optional. Airline pilots have to communicate using uniform language with airport towers worldwide. They don't get to make up their words. There is a specific terminology and it is very precise. Imagine the consequences otherwise. Lawyers have to be precise. Each word in a legal document has meaning and it matters how those words are written. In the case of doctors, prescriptions are written in a way that many of them are not readable. Pharmacists often have to call physicians to clarify a drug or a dose, and sometimes if they guess instead of call, a tragic result could occur. Adverse drug events result in more than 770,000 injuries and deaths each year and add billions of dollars to the cost of healthcare.[202] Paper based prescribing should no longer be acceptable. Newt Gingrich, in *"Health Care - the Cure for What Ails Us"* said, "With all of the information technology available today, we can no longer accept suffering and death because of prescription errors or any other preventable errors".[203] Fortunately, e-prescribing is on the right trajectory to make Newt's 2003 challenge a reality.

Health Records In The Cloud

Seems like everything is in the cloud or on the way to the cloud including our money, travel plans, music and pictures, email, contacts, calendar, documents, and spreadsheets. There has always been something about clouds that brings the term into our daily lives. We say, "it is a cloudy day", or "there is not a cloud in the sky", or if we feel especially elated or happy, we might say, "I feel like I am on cloud nine". Nowadays, many are talking about "cloud computing", or we just say something is "in the cloud". It means different things to different people.

In the early days of the Internet, technology leaders thought of the Internet as consisting of three parts. First, there were a large number of specialized computers called routers that moved information between origin and destination. Second, was another set of computers called servers containing emails, documents, and web pages. Third, the networking infrastructure including telephone wires, modems, and various networking devices that tied everything together. Most users of the Internet today are not aware of the technical aspects of the Internet infrastructure. They don't have to think about it. Most know the Internet for its most popular application, the World Wide Web. In a sense, the web is a "place" containing all of the information and applications we want to use.

Currently, the larger web application providers, such as Amazon, Apple, eBay, Dropbox, Google, Microsoft, and Yahoo began to refer to their infrastructure as clouds. If you create a spreadsheet at Google Docs and then save it, where is it actually saved? It is in the Google cloud. We don't know exactly where it really is. It is just there at docs.google.com in the cloud. There are millions of servers connected to the Internet, but to most people there may as well be just one. That is the beauty of the Internet. You don't have to know what the infrastructure is or how it works.

The advantage of having your data in the cloud is cloud-computing centers can make your data available to you in multiple places using multiple devices. For example, if you take a picture with an iPhone, the picture immediately travels over the Internet to iCloud, which consists of a large number of Internet servers that Apple operates in North Carolina. The iCloud servers know about all of your other Apple devices you have registered with your Apple ID. As soon as the picture you took arrived in iCloud, it immediately was sent to your iPhone, iPad, MacBook, iMac. If you setup sharing, the picture could go to all the devices of your friends and family. The power of the cloud is you can have access to your data whenever you want, wherever you want, and using whatever device you choose to use.

Suppose the data you send to the cloud includes your blood results, the pathology report from a biopsy, or a spreadsheet with your personal financial plan with income, taxes, assets, liabilities and estate plans. Can you trust Apple or Google with this information? Apple and Google have a lot at stake with their clouds. If iCloud or Google Drive is hacked and data is stolen, entire multi-billion dollar businesses are at risk. The major companies hire top technical talent and spend millions to protect their infrastructure. Most cloud providers are encrypting their data so even if someone breaks into the cloud and steals data, they will not be able to decipher it.

The security of the cloud may be superior to what most people have with their PCs and Macs. Hard drives do not fail frequently, but they do fail. When failure occurs, people lose all their data. If your laptop was stolen or left in a taxi, cloud based storage facilitates retrieval of your data. Encrypted healthcare data stored in the cloud, authenticated, and properly authorized for access will be safer than the millions of manila folders currently guarding our sensitive information.

Google.com/health made a bold move to provide a universal repository for storing health records. I was one of the early users and came to depend on it. When did I get the flu shot last year? What was my blood pressure at last year's physical? What test results and medications do I have? All of the specific information was provided for free by Google Health. Consumers could authorize CVS, Medco, Quest Diagnostics, and others to automatically send prescription data and test results to Google Health. If you got a blood test, a graph of how those results compared to results over the past five years would appear in a couple of days. Google Health was a very helpful service, but unfortunately, the company shut it down permanently in January 2012 and deleted all the data it had collected. They gave users instructions on how to download their health data to their own computers and requested it be done within 18 months. Google decided Google Health was not having the impact they anticipated so they decided to focus their efforts in fewer areas.

Google Health may have been ahead of its time, but it did a poor job reaching out to a growing ecosystem of developers focused on healthcare. Microsoft launched a similar effort in the cloud called HealthVault. The company says they are committed to it. Apple appears to have the most strategic view of the opportunity, and a significant collaboration in the industry. The EHR vendors, such as Allscripts, eClinicalWorks, and Epic are in the best position to dominate providing healthcare databases for consumers, but so far their patient portals to access EHRs have proved to be difficult to use. This may change as they work with Apple and IBM.

Selecting Your EHR Provider

It is still early in the game and there are many possibilities as to who may become the preferred EHR provider for consumers, or if there will be one universal provider. First movers will not necessarily be the winners, as demonstrated by Google. Microsoft HealthVault has some advantages compared to Apple Health. The free HealthVault database includes records of medications, allergies, immunization, test results, surgeries, procedures, conditions, doctor visits, health insurance policies, and appointments. You can enter any of hundreds of blood chemistry measurements from lab reports or link directly to Quest and other labs to have your results automatically imported. Despite a very comprehensive database compared to Apple's free Health database of 60 items, Microsoft has so far not been able to get significant traction.

Apple is making a major strategic investment with their HealthKit and Health app, but the small database may limit adoption. The 60 database record types are mostly related to health and fitness, but do not include common clinical measurements such as AST and ALT, which are considered to be two of the most important tests to detect liver damage. The Health database does not include TSH or CBC, which are typically used as a broad screening test to determine our general health status. The CBC includes nearly 20 different measures. None of these results are included in Apple Health. I think it is likely Apple has plans to expand beyond the 60 fitness-oriented measures, especially as the FDA approves more devices to enable consumers to do their own blood tests.

Technology companies are not the only potential actors in the race to make EHRs ubiquitous. Our health insurance provider may decide not to share the vast amount of information they have about us with the EHR vendors because they may want to be your EHR provider. Then there are the hospitals and large physician practices. They are logical providers for an EHR service in the cloud, but will they have the resources and skills to launch a user-friendly, scalable, secure cloud based service? There is CVS, Drugstore.com, Walgreen, Walmart, and other retailers. They may all want to be your EHR provider as an integrated service with their pharmacy operations. We cannot rule out Big Pharma. GlaxoSmithKline, Merck, Pfizer, and others have large numbers of chronically ill patients who depend on certain medications. The drug manufacturers want to have a direct relationship with patients by providing an EHR service tailored to monitor, sell, and communicate about their drugs.

Medscape, WebMd, and the many other e-health sites are logical providers of an EHR based on the wealth of medical information they provide. Finally, there are The Centers, the largest healthcare payer in the world. Will just a few giant EHR providers dominate the field? Will the government step in and mandate standards to insure compatibility? Will the technology companies develop a technical solution allowing multiple incompatible EHR systems play nicely together? At this stage, there are many opinions and no certain answers.

Security and Privacy

During a scan of the news one day, I saw two articles related to healthcare security. One reported an employee of the National Health Service in the United Kingdom had a PC with patient data on it he or she put up for sale on eBay. The second story was about an inquiry by the Illinois Attorney General to eight health-related websites asking what data they had collected about site visitor queries and what they did with that data. Both of these situations could potentially involve data from EHRs and present threats to our privacy.

In the first case, there are a number of questions to ask. The main question is why was there patient data on the PC? This situation demonstrates the benefit of cloud computing, where major companies such as Allscripts, Apple, Dropbox, Epic, Google, and Microsoft take extraordinary measures to keep data secure. With their entire cloud business built on excellent security features, they have more to lose than a user. These companies apply the best people and technology to achieve high levels of security. Having data on a computer in a health clinic or hospital used to be essential, but no longer. With the advent of smartphones and tablets, hospitals are implementing software to allow clinicians and staff to access healthcare data while at work or from home, but the data remains on protected servers, not on the smartphones or tablets.

In the second case, the issues are more complex. No doubt, the web companies have a lot of data about who inquired about what. I am sure that WebMD, for example, knows how many people inquired about diabetes. They know what time of day the inquiries were made and the Internet protocol addresses of the devices from which the inquiries were made. If the user logged in, WebMD would know the names and email addresses of the persons, and potentially much more. The question the Attorney General is asking is: What do WebMD and others do with this data? If they make it available to insurance and pharmaceutical companies, the data should be anonymized. Anonymization is a process that separates healthcare data from personally identifiable information such as name and address. However, with the power of big data analytics, can even anonymized data provide a trail to the persons who inquired? That is the question that websites will need to explain to the Attorney General.

Standards

There are many hurdles to making EHRs interoperable so a collaborative approach to our healthcare becomes routine. A key element of the solution is standards. The Internet works exactly the same way in every part of the world because it is built on global standards. There is only one Internet. Health records have standards too. The problem is there is not one standard – there are many. A single central provider of EHRs could have many advantages, but I don't believe consensus could be reached on how to do it. Healthcare.gov has shown us one large system for hundreds of millions of people is not easy to manage with good reliability. I believe the government has an important role here. It should either mandate a standard for EHR data sharing or broker an agreement to use one of the existing vendor's software as the standard. With a national standard, hospitals and providers of all kinds would be able to build local and regional solutions for their EHRs and use HIEs to exchange data with all other providers. I believe there will be many developments on the subject of standards soon.

Various healthcare industry standards initiatives have been launched in the last ten years. Few of these initiatives have been effective because there was insufficient support behind them. Many hospitals want to maintain the systems they have rather than convert to a new mandated standard. EHR vendors resist the idea of adopting a national standard unless it is their own. They claim to follow standards and maintain interoperability, but it is not the case. Some experts claim a single national standard is too complex, but many examples demonstrate standards can work nationally and globally. The wired and wireless Internet works the same everywhere in the world. The financial services industry can dispense cash from ATMs with your credit card almost anywhere in the world. Money can be wired from anyone to almost anyone. UPC bar codes are consistent wherever food is sold. There is no reason we cannot have a national standards for EHRs.

The United States Department of Veterans Affairs (VA) healthcare system includes 163 hospitals, 800 clinics, and 135 nursing homes. In the mid 1990s, the VA adopted a comprehensive EHR system enabling instant access to patient records across all VA and Department of Defense treatment facilities. Despite recent criticism about wait time for patients, the VA has made significant accomplishments as a result of having a standard for EHR implementations for all healthcare organizations under its control. The VA's use of a computerized provider order entry system decreased adverse drug events and increased prescription accuracy rates to Six Sigma (99.997%) compared to the national error rate of three to eight percent (92-97%).[204] The system has stabilized costs per patient despite increasing price inflation, largely by using its centralized EHR system to eliminate repetitive lab tests and paperwork. A standardized system has enabled the VA to provide two-thirds of the care recommended by national medical standards in comparison to only half provided by non-VA providers nationally.[205]

Sao, Gupta, and Gantz are experts in law and computer science. They studied the issues, barriers, and benefits of a single national standard for EHR interoperability. They published their findings in The *Journal of Legal Medicine* in 2013. Their conclusion was the United States could obtain the same benefits achieved by the VA with the adoption of a single national EHR standard. While acknowledging the many barriers, they concluded federal legislation mandating a single standard had numerous precedents, was achievable, and could withstand any legal challenges that might arise.[206]

Ease of Use

EHR systems can be difficult for patients and doctors to use. When Apple developed the Health app, it started with a clean slate. Like most iPhone apps, they were able to design it to make it really simple for users. The mainstream EHR vendors like Allscripts, Cerner, Epic, Siemens, and others did not have the luxury to start from scratch. They all had earlier software, some designed in the 1970s, which had to be included in the EHR software in order to provide compatibility with customers existing software. The vendors all converted their software to be accessible via the web, but unfortunately, the legacy they brought forward was not readily adapted to the web. Consequently, it is not easy to use.

The Internet used to be very hard to use, and it took years before non-technical people learned how to use it effectively. Many of the 250+ EHR technology providers have systems built years ago on old technology platforms. In the payment arena, PayPal has the same problem. It is not built on the latest technology. At least a dozen new alternatives to PayPal such as Amazon payments, Bitcoin, Braintree, Stripe, and WePay have sprung up having no legacy and therefore the PayPal competitors can exploit the latest technologies. It is hard for startups to break in to the EHR market, but hopefully competition will heat up and new capabilities will be introduced using interoperable standards.

Data entry for EHRs needs improvement. Many questions are not relevant to a particular patient or to the particular reason for the doctor visit. EHR software should be smart enough to only ask for what is really needed based on various patient and diagnostic factors. A New York startup called Hiteks has developed an analytics engine that works at the point-of-care. The Hiteks software converts the narrative portion of the clinical note, which each doctor has his or her own style of entering, into highly structured, organized, and coded data. The structure reduces double entry, auto-reconciles with other data in the chart, increases claims capture, and improves management of Medicare inpatients. As of October 2014, Hiteks was already live at Hackensack University Medical Center and the Clearview Cancer Institute.

EHR data entry should be taking better advantage of voice recognition. Nearly 200,000 physicians make some use of medical dictation software such as Nuance, but the technology is not completely integrated with EHR software. It works quite well for dictating notes about a patient consult, but to enter structured data into many data fields of an EHR requires more than just recognition of the words. Smartphones have voice recognition and accurate dictation, but much closer integration is required with the EHR software. Skype's real-time translator shows the potential. For example, a German and an Italian can have a conversation in their native languages. The Skype technology translates in real time what the German person says into Italian and what the Italian person says into German. If Skype can do that, why can't EHR vendors automate the data entry process for doctors? The combination of better-designed workflow, voice recognition with dictation, and analytics to interpret what the doctor says should be able to make the data entry process a by-product of a conversation between patient and doctor. I am optimistic this will happen.

Another approach to reduce the time physicians spend entering data is to offload much of the data to the patient. In effect, patients could be their own scribes for entering healthcare data into the EHR. Distributors of products used to receive orders on paper and then use data entry clerks to enter the data from the order into computers. Does Amazon have data entry clerks? No, we are the data entry clerks. Amazon offloaded data entry to the customer. ZocDoc has done this very nicely with patients. You fill out your information online, and ZocDoc sends you a reminder of your appointment. When you arrive at the physician's office, the staff doesn't greet you with a clipboard. Patients will be able to share the data captured in their Health app or the various mHealth apps plus a preliminary diagnosis from the Isabel app so the doctor has a clear understanding of the purpose for your visit.

Getting the Data

From the previous example of Frank and Alex's quest for prior medical records, we see obtaining healthcare data can sometimes be a challenge. I had a recent experience equally frustrating, although certainly not as threatening. I had a blood sample drawn, and was told I could go to the laboratory website and request a copy. I filled out the online form and a few days later received an email, "Dear John, we are unable to locate your recently requested lab test results. This may happen if any of the following information does not match what is on the order in our systems: the personal information you provided in your account, the date collected, the physician or practice name, and the physician practice phone number." Needless to say, I knew the correct answer to all of those items and had entered them accurately. I called my doctor's office and got the results faxed to me.

In addition to technology glitches, there is the question of who owns laboratory and imaging study results. Medscape and WebMD collaborated on a survey to determine how physicians and patients viewed questions about the use of mHealth and the ownership and access to EHRs and laboratory and imaging test results. The study was unique in that it asked exactly the same questions to two very different audiences. The Medscape survey went to physicians and other health providers via an email invitation and 1,406 responded. The WebMD consumer survey was obtained from 1,102 random WebMD site visitors where all site visitors had an equal probability of answering the survey. The surveys were conducted during August 2014.[207]

The opening question in the survey asked whether technology, such as smart phones and add-on devices, should be used by patients to assist in the diagnostic process. 84% of patients said yes, while 69% of physicians said yes. When asked whether patients should be allowed to self diagnose without provider input, only 17% of physicians said yes. Approximately 67% of patients and physicians thought smart phones should be used for routine blood tests. This does not bode well for hospital laboratory revenues. Most patients thought smartphones could replace office visits for checking of heart rate and rhythm, skin problems, and eye and ear exams. Doctors agreed heart rate and rhythm could be measured with smartphones but were much more skeptical on the other tests.

More than 95% of both physicians and patients believe patients should have access to their EHRs, but when it comes to the rights of patients to see all of the notes taken by their physicians during an office visit, 89% of patients agreed they should be able to see the notes compared to 64% of physicians. When asked the question of whether doctors should share only the notes they deem appropriate, just 11% of patients said yes and 36% of physicians said yes.

Who owns medical records? More than half of patients said they owned them while 38% of physicians claimed ownership. I was surprised just 34% of patients and 15% of physicians believe they should be given immediate access to lab results. 75% of physicians and 58% of patients said doctors should review results before patients are given access in case a discussion is needed.

The U.S. Department of Health and Human Services (HHS) published new rules in early 2014 to give patients the ownership of data collected from blood work and imaging studies. HHS then Secretary Kathleen Sebelius believed patients should be informed partners with their healthcare providers. "The right to access personal health information is a cornerstone of the HIPAA privacy rule," she said.[208] "Information like lab results can empower patients to track their health progress, make decisions with their health care professionals, and adhere to important treatment plans."[209] The new rule gives patients or a person designated by the patient a means of direct access to the patient's completed laboratory test reports.

A new rule amends the Clinical Laboratory Improvement Amendments of 1988 to allow laboratories to give a patient or a person designated by the patient, access to the patient's completed test reports. While patients can continue to get access to their laboratory test reports from their doctors, these changes give patients a new option to obtain their test reports directly from the laboratory while maintaining strong protections for patients' privacy. Quest Diagnostics and other laboratories can automatically release results, with patient agreement, directly into smartphone apps, patient portals, and EHRs.

The laggards have an out to be less responsive than Quest. The rule has a provision that the patient or the personal representative may have to "put their request in writing and pay for the cost of copying, mailing, or electronic media on which the information is provided, such as a CD or flash drive."[210] In most cases, copies must be given to the patient within 30 days of his or her request. This is not exactly real-time. As consumers learn they own the data, they will make increasing demands to get it electronically and immediately.

Medical Tourism

Medical tourism is now a global industry exceeding $40 billion in 2013.[211] The Centers for Disease Control and Prevention (CDC) estimated up to 750,000 US residents travel abroad for care each year.[212] There are various reasons for Americans to go to another country for care. Many people make the journey because treatment is significantly less costly. Many immigrants to the United States return to their home country for healthcare. The CDC says the most common procedures medical tourists receive are heart surgery, dentistry, and cosmetic surgery. Since interoperability of electronic health records has not yet been achieved between hospitals in America, it is safe to assume if you decide to go on a medical vacation to India for heart surgery, your home hospital will not allow the Indian hospital to have access to your EHR.

Summary

A large part of the future of healthcare centers on the adoption of electronic health records. There are numerous challenges associated with EHRs, for the doctor and the patient. I am optimistic about increased adoption which will help reduce the cost and improve patient safety and outcomes. In the mid 1990s, the web was really hard to use. It was not very reliable, nor secure. It took years for the web to become something non-technical people could easily use, rely upon, and subsequently find indispensable. Compared to the evolution of the web, EHRs are at about the year 2000 in their development.

Great progress is being made to eliminate prescriptions written on a piece of paper which can result in deadly medication errors. Physicians are using e-prescribing to make prescriptions safer, and are beginning to collaborate by sharing access to EHRs. Heart failure patients discharged from the hospital are no longer left adrift with new prescriptions they don't understand. EHRs address these issues and many more. The government's meaningful use challenge is causing healthcare providers to accelerate implementation of EHRs. A health attitude which accepts the changes necessary to adopt EHRs will improve healthcare for all patients. EHRs are not the complete answer. They need to be supplemented with a new attitude about the practice of medicine.

CHAPTER 9

Health Attitude in the Practice of Medicine

Attitudinal shifts in healthcare providers will improve healthcare delivery. Changes in the practice of medicine include a shift to patient centered medicine coordinated across the continuum of care and a focus from the Centers for Medicare & Medicaid Services on population health. This chapter concludes with a discussion about end of life care.

For many years, healthcare providers have been compensated on the basis of the services they provided. Providing more was good because it meant more revenue. For some providers, fee for service became an entitlement – provide a service, earn a fee. Treatments due to an error were compensated the same as any other treatment. There was nothing immoral or unethical about the old model. However, it has become unaffordable, and it lacks incentives for collaboration, focus on cost reduction, improved patient safety, and innovation in the delivery of healthcare. The models described above must be changed. Part of the solution is policy oriented but it also will take a new attitude, health attitude, to move to new models I present.

The Affordable Care Act (ACA) is designed to change the healthcare model and introduce incentives to improve outcomes and patient safety while reducing cost. Through the concept of value based purchasing, which is a strategy to measure and reward excellence in healthcare delivery, the ACA breaks the old model and begins a course to affordable healthcare. The accountability under the new ACA reform shifts risk from the payer to the provider in a way that provides financial benefits to providers who have high quality and efficient operations. All of the ACA changes are significant and will take years to fully implement. Enhancements and fine-tuning of the provisions of the Bill will need to be made, but the shift from an entitlement oriented, fee for service model to an accountability oriented, fee for value model is fundamental to healthcare reform. The changes will begin with adopting a new health attitude.

Continuum Of Care

For every physician and surgeon in the United States, there are four nurses and 16 assistants, technicians, therapists, and other support personnel who provide essential healthcare services. Table 4: United States Healthcare Workforce shows the makeup of the more than 11 million people in the healthcare workforce.[213] The numbers make it clear those delivering our healthcare include more than doctors and nurses.

Table 4: United States Healthcare Workforce		
Area: National		
Period: May 2013		
Occupation	Employment	%
Home Health Aids and Nursing Assistants	3,924,390	34%
Health Technologists and Technicians	2,849,330	24%
Registered Nurses	2,548,520	22%
Physicians and Surgeons	623,380	5%
Therapists	600,660	5%
Pharmacists	287,420	2%
Nurse Practitioners	113,370	1%
Dentists	112,300	1%
Physician Assistants	88,110	1%
Other Practitioners and Technical Support	532,720	5%
Total	11,680,200	100%

Source: http://www.bls.gov/soc/home.htm

Until now, providers worked independently, seeing patients as requested and charging fees for the services they performed. The emerging model of care replaces the independent silos of care with a continuum of care. The continuum of care is a concept involving an integrated system of care guiding and tracking patients over time through a comprehensive array of health services spanning all levels of care from home health aid to surgeon. Think of the continuum as a team providing whatever care the patient may need.

Patient-centered Medical Home

Coordination is the key to success across the continuum of care. The Patient-Centered Medical Home (PCMH) can have a major impact in this area. The home in PCMH is not a place. It is a concept in which the primary care physician coordinates the care of a population of people and recommends the care needed to keep that population healthy. Under the PCMH model, the PCP focuses on health instead of treatments, and uses a full range of procedures and providers to achieve improved health. These include alternative medicine, home healthcare, follow-up calls to ensure medication compliance, and follow-up appointments to monitor progress. The PCMH has a major impact in providing coordination of services.

As more electronic health records and associated patient portals improve, patients will eventually be able to use secure email communications to ask the doctor a question in lieu of an appointment. The focus on health is more likely to keep patients out of the hospital where costs are significantly higher. Many major employers like the idea. My former employer, IBM, has more than 400,000 employees and consequently a multi-billion-dollar healthcare expense. Dr. Paul Grundy, Director of Healthcare Transformation at the Patient Centered Primary Care Collaborative urged the company to embrace the PCMH concept and urge providers to adopt it. IBM looks at healthcare as a service it purchases. With the purchasing power of such a large company, providers listen to what the company says. IBM insisted providers shift from volume to value. IBM sees the PCMH as a way to make the transition.

Congestive heart failure (CHF) is a good example of how a hospital and patient-centered medical home can work together to the patient's benefit. Under the traditional model of care, a CHF patient would go to the ER with swollen ankles, shortness of breath, or dizziness. The ER would stabilize the patient and then admit him or her to the cardiac floor of the hospital. After 3 to 4 days, the patient would be discharged and essentially be on his or her own. Within 30 days, 25% of such patients are readmitted. The new model of care is integrated across the continuum. At the time of hospital discharge, a nurse navigator ensures a primary care appointment is established within seven days and confirmed before the patient leaves the hospital. A care manager in the PCMH works with the patient to ensure medication reconciliation. The PCMH provides ongoing assistance with all forms of care the patient may need. This may include alternative services such as acupuncture; massage therapy, or dietary counseling. The PCMH does not wait for the patient to have a medical problem – they reach out and ask the patient how they are doing. This more integrated approach is expected to reduce readmissions substantially.

One of the reasons for high hospital readmission rates for CHF patients is the lack of follow-up and coordination after a patient is discharged. Studies have shown an appointment with the patient's PCP within seven days to reconcile and update medications reduces the likelihood of a readmission. Likewise, coordination with skilled nursing facilities and other caregivers can improve the quality of life for patients and families. The PCMH can serve this purpose. Although still in the early stages, hundreds of PCMHs have been rolled out and the results look promising.

Provider Ladder

When we think we need medical advice, we normally think of our doctor. The hierarchy begins with the receptionist or secretary and ends at the doctor. As shown in Table 3, doctors and surgeons represent only 5% of the healthcare professionals in the United States. If our attitude would change from depending only on doctors to trusting our care to the other 95% of qualified healthcare professionals, healthcare costs could be reduced.

Surveys show people trust the judgment of physicians more than other providers. Opinions may change as we get to know the other resources available such as the advanced practice registered nurse (APRN), clinical nurse specialist (CNS), nurse practitioner (NP), and physician assistant (PA). These healthcare professionals are informally referred to as physician extenders. Extenders leverage the amount of resource available to care for the population. Following are descriptions of certified extenders who are part of the healthcare continuum.

An APRN has completed advanced education such as a Masters in Nursing or a Doctor of Nursing Practice (DNP); and has acquired advanced clinical knowledge and skills to prepare her or him to deliver safe, competent, high quality care to patients. APRNs are able to diagnose and treat health problems, prescribe medications, perform procedures, order and interpret laboratory tests, counsel patients about health promotion and prevention, coordinate care, refer patients to physicians and other healthcare providers. They can advocate for patients as they traverse the continuum of care. The NP and CNS are classes of APRNs. They are similar, but have some variations in their areas of focus and the certification they must have.

NPs have passed at least one nationally recognized certification exam in their area of focus such as adult and geriatric care, pediatrics, or women's health. NPs offer high quality healthcare services. They can diagnose and manage acute and chronic conditions and provide advice for health promotion and disease prevention. NPs can order, perform and interpret diagnostic tests such as lab work and x-rays, diagnose and treat acute conditions such as chronic conditions, infections, and injuries.

Like the NP, a CNS is a registered nurse who has completed advanced education at the Masters or Doctoral level and passed a nationally recognized certification exam. A CNS is an expert clinician who usually practices in a specialty area, such as cardiovascular, diabetes, geriatrics, or mental health; and provides direct patient care, as well as consultation and education to nursing staff. Some CNSs focus on research evidence to develop standards of care and related policies and procedures for hospitals to help them improve the quality of healthcare.

Both NPs and CNSs can prescribe medications, but there are some differences because of state regulation. For example, in 36 states, psychiatric and mental health clinical nurse specialists have prescriptive authority, but in other states they do not. NPs have the authority to prescribe medication in all 50 states, but only 13 states including the District of Columbia allow nurse practitioners to prescribe medication independently without the oversight of a physician. There is some debate about how much autonomy APRNs should have. The nurses believe supervision is not required, and many physicians agree. However, some physician groups argue having no supervision introduces a patient safety issue. Some nursing groups respond the physician concern is motivated out of concerns for job security and income.

The PA and APRN are very similar in terms of their skills, education, and certification. The practice of APRNs varies by state while the practice of a PA is defined by agreement with the physician he or she is assisting. Supervision of APRNs varies by state. PAs are always supervised by the physician. APRNs and PAs provide healthcare services including assessment, diagnosis, prescribing for treatment of acute and chronic illness and health maintenance and thereby extend the amount of coverage available for patients.

A Harris Poll conducted in 2014 showed the public has a high regard for doctors and for the increasing number of physicians' assistants and nurse practitioners. The majority of patients gave their physicians an A (62%) or a B (29%) for the quality of care they received. Only a handful of patients gave them a lesser rating. These numbers are almost the same as they were in 2012. Substantially more patients give As to physicians than to the other categories of healthcare professionals. A majority of Americans (70%) polled said they trust the advice given to them by physicians, while just 33% said they trust the advice from the physician extenders.[214] These numbers are likely to change as we get more experience with the extenders.

A few years ago, when I was having a lot of difficulty with my knee that was badly worn from too many marathons, the orthopedic surgeon suggested a series of five injections of Supartz. The medication targets inflammation and stiffness in the knee joint. When I called for the first appointment, I was told I would be seeing Bill, the surgeon's PA. I admit to being a bit concerned about this, but after getting to know the PA, I trusted him completely. Bill was more patient and sensitive to someone like me who does not like needles. Previously, I had injections from a surgeon. The surgeon always was in a hurry and not sensitive to the pain I might experience from the injection. I also found Bill knew a lot about knee problems and took the time to discuss my knee condition during each visit. I would give him a 100% customer satisfaction rating.

The American Nurses Association said that Nurse Practitioners can deliver as much as 80 percent of the health services, and up to 90 percent of the pediatric care, provided by primary care physicians, with equal quality and at lower cost.[215] A review of 19 recent studies in the May 2010 issue of *Health Affairs* confirmed Nurse Practitioners delivered care equivalent to physician-provided care, and in some studies, more cost-effective care in certain areas than provided by physicians.[216] NPs also consistently demonstrated better results for patient follow-up, satisfaction, consultation time, and providing screening, assessment, and counseling.

Care provided by APRNs and PAs is cost effective and safe. Mary Naylor and Ellen Kurtzman, authors of "The Role Of Nurse Practitioners In Reinventing Primary Care", recommended that APRNs should be permitted to practice in all states with consistent standards.[217] They also said that NPs should receive equivalent compensation for comparable services regardless of practitioner. The authors added that outcomes achieved should be transparent to the public. Permitting APRNs to provide care consistent with their education and training will provide positive outcomes for patients and help reduce the cost of American healthcare. As the ACA reform moves forward, tens of millions of new patients will be joining the rolls of insured Americans. They can obtain care only if there are sufficient providers. Including APRNs and PAs who can diagnose and treat patients would add 40-50% more providers.

Home Healthcare

The need for senior care will increase greatly. Between 2010 and 2050 the senior population is expected to reach 88.5 million or 20% of the U.S. population.[218] Home healthcare will then become an even more significant element of the continuum of care, as our elderly population increases and requires higher levels of healthcare which are more affordable at home. Seniors also have a strong preference for where they want to receive care. A 2011 survey conducted by the National Conference of State Legislatures and the AARP Public Policy Institute showed 90% of seniors prefer to age at home.[219]

Fernand Sarrat is the owner of Home Helpers & Direct Link, a home healthcare service in Austin, Texas. He said,

> Senior citizens not only prefer a familiar environment, but want to retain as much independence as they can. Hospitals, nursing homes and increasingly, assisted living facilities, tend to require adherence to schedules and usually offer less privacy. Additionally, patients' contact with caregivers like nurses is limited. Financially, home health care is less expensive than live-in facilities.[220]

For these reasons, home healthcare increasingly will play a role in healthcare at large. Hospitals will benefit from reduced readmissions and government penalties. Family members who cares for their elders often experience a burden. Home healthcare will provide much needed respite. For elderly people limited in their daily activities, home care offers benefits. Toileting and bathing are easier. They have better mobility and they can enjoy cooking and companionship. They can live in a familiar environment where they feel independent, relaxed, and secure.

For many, home healthcare may be an interim step to home medical care and then nursing homes. But if the elderly have their way, they want to stay home. The Giraff Plus, robots, and other technologies described in Chapter 7 will make it easier for seniors to do so.

An April 2012 Pew Research Center survey found for the first time more than half of older adults (defined as those ages 65 or older) were Internet users. As of 2013, the number had grown to 59%, a six percent growth in one year.[221] In addition, 77% of older adults have a cell phone, up from 69% in April 2012. Seniors have adopted tools which help promote a positive health attitude.

Medicare's coverage for home health care doesn't match the demand. Non-medical home care largely is not covered, and medical home care is quite limited. The Centers should review policies in this area in light of the lower cost of home healthcare and the preference seniors are expressing for it.

Accountable Care Organizations

A definition of accountable includes "as required to explain actions" or "required to be responsible for something".[222] The concept of an Accountable Care Organization (ACO) was first described in 2006, but the definition has been vague and highly debated.[223] The intention of the ACA, signed into law by President Barack Obama on March 23, 2010, was clearer. An ACO must be accountable for the quality, cost, and overall care of a population of people who are enrollees in the ACO. The payer behind an ACO can be either Medicare or a private health insurance company. In either case, the providers who operate the ACO select a specific population of people for which they will be accountable. The driver behind the ACO model is to reduce the cost of healthcare by shifting the financial risk of caring for patients from the payer to the provider.

The ACO takes the PCMH to a higher level by changing the reimbursement model to apply to the population instead of the individual.[224] Under the ACO model, a payer such as Aetna or Blue Cross would enter into a contract with a community hospital to cover the entire population of a city, town, zip code, or specific policyholders except for those on Medicare. Medicare might similarly enter into such a contract for those who are Medicare-eligible. Under an ACO model, the community hospital or physician group would receive a fixed payment, say $350 per month for each person enrolled in the ACO. As a result, the hospital becomes highly motivated to understand the population at a very detailed level. They will utilize big data and analytics to determine what diseases are prominent in the population and they will develop preventive care and clinics to address those diseases. Because of the fixed payment per person in the population, the more effective preventive care the hospital can deliver, the better their financial results will be.

The big change in the ACO model will be risk based reimbursement; in effect, shifting the risk from the payer to the provider. The effect of the population model carrying over directly into the financial model can be significant. For example, under the risk based model, an ACO may get $10,000 to provide a hip replacement regardless of how many MRIs, tests, and treatments for infection may arise. If the patient gets an infection or requires a reopening of the hip for any reason, the cost rises dramatically, but the reimbursement is fixed.[225] On the other hand, a well-managed hospital with good teamwork and alignment among the caregivers may do the replacement for $6,000 and keep a portion of the incremental profit.

The Dartmouth Medical School was one of the first organizations to implement the ACO model. Two important lessons arose from their experience. The first was information technology is the most important tool to make an ACO work. The whole concept revolves around knowing which patients to include in the population model based on data about them, and collecting all the details associated with their care once they are in the program. Dartmouth used data warehouse technology to gather and analyze their data. Hospital administrators should begin the task of data gathering and analysis as soon as possible even if they are not ready to implement an ACO. The second lesson Dartmouth learned suggested hospital administrators should focus on coding charges. This would ensure the proper reimbursement to cover their costs and would allow them to participate in sharing of any cost savings.

Organizational Trends

According to the American Medical Association, about 60% of family doctors and pediatricians, 50% of surgeons, and 25% of subspecialists such as ophthalmologists and ear, nose and throat specialists are employees rather than independent practitioners.[226] The number of doctors who practice as salaried employees of hospital systems nearly has doubled in ten years. The number will continue to grow. With reduced reimbursements, single and small practices face a financial challenge since their overhead is significant. A physician specialist I know has two employees; a nurse and a receptionist. He cannot afford to implement an EHR system. Although he is an outstanding physician with high patient satisfaction, it will become increasingly difficult for him to support the overhead costs without other physicians to share it with. Patients may begin to demand electronic communication and access to an EHR. Some physicians say they will not bother implementing an EHR because they plan to retire soon.

My primary care physician recently joined a large practice of family physicians with more than 50 offices. A large group can easily afford to make the investments in an EHR system and numerous other resources shared among a large number of physicians. Many other physicians have decided to join a Physician Hospital Organization (PHO). A hospital in New England formed a PHO with 500 physicians, half employed by the hospital and half community doctors who the hospital recruited to join.

There are several aspects of the PHO that have created better alignment of goals between the hospital and the physician. First is the negotiation of reimbursement rates with the payers. A PHO with a large number of physicians has more leverage and can get better reimbursement rates than the doctors could get on their own.

The size of the hospital provides numerous other benefits to member physicians. PHO members benefit from hospital IT investments in EHR and HIE systems. These systems are unaffordable by small physician practices. The hospital can use its buying power to provide software, services, and educational programs at discounts to the physician members. The large employed medical group shares evidence based medical practice information with all members, and the benefit is the shared goal of improving patient safety and satisfaction. By following a consistent care delivery process, collaboration can lead to better healthcare across the community.

Hospitals are examining other organizational models to work more closely with community physicians. For example, some hospitals have formed co-management agreements with several specialized physician practices such as a spinal reconstruction group. Such an agreement calls for gain sharing where the hospital and the specialists base savings on the cost of surgical implants and devices and achievement of various quality related factors. Not that long ago, agreements such as these were considered anti-competitive and illegal, but policymakers now see the potential for cost reduction and encourage them.

Leveraging Specialists

As of September 2014, there were 893,851 physicians in the United States. Fifty-two percent were specialists and forty-eight percent were primary care physicians. Specialists create tremendous value as a result of their highly focused training, experience, and treatment capabilities. However, the overuse of specialists adds extra cost, and can cause unintended side effects. An example is the frustrations of the merry-go-round phenomena such as my mother experienced.

The New York based healthcare start up, RubiconMD, has an information technology based solution. A typical PCP office visit has an $80 reimbursement, while a specialist visit might be as high as $250. If the difference could be saved without impacting the outcome for the patient, a significant reduction in healthcare cost could be achieved. The RubiconMD solution provides clinical specialist advice and support to the PCP through its website.[227] The PCP then is able to make a request based on his or her diagnosis; a specialist is assigned and reviews the case, and provides clinical guidance to the PCP within hours. The PCP is then able to make a better informed decision on patient care. The business model includes the specialist receiving $50 or so for their advice. The online consult can be done anytime, anywhere, from any device, and the time commitment is typically 10-15 minutes. From the PCP perspective, he or she is getting expert advice enabling them to maintain a position of managing the healthcare situation for the patient.

RubiconMD would receive a small fee for managing the referral and advice between PCP and specialist. Gil Addo, co-founder and CEO of RubiconMD said that hospital and provider groups migrating to the accountability oriented, fee for value model are very interested in reducing the utilization of specialists and gaining the resulting savings. As for the PCPs using the RubiconMD platform, Ado said, "They are delighted to gain the expertise of the specialists without stepping out of the loop. The RubiconMD approach does not eliminate specialists – it leverages their capabilities for the benefit of the PCP and the patient."[228]

Evidence based Medicine

Anecdotal evidence is based on observations or reports. It is not based on science or research based information. Anecdotal medicine has served us well for more than a century, but it is possible to get much better healthcare outcomes with evidence based medicine. When we see our trusted doctor, he or she often diagnoses and prescribes based on decades of experience. We are fortunate there are great doctors with substantial experience, but there is a better way.

With the anecdotal model, the patient sees the doctor with certain symptoms and the doctor recalls a similar patient with similar symptoms and prescribes what he or she recalls worked previously. With evidence based medicine, the patient sees the doctor and the doctor consults with a database containing anonymized information on similar patients and what treatments produced what outcomes. Evidence based medicine gives the doctor access to data about thousands and eventually millions of patients and outcomes, not just the ones he or she has seen.

Personalized medicine takes evidence based medicine to a higher level. IBM is now positioning Watson, the IBM supercomputer that won Jeopardy, as a solution to many complex challenges, healthcare in particular. The company is working with the healthcare industry to use the massive amount of anonymized medical data collected from EHRs. It combines the data with advanced analytical tools to provide a personalized treatment recommendation based on matching a patient not to all patients, but to one particular patient. The recommendation would take into account, based on DNA, how a certain medication would be assimilated by the patient and exactly how much of the drug to take and when to take it.

Following is an example of a doctor using the tools of personalized medicine. The doctor would make a phone call to IBM's Watson with the following question. "I have a patient here who is a 43 year old, African-American female who has symptoms a, b, and c, and is taking medications x, y, and z. What do you recommend?" In the following few seconds, Watson would examine millions of anonymized EHRs plus thousands of relevant scholarly journal articles, and provide a recommendation based on scientific studies and an examination of the diagnoses and outcomes for 250,000 similarly situated persons. In evidence based medicine, the doctor decides, but is guided by substantial evidence.

The healthcare.gov website dominated healthcare news, but the U.S. Department of Health and Human Services has many other websites. One of them is provided by the Patient-Centered Outcomes Research Institute, an advisory committee chartered under the ACA to implement a new approach to medical care based on comparative effectiveness research (CER). The purpose of CER is to inform healthcare decisions by providing evidence on the effectiveness, risks, and benefits of different treatment alternatives. The source of the evidence is research comparing drugs, tests, procedures, medical devices, and methods of healthcare delivery. *The Washington Post* called CER a "rigorous review of what works and what doesn't".[229]

When a doctor is not sure of a diagnosis, and no doctor can know everything, he or she often orders tests. Many of the tests can be duplicative or unnecessary and add hundreds of billions of dollars to the cost of American healthcare. The concept of CER seems simple but it will face political hurdles. Congress passed legislation backing CER and provided funding for it. Congress then barred the government from using the results of what it had funded to examine the cost effectiveness of medical practices.

What are some of the reasons for concern about the use of CER? Is it possible The Research Institute may find ineffective tests, procedures, or drugs? I believe the answer is yes. Is it possible the revenue streams from such tests, procedures, or drugs are associated with a business whose lobbyists influenced the legislation? Once again, I believe the answer is yes. The Editorial Board at *The Washington Post* said the incentives for healthcare providers must be reformed. With regard to the use of CER, the Board said:

> The Institute will encounter its share of political dogfights. Republicans will invoke the specter of government imposed rationing. Some have already tried to ax the panel. Democrats will balk at the committee's research as heartless number crunching. Removing ineffective treatment from the healthcare system will be far from painless.
>
> But the alternative — throwing money into the cash-gobbling health-care industry with little measurement or accountability — should be much less tolerable. In fact, the Affordable Care Act's comparative effectiveness provisions don't go far enough; the law bars the government from examining the cost effectiveness of medical practices in the most straightforward way. That analysis should at least be available for the public to consider.[230]

Evidence based medicine is one of the largest areas of opportunity to improve healthcare outcomes for patients. There is a massive amount of data that gets captured and stays captured. Business intelligence (BI) is an analytical tool that operates on the concept of letting the captured data "escape" and become useful. BI software is used for extracting, identifying, and analyzing business data. BI software and services are available from mainstream software vendors including IBM, Oracle, and SAP, and from numerous smaller vendors. *Information Week* reported 50% of healthcare organizations would be using BI systems in 2015.[231]

BI can support clinicians, administrators, and patients. For example, a hospital analyst might use BI to analyze patient satisfaction data collected from surveys. The analyst might find patient satisfaction seems to dip on Tuesdays. Looking further, it may become evident on those Tuesdays with low satisfaction, there is a higher than normal amount of activity in the radiology department. With further study, BI may show a certain technician worked one day a week – on Tuesdays. There is a good chance this technician was the source of the patient satisfaction issue. This is just a hypothetical example, but it illustrates the potential of BI relative to patient satisfaction.

Much larger opportunities are on the horizon. In addition to improving patient satisfaction, BI tools can be used for data modeling, forecasting, and predictive analytics. It also can be used for trending of financial, operational, and clinical data. The time is near when all existing healthcare data will be able to be stored and analyzed by systems such as Watson. A primary care physician will be able to operate much like Captain Kirk and the crew of the starship Enterprise at the ship's computer on "Star Trek". IBM said the input will be expressed in human terms and the output will be accurate and understandable. Diagnoses will no longer have to be anecdotal. The transition from traditional data analysis to the use of more advanced tools such as BI will require an attitude change toward a more expansive use of data. Data is much more than it used to be.

Doctor Shortage or Surplus

One of the issues confronting the American healthcare system is the impending addition of tens of millions of previously uninsured people. Many people think this extremely large growth of patients will result in a large shortage of physicians. This likely will be true in the short run, but some believe the long-term supply of physicians may actually be a surplus. Dr. Eric Topol, an American cardiologist, geneticist, and researcher, believes the rapid growth of mHealth devices, and apps that can perform sophisticated algorithms, will enable consumers to help in the diagnosis of disease. At a minimum, physician productivity could be increased. In some cases, consumers will be able to self diagnose. Topol believes that 75% of echocardiograms can be eliminated by the use of an mHealth app. He said, "Since at least 50 percent of office visits may not be necessary, video visits could prove to be important for increasing the efficiency and productivity of both patients and doctors."[232] Topol's conclusion is physician productivity will be increased substantially through the use of new technology. Perhaps the shortage of physicians some predict may not happen.

Patient Safety and Quality

Patient safety and quality have not always been visible in healthcare. That changed when the Institute of Medicine published "To Err is Human: Building a Safer Health System" in 1999 reporting up to 98,000 people die in hospitals each year from medical errors which could have been prevented. Eliminating the unacceptable errors requires leadership, new tools, and new attitudes. This section describes the new attitudes required and describes some tools to translate the new attitude into results.

Patient safety and quality programs begin with leadership and a health attitude from the top. John Byrnes, author of "The Drive for Value: Key Roles for the CEO", said that quality and safety programs can only work effectively if the CEO follows a proactive approach. Byrnes said:

> CEOs should be the leading spokespeople for quality programs - passionate leaders for improvement, almost evangelical about the cause. They should use every available avenue and forum to reinforce that quality is their organization's top priority. This role cannot be delegated even if a chief medical officer or cheif quality officer is in place to manage the overall strategy and daily execution. What the CEO endorses publicly and privately is what gets done. If the CEO is silent on an issue, the message to the entire organization is that the issue is unimportant. Nothing is more impressive or galvanizing than a CEO who demonstrates a deep understanding of quality and safety from the podium to the hallway.[233]

The CEO has many opportunities, public and private, to reinforce a quality attitude as the top priority of the organization. During the Ebola crisis in October 2014, the CEO of Texas Health Presbyterian Hospital remained silent publicly for weeks after the Ebola care problem was identified and reported by the press. This seemed to be a missed opportunity to send a strong message to the entire organization.

The key steps Byrnes outlined for the CEO to achieve the best patient safety and quality possible are to instill accountability, effectively utilize committees at the board and organizational levels, and ensure availability of appropriate resources. At the hospital where I served as a board member for nine years, the CEO led generative discussions about patient safety and quality at every board meeting. He would take a few minutes at the beginning of the meeting to describe two events since the prior board meeting. One would be a "miracle" event representing an outcome far more positive than could have been expected. The other would be a "sentinel" event representing a poor outcome that should never have happened.

The Joint Commission, an independent, not-for-profit organization that accredits and certifies more than 20,000 healthcare organizations and programs in the United States, defines a sentinel event as an unexpected occurrence involving death or serious physical or psychological injury, or the risk thereof. The Board reviewed the top 50 patient safety and quality measurements at least quarterly. Each month the Board approved physician credentials and appointments or renewals to the medical staff of the hospital, thereby giving them the ability to admit and treat patients. The Board had an attitude that quality was its responsibility.

Coordinating healthcare for patients in the many departments of a hospital is similar to managing an automobile assembly line. The analogy extends further to the quality of healthcare. Hospitals are learning to use a quality control tool other industries have known for decades – Six Sigma. Six Sigma is a set of statistical techniques and tools used to improve the quality, efficiency, and productivity of processes. The idea of measuring quality is not new. One of the great pioneers of quality was Dr. Joseph Juran. Juran immigrated to Minneapolis in 1912 and was an engineering graduate from the University of Minnesota. Juran's *Quality Control Handbook* was published in 1951and represented the beginning of a new approach to manage quality.

Quality has been highly integrated in manufacturing for 50+ years; it is late in coming to healthcare. The Malcolm Baldridge National Quality Award recognizes extraordinary quality efforts in an organization, giving its first award in 1988. Two hospitals won the award in 2003, and the focus on quality in hospitals is increasing. Seventeen hospitals have won the Baldridge out of a total of 95 that have been awarded. The Magnet Hospital program, which recognizes positive work environments and professional development opportunities for nurses, includes the effectiveness of quality programs as criteria for award nominations.

Many hospitals have specially trained Six Sigma experts known as Black Belts who are experts at examining processes and suggesting measurements and improvements to remove defects and improve outcomes or reduce cost or both. NewYork-Presbyterian Hospital has embraced Six Sigma tools to find solutions to difficult problems. A 2006 study published in the *Journal of Organizational Excellence* reported a 2,224-bed hospital made a significant investment in people and systems to employ rigorous process measurements. As a result, quality and effectiveness were improved and paid for the investment many times over. At NewYork-Presbyterian, anyone in the hospital can nominate a project where they believe process improvement would enhance patient safety and quality.

One of the key tools of Six Sigma is called DMAIC, which stands for define, measure, analyze, improve, control. The Black Belt teams applied the technique to more than 100 projects. One of them was focused on a problem faced by every hospital -- reducing patient room turnaround time. When a patient enters the hospital through the ER, the clock starts ticking for an available bed. Like a hotel, the number of beds is fixed and to make one available usually means someone has to vacate the room and then the room has to be cleaned. The cleaning time is a key part of the process. If there is a backup, the ER becomes overcrowded and patients and doctors become dissatisfied.

The Black Belts designed what they called the Housekeeping Turnaround Time Project designed to find ways to reduce bed-cleaning time and move the patient more quickly through the continuum of care at the hospital. The cleaning process includes three steps: (1) the patient care unit notifies housekeeping the bed has been vacated and is ready to be cleaned, (2) housekeeping cleans the bed, and (3) housekeeping notifies the nurse's station the bed is ready for the next patient.

The Black Belt's initial measurement found the three-step process took an average of 101 minutes. However, a second measurement showed a thorough cleaning only took an average of 25–30 minutes. The Black Belt team analyzed the gap between the two notification points, and found it was caused by lack of staff availability and communications. A further analysis showed cleaning staff was not available during shift changes and lunch breaks, and the notification process for a vacant bed was not consistent.

The Black Belt team devised some simple process changes to improve the housekeeping turnaround time. Lunches and shift changes for housekeeping staff were placed on a staggered schedule to enable continuous coverage. The second part of the solution deployed an electronic bed-tracking system in which housekeepers carry a pager so the nursing station can notify them immediately when a bed becomes empty and ready for immediate cleaning. The Housekeeping Turnaround Time Project resulted in a 50% reduction in the average housekeeping turnaround time, and the improvement has sustained at that level for more than a year. The hospital projected the value of the new process at more than $700,000 annually, in addition to increasing bed capacity and improving patient and physician satisfaction.

The operating room (OR), in many ways, is like a manufacturing environment with a lot of complexity and moving parts. Dr. Atul Gawande, a surgeon and author of *The Checklist Manifesto: How to Get Things Right* described the OR as a theatre where, in the past, the surgeon was totally in charge, and everyone else took orders. Dr. Gawande uses examples from medicine and aviation to make the point about how easy it is for people, even brilliant surgeons, to forget things which can jeopardize the lives of others.

Being a pilot, I greatly appreciate the importance of checklists. When learning to fly, the checklist is fundamental. You learn to use the checklist before every flight, every time, no matter how much experience you have, even if you have flown the airplane thousands of hours. Dr. Gawande's book explains the numerous errors occurring when a simple step is skipped in a medical setting due to the frenetic pace of the operating room, possible distractions, and interruptions. Dr. Gawande believes the checklist can be applied to healthcare as it has been for decades in aviation. In some respects, healthcare providers have considered themselves unique and not subject to the processes of other industries. Now, providers understand there are direct benefits from studying other industries.

Although the surgery error rate is difficult to discuss, the numbers of errors are in the thousands. Dr. Gawande believes simple checklists of steps needed to ensure high quality surgery can dramatically change the numbers, and he cites studies where this is proven. I was impressed with the great respect Dr. Atul Gawande shows toward nurses in his book. In addition to promoting the checklist, he highlights the critical role nurses play, participating equally with the surgeon as part of a team taking care of a patient.[234]

I was fortunate to witness checklists in action. A spinal reconstruction surgeon invited me to visit the OR and see how quality arises from teamwork and processes. I was in several ORs for seven hours and witnessed open heart, brain craniotomy, neck repair, middle-back repair, and major spine reconstruction surgeries. I never will forget the incredible experience. In each of the ORs there was a big poster on the wall labeled "Teamwork for a Timeout". After the patient was in position and prepared for surgery, the lead nurse led an interactive checklist. She asked: Who is the surgeon in charge? Who is the anesthesiologist? Each person responded with his or her name. She then asked the surgeon for the name of the patient, the reason he or she was there, what procedure was going to be performed, and what medications the patient would be taking after the surgery. After the last item, the nurse said, "Does everyone agree?" There was a brief silence. The scalpel did not touch the patient until the timeout was complete.

Many technologies used for years in manufacturing and distribution could also be used by hospitals and have a positive impact on patient safety and quality. For example, radio-frequency identification (RFID) is an innovative technology that can have major implications for healthcare organizations. An RFID tag contains a chip that can respond to a radio frequency signal, much like a Mobil Speedpass for gasoline purchases or a highway and bridge toll tag on a car windshield. RFID tags in surgical sponges could enable the OR team to see a precise sponge count on a video display throughout a procedure.

One of the many new policies contained in the ACA is the intent to introduce incentives for improved healthcare. The Centers withhold 3% of hospital Medicare reimbursements and redistributes the withheld funds based on a hospital score. Three percent of Medicare reimbursements is billions of dollars, so hospitals pay attention to the new method of reimbursement. The score is 70% based on quality measurements and 30% on patient satisfaction.

Quality measurements include patient safety and quality-related items such as hospital-acquired infections, improper needle sticks, ventilator-associated pneumonia, and patient falls. The patient satisfaction score is based on a hospital consumer assessment of healthcare providers. The score is derived from a survey containing 21 patient perspectives on care and rating of items in nine key areas: (1) communication with doctors, (2) communication with nurses, (3) responsiveness of hospital staff, (4) pain management, (5) communication about medicines, (6) discharge information, (7) cleanliness of the hospital environment, (8) quietness of the hospital environment, and (9) transition of care. The questions asked in the survey are very specific about the hospital and staff. They include: Was the room clean? Was the room quiet? Did you understand the conversations you had with the doctors? Could you understand the nurses' directions?

Some hospitals are becoming Planetree hospitals, a concept to improve patient satisfaction and gain good survey scores. Planetree is a model of care putting the focus on the patient as never before. Physicians, nurses, and management are trained on the Planetree model and learn the importance of treating patients with respect and ensuring their communications with patients are clear and unambiguous. Planetree studies show by asking the patient if they understand what has been explained to them, there is a net savings of time by avoiding follow-on questions.

Population Health

As millions of consumers and providers add data to patient EHRs, a multitude of data will become available for the greater good. Researchers can anonymize the data and combine it with a large database containing vast amounts of information about the health of the population at a community level, nationally, or globally.

In order to create large databases, providers and state public health organizations must input and share information. To make that happen, the Office of the National Coordinator for Health Information Technology within the U.S. Department of Health and Human Services issued $548 million in grants to help states develop health information exchanges for sharing health data among providers, Medicare, Medicaid, and public health agencies.[235] For healthcare providers to receive the incentives, their EHR systems must interface with immunization registries to transmit electronic data public health agencies deem important, electronically record and submit clinical surveillance data and laboratory results, and identify and report cancer and certain other cases to a state cancer registry.

A thorough understanding of the demographics and medical condition of a population subset could enable hospitals to develop community based preventive care programs and clinics to address the needs of chronically ill patients in the community. The combination of big-data and analytics can enable researchers, public health officials, and healthcare leaders to ask previously difficult to answer questions, and focus on population health.

An example of focusing on population health was documented in a 1981 Massachusetts Department of Public Health study confirming a cluster of childhood leukemia in Woburn, Massachusetts. While the treatment of each child was vitally important, of equal importance to the population at large was gaining insight about why Woburn was experiencing a higher than expected incidence of childhood leukemia. Woburn has a 130 year history as an industrial city. Part of the recent history included the deposit of tannery and chemical manufacturing waste into the local environment. Tests in 1979 revealed contaminants in two of the city's drinking water wells. The wells were closed. By 1986, 21 childhood leukemia cases were reported. Based on the population size, less than six cases would have been expected.[236] Analysis of water distribution models and neighborhood locations, it was possible to identify possible cases of the disease. The big data and analytics tools available today make it possible to examine phenomena such as the leukemia cluster on a much larger scale and with greater precision.

As the ACO model of care causes providers to think about the population for which they are caring, gaining insight from data about that population will become essential. Cardiologists may see data from a CHF research study as a way to develop care plans that are more effective than plans developed at an individual level. For example, detailed data from CardioNet or other monitoring technologies could enable cardiologists to make changes in a drug, drug dosage, or frequency of taking a drug, and then see the impact on the activity of the heart of the patient. Likewise, home healthcare services may be able to use data from a CHF study to help them refine their care delivery programs. PCPs participating in PCMHs are beginning to see the benefits of gaining more data about CHF patients.[237] PCPs, cardiologists, and home healthcare services could encourage their regular patients to participate in research studies. More participants would increase study size and provide greater statistical power to validate or disprove various hypotheses.

Benefits of Population Health

The shift to the ACO model will require providers to understand as much as possible about the population for which it provides care. Researchers Kayyali, Knott, and Kuiken said that the use of big data could provide transparency to the health of a community, and drive improved patient outcomes, reduce readmissions, and eventually reduce American healthcare cost by $300 billion to $450 billion.[238] Healthcare leaders need to ensure they have robust plans for exploiting their data. Focusing on the population at large is essential when you consider the demographics. Dr. David Nash, Dean of the Thomas Jefferson University School of Population Health said that the sickest 5 percent of the population costs 50 times as much per capita as the 75 percent of people who are healthy. The reason physicians do not focus on the population at large is related to incentives. Dr. Nash pointed out his hometown of Philadelphia has five outstanding medical schools that combined train five percent of all United States physicians nationwide, yet Philadelphia is in the least healthy county in Pennsylvania. Dr. Nash said, "Medical schools aren't focused on the health of populations, they focus on episodic acute care, because that is where the money is today. When the incentive system changes, physicians will change the way they practice."[239]

Wearable, health information devices such as the Fitbit represent the beginning of a new age in personal data collection. The data can benefit both the individual and the population at large. Treatment of individual patients is important, but the larger opportunity is to gain an understanding of the epidemiologic factors affecting the community population. The resulting insights could provide a basis to develop new standards of care and lead to improved patient safety and a higher quality of care. These factors result in improved quality of life for patients and their families.

For example, a cardiologist may ask what percentage of all congestive heart failure (CHF) patients in the community served by the practice are males over 65 who have been readmitted at least once in the past year and are taking a beta-blocker medication. A healthcare planning analyst may develop a model to predict the number of CHF readmissions to expect in the coming year. A descriptive statistics study of the CHF population may serve as the basis to design new studies and formulate hypotheses. Such studies may answer key research questions relevant to the hospital's mission to care for the community it serves. Such studies, combined with epidemiologic data, could help healthcare leaders to develop programs to replace patient-by-patient treatment with preventive medical programs. Clinics can address health problems on a community basis.

Healthcare leadership should evaluate the role of epidemiology in the organization's strategic planning. An epidemiologic approach would use the science of public health and prevention as a tool to examine the etiology of disease on a population basis. The data exists. The next step is to build an analytics platform to extract information and understanding from the data for the benefit of the community.

Analytics also can help doctors see trends in patient populations. For example, by showing among 2,000 patients how many have uncontrolled diabetes, or how many women haven't had their mammography screening, healthcare planners gain a snapshot they haven't been able to see before. All of these things combined move us one step further away from anecdotal medicine toward information based medicine. The result will be better outcomes at lower cost.

End of Life Choices

The changes in health attitudes I have proposed must include a discussion about end of life care. The recent passing of my mother-in-law at 93 caused me to think about end of life. The first thoughts were about reverence and respect. Grandma was a wonderful person. Her three children, five grandchildren, and eight great grandchildren loved her. Grandma was also the last of our four parents, and elevated my wife and I to the position of elders, a role we feel too young to hold. Grandma died peacefully in her sleep after being in hospice care for two months. The hospice care was thoughtful and caring. Unfortunately, my wife's father and both of my parents did not experience peaceful days as they approached the end of their lives, but they could have.

One beautiful Fall day in 2012, I drove to Manhattan to have breakfast with a dozen physicians and healthcare executives. We had a discussion with Dr. Atul Gawande, a surgeon, staff writer for the *New Yorker*, and author of three best-selling books about healthcare. After the breakfast discussion, we went to the packed School of Visual Arts Theatre at the annual New Yorker Festival to hear Dr. Gawande's talk titled "How to Live When You Have to Die". He expanded on the subject in his new book, *Being Mortal: Medicine and What Matters In The End*, published in October 2014.[240]

End of life is a subject deserving more discussion. Dr. Gawande cited figures about the staggering cost of healthcare expended in the final days of life for millions of people. Medicare spends six times more for persons who are in their last year of life than for a survivor. Out-of-pocket expenses for Medicare beneficiaries averaged $38,688 during the last five years of life compared to $23,000 for survivors.[241] The cost difference in the last month is even more pronounced. Of the

$554 billion Medicare spent in 2011, 28 percent, or about $170 billion, was for patients' last six months of life.[242]

Dr. Gawande believes part of the challenge in changing attitudes about end of life is doctors often are not candid about the prognosis for a patient, and family members do not want to discuss end of life. In his book, he suggested what is needed is what he called a breakpoint discussion with the terminally ill patient centered around four simple principles. First is an honest assessment of the condition and prognosis. Second is to ask about what fears the person has. Third is to ask the patient about his or her goals — what do they want for themselves and for their families? Finally is the question of what tradeoffs the person is willing to make — for example, what degree of pain and suffering versus comfort?

At the conclusion of his one-hour talk, Dr. Gawande entertained questions. A young woman in the audience told of her experience of losing her husband to cancer six months earlier. She described how they had discussions very much along the lines Dr. Gawande had outlined. She praised the approach and brought the audience to tears.

The largest components of end of life costs are inpatient hospital stays, the use of physician services, and stays in skilled nursing facilities. An increase in medical care near end of life is expected, but the dramatic cost of it raises the question, Is there is too much care near the end of one's life? Dr. Dempsey Springfield, an Orthopedic Surgeon in Boston, MA, said, "In the 1970s, it was difficult for a physician to do much for some seriously ill patients near the end of life, so excessive treatment was rare. However, because of advances made in medical care over the last 35 yeas, it is now extremely easy to provide excessive care, and in fact, it is usually expected for a physician to do as much as is humanly possible near end of life. The result is too much testing, too much treatment, and too much cost."[243]

Even though palliative care, relieving pain and providing comfort without treating the underlying cause, can result in living longer with better quality of life, there is often an unstoppable momentum by physicians and family to do more. Our impulse is to try anything and everything to preserve the life of a loved one when at times this approach results in a nearly unbearable quality of life. This is followed by significant trauma to family members when the end of life eventually comes. Hospice care is often shunned out of fear of the implications. It provides comfort to all it serves. The hospice staff helps reduce trauma for family members and moderate suffering for the terminally ill.

After two trips to the ER, it became clear how traumatic the trips were for Grandma, my mother-in-law. The care she received did not cure her, but rather stabilized her condition interim to the next ER visit. At 93, her CHF would not be cured and her strength was on the decline. The assisted living home nursing staff recommended hospice. Hearing the term automatically conjures up end of life, but my wife, a former registered intensive care nurse, decided to learn more about what the nurses were proposing.

Grandma would be able to remain in the same room at the assisted living home she had been living in for nearly four years. The same staff would see her, but additional hospice nurses from a separate organization would be assigned. There would be a hospice physician who would make any needed medical decisions. A hospice chaplain would provide spiritual support to Grandma and my wife. What Grandma would not receive was any more trips to the hospital. If an acute situation should arise, the hospice physician would decide what palliative care would be applied. My wife considered all these factors and discussed hospice with her mother. They both agreed it was the best path forward.

Hospice care for Grandma lasted three months. She had some episodes, and the nurses handled them. Then, she began to fail. The hospice staff adjusted medications to relieve her pain and agitation. Grandma was 200 miles away, but my wife visited her more regularly than before hospice. She received daily phone updates from the hospice nurse. My wife described the care her mother received as "compassionate and appropriate". When the end came, it was not a surprise. Medicare paid for 100% of the hospice care, but spent much less taxpayer money than the traditional care would have cost.

Having the end of life discussion with a terminally ill patient can become emotional and distressing for the patient and family. Putting a structure behind the discussion can make the task a little easier. Elizabeth Puffenbarger, a liaison for the Center for Connected Care at the Cleveland Clinic Hospice and Palliative Medicine at Home in Independence, Ohio, wrote, "When To Refer Patients For Hospice Care", which was published in *American Nurse Today*. To structure the end of life discussion, Puffenbarger recommends a framework called SPIKES which stands for setting, perception, information, knowledge, empathy, and summarize.[244]

About 3,500 hospice organizations delivered Medicare hospice services to 1.1 million Medicare enrollees in 2010, a jump of 53 percent in 14 years, according to the Medicare Payment Advisory Commission MedPAC. Forty-four percent of beneficiaries who died in 2010 used hospice, up from 42 percent in 2009 and 23 percent in 2000. The average length of stay in hospice increased to 86 days, up from 84 days in 2009 and 54 days in 2000. Medicare is encouraging the use of hospice and paying for it. It is a major tool for containing the growth of American health-care cost.

A study published in the *New England Journal of Medicine* found cancer patients receiving palliative care lived almost two months longer than those who received standard care.[245] The researchers also found the patients receiving palliative care reported a higher quality of life as they approached their end of life. Health attitudes about hospice are changing in a positive way. Patients and physicians are more receptive to the concept. Hospice care is losing the stigma of "giving up" on a chronically or terminally ill person. One regional hospice organization describes their service as, "Care beginning with dignity, propelled by hope, and accomplished with grace."[246]

Summary

This chapter included many health attitude changes suggested for health-care providers. It starts with the shift from an entitlement oriented, fee for service model to an accountability oriented, fee for value model. Shifting away from fee for service is not easy, but the cost of continuing with it is unbearable. Coordination of care through the PCMH and leveraging of physician extenders can improve care and reduce the cost of care. The ACO shift of risks to providers can also be difficult. It not only can reduce costs, but also can lead to higher quality healthcare. New models such as PHOs create better alignment between the goals of hospitals and physicians. Specialists are vital to healthcare, but perhaps PCPs could have other options in the way they use specialists which would be less costly. Evidence based medicine can lead to better outcomes and less unnecessary testing. Patient safety and quality are taking a higher profile, as they should. Another shift underway is the focus on the care of populations, not just individuals. Finally, end of life care needs a higher priority. It must become part of the discussion between terminally ill patients and their physicians and families. All of the changes and improvements in healthcare described in this chapter require new health attitudes. Providers also need new tools to exploit technology developments that can improve healthcare.

CHAPTER 10

Leveraging Health Attitude with Provider Tools

O ne of the reasons people are taking more responsibility for their health and healthcare is the availability of easy to use fitness and health monitoring equipment. The use of these tools and a new health attitude are key ingredients in the transformation to a better healthcare system. Providers need to consider their health attitude and to what degree it is centered on the health of patients and less focused on fee-for-service. Patient-centered care supports and encourages active involvement of consumers and their families in treatment decisions. This care embraces patients participating in the diagnosis using the numerous mHealth devices and apps that are available to consumers.

This chapter includes a discussion about the practice of medicine across the continuum of care and a shift to population based healthcare. I will describe many tools available to providers including additional mHealth devices and apps, telehealth, genomic based personalized medicine, big data and analytics, algorithms, and the World Community Grid.

Tablets, Phablets, and Apps

Bertha Coombs at CNBC reported how our attitudes are changing about the use of tablet computers. She said that there are two things Dr. Larry Nathanson,

Director Of Emergency Medicine at Boston's Beth Israel Deaconess Medical Center, can't work without when he's on duty: his stethoscope and his iPad. "As I am walking from room to room, I know who I need to see next," he explained, scrolling through a list of patients in his virtual emergency room on the iPad. [247] Early adopting physicians have been embracing the iPad since its introduction, but now the iPad is mainstream. Not only can a doctor scroll his or her list of patients to be visited, but also he or she can share information with patients.

Dr. Henry Feldman, a surgeon at Boston's Beth Israel Deaconess Medical Center, told Coombs that when it comes to treating surgical patients, being able to pull up diagrams and x-rays at their bedside has been a real game changer. Feldman said patients have told him more than once, "That's the first time I've understood my disease". [248]

ITG Market Research conducted a survey of 500 physicians and hospital professionals in 2014. When asked to identify the devices they use for professional purposes, the respondents indicated 68% use an iPhone and 43% use an iPad. [249] Do these statistics mean Apple will dominate healthcare mobile computing? What about Samsung, Microsoft, the Blackberry, and other Android tablets? We are still at the early stage of the shift to tablets. The market is certainly large enough for a lot of players, but Apple has some distinct and relevant advantages. It offers ease of use, integration across multiple devices using iCloud, and the Apple Health app. An additional subtle factor is Apple vets all apps before they are released in the app store. Many doctors believe this adds some creditability to the apps compared to the millions of apps available on Android where there is no vetting.

Although tablets are a natural device for handheld apps in healthcare, they are not the only solution. When Samsung introduced the Galaxy Note Smartphone with a 5.7 inch high definition display, the common reaction by many was that it is "huge". However, consumers who bought them loved the large display and found it more pleasing to browse the web and use mobile apps. Samsung's market share began to grow significantly. Apple responded with the iPhone 6 Plus, which is even bigger. The large screen smartphones are referred to as phablets – larger than a normal smartphone and smaller than a normal tablet. What is normal for one person is not normal for others, but the rapid acceptance of the iPhone 6 Plus indicates large is the new normal. For healthcare providers, phablets are a good fit. In addition to phone capabilities, providers find the device small enough to fit in a pocket and large enough to use healthcare apps productively.

An example of an app that may not have been useful on a small smartphone but surely is with a phablet is Muscle Systems Pro. It is an interactive tool that allows a physician to completely explore the muscular anatomy of the human body. It uses photorealistic 3-D models you can select, view, rotate, explore, and study. You can strip away muscles layer by layer, and view the underlying skeletal structure. You can look up 433 of the major muscles in the human body. With the normal finger swipes, you can rotate any part of the human body model and see its anterior, superior, inferior, or lateral views. Zooming in on a specific muscle reveals the direction the muscle and fascia fibers are running. If you want to learn more about a particular muscle, just tap on a graphical flag on the muscle and a pop-up shows the muscle's name, its origin, and what it does. You can even add a note to the muscle to record your thoughts or comments about it. One physician I showed Muscle System Pro to said he would have had much better grades in medical school if he had this tool.

While most iPad apps cost a few dollars or less, Muscle System Pro is $9.99. Michael Grothause, a technology writer, said in his blog, "This isn't your run of the mill app." In his review, he called it, "A 3-D powerhouse of interactive anatomy that every doctor, chiropractor, nurse practitioner and massage therapist should own, not to mention every medical student or anyone interested in human anatomy."[250] Grothause described a really big market segment. He added that when you use an app like this, it's easy to tell tablet computers are not just the future of consumer computing, but for learning and medical reference as well. I agree. I can imagine an orthopedic surgeon using this in his or her office to describe your knee pain to you instead of showing the plastic models of old. The app could be a great bedside aid for a physician to explain to a patient why they hurt, where they hurt, and what exact intervention is proposed to make things better.

One of the big unknowns in the early days of the iPad was how federal regulators would respond to the grass-roots demand for healthcare related apps. There are many questions to be answered. If a doctor takes a picture of a patient with the iPad, does that make the iPad a medical diagnostic device? A similar set of questions was raised in the field of aviation, but the demand from pilots was so strong the FAA found a way to certify the iPad for paperless flight charts. The Center for Devices and Radiological Health within the FDA regulates and approves any equipment they deem to be a medical device. For example, the Kinsa thermometer described in Chapter 7 provides a consumer with their temperature. This is considered an important piece of medical information that must be accurate. The Kinsa app is not regulated, but without the device, the app is useless. The FDA has already cleared more than 150 mobile device apps for smartphones, but it isn't just consumers who have access to the growing number of mobile health apps and devices. There is an explosion of mHealth apps and devices for doctors, nurses, and hospitals.

In a November 2014 Medscape Multispecialty e-newsletter, read by thousands of doctors, Dr. David Lee Scher and Neil Chesanow described "15 Game-Changing Wireless Devices to Improve Patient Care".[251] The technologies described can help doctors better manage and care for patients.

Table 5: Game-Changing Wireless Devices

AliveCor® Heart Monitor. An ECG in Your Pocket	Attaches to a smartphone and records accurate ECGs and heart rate in 30 seconds. Can monitor effects of medications, track palpitations and shortness of breath, and record the cardiac effects of alcohol or caffeine consumption.
AirStrip®. Monitoring inpatients when you're not in the hospital	Monitors inpatient's vital signs remotely. Retrieves patient's temperature, blood pressure, CT scans, ultrasounds, labs, radiographs, medications, and EHR from hospital on a doctor's tablet or smartphone.
Glooko MeterSync™ device. Checking All Your Diabetic Patients at Once	Connects over 30 non-wireless glucometers to patient smartphones. An app shows doctor data on multiple patients including date of birth, diabetes type, and blood glucose readings. Flags patients who may be trending toward risk. Helps doctor manage his or her patients.
Proteus Digital Health. A Foolproof Medication Compliance Monitor	Stomach juices activate tiny chip on ingestible pill. Digital signal sent to Band-Aid® like monitor worn on the patient's arm or stomach. Records medication taken, ingestion time, heart rate, body temperature, body position, and rest and activity patterns. Data are wirelessly transmitted to an app, which in turn relays it to monitoring doctor or family member.
Propeller Health. A Symptom Tracker for Patients With Asthma or COPD	Patients with asthma or chronic obstructive pulmonary disease (COPD) use device that fits onto an inhaler and wirelessly syncs with an app to record trends. Helps doctor manage asthma patients and their medications based on time of day and air conditions.

Echo Therapeutics. An Advance in Insulin Administration and Glucose Monitoring	A non-invasive monitoring system for patients with diabetes. A pen-like device administers insulin by pain-free permeation of skin. No needle. Biosensor placed on finger, much like a Band-Aid®, transmits blood glucose level every minute to a monitor that tracks glucose levels and rate of glucose change. Not yet FDA approved.
Medtronic's Seeq™ Mobile Cardiac Telemetry System. Precise Monitoring of Cardiac Patients With Frequent Symptoms	A wearable peel-and-stick sensor with wireless transmitter for up to 30-day cardiac monitoring. Medicare-certified diagnostic testing facility monitors data and notifies physician of relevant events. Records events and every heartbeat.
Withings Smart Body Analyzer. A Scale That Measures Much More Than Your Weight	FDA approved Bluetooth device monitors fat mass, lean mass, body mass index, pulse, and air quality. Companion app tracks running, weight loss, activity, calorie levels, and cardiovascular fitness. Physicians can monitor weight gains for congestive heart failure patients.
Zephyr Technology BioPatch™. A Smart Way to Monitor Cardiac Patients	Continuously monitors heart rate, R-wave interval, respiration rate, activity level, position, and posture from home or hospital. Doctor can remotely monitor vital signs that are updated every minute.

GrandCare Systems. A Wireless System to Improve Seniors' Health and Wellness	Tablet-like device can allow elderly patients at home or nursing home to enjoy higher quality of life. The app displays medication schedules, reminders, and notes from family or doctors. Connects to weight scale, pulse oximeter, glucometer, blood pressure cuff, thermometer, motion sensors, door and window sensors, and pressure sensors to detect use of chair or bed. A web portal allows video chat, photo sharing, email, music, and videos.
EarlySense® All-in-One System. An Early Warning System for Monitoring Inpatients	Sensor inserted under the mattress of the patient's bed monitors heart rate, respiration, and body movement. Continuous instead of nurse check every 4-6 hours. Nurses are notified of a change in patient status. May prevent falls and pressure ulcers.
Viatom Technology Checkme™ Health Monitor. A Real-Life Tricorder	Small wireless device monitors heart rhythm, blood oxygenation, sleep patterns, temperature, blood pressure, and footsteps. Allows daily reminders, voice memos, and health information sharing with family and friends via email social media sites.
MIT's Media Lab. Patient-Generated Eyeglass Prescriptions	Plastic eyepiece clips onto a smartphone screen. Patient views the screen through the eyepiece, sees several parallel lines, and presses the phone's arrow keys until the lines overlap. Results in a prescription for eyeglasses in two minutes. Pending FDA approval.

Moticon OpenGo wireless insole sensor. The Sole of a New Machine	Thin as a normal insole, it wirelessly transmits data on a patient's plantar pressure distribution and gait to smartphone app. Useful for clinical research and sports science, analysis of training, and optimizing rehabilitation after a foot injury. Can predict Parkinson disease or risk for falling.
WoundRounds®. Reducing Pressure Ulcer Risk in Bedridden Patients	Software tool for doctors to automate wound assessment, simplify wound treatment, and identify bedridden risk of pressure ulcers. Allows doctor to track progress of wound healing and data to provide a referral to specialist if needed.

A Perfect Storm

Thirty years ago corporations were focused on solidifying their mainframe computer applications. Department Heads wanted their own solutions and they opted for local area networks of PCs. It took Chief Information Officers (CIOs) a couple of decades to regain control of the organization's information technology. The cycle is now repeating itself – doctors and patients alike want easy to use mobile apps, not the often more complicated apps that use web browsers on desktops. The missing link is to allow providers to use devices and apps while the hospital or provider organization maintains control over the central repository of data. CIOs refer to this as the "backend". For music, the backend is iTunes. For healthcare, the backend will be the health information exchanges and patient portals springing up around the country. When the linkage is made, the tablets and phablets will become the windows into our health and be a tool for improved outcomes.

Dr. John Halamka, Chief Information Officer of the Beth Israel Deaconess Medical Center in Boston, summed it up for CNBC. He said, "I would call this [transition to mobile devices] a perfect storm for medicine. You have alignment of funding; a cultural change where doctors want to use devices to improve quality; you also have new devices and new software that is much easier to use.[252] It is common knowledge errors are made in healthcare and patients can be harmed. I believe a major contributing factor to these errors is imperfect communication of information. Mobile devices can greatly improve communications between patients and providers. The apps and devices described here are the tip of the iceberg leading to better outcomes and reduced cost.

Telehealth

Telehealth is the use of telecommunications technologies and the Internet to support a broad range of healthcare services for consumers and professionals. The services include the distribution of public health information, availability of health-related education, and long distance clinical healthcare diagnostics and monitoring. The technologies include land based and wireless communications, the web, streaming media, and videoconferencing.[253] Telemedicine is a more specific subset of telehealth that uses telecommunications and the Internet to provide access to online consultation, diagnosis, health assessment, intervention, coordinated care plans, and the ability to exchange information with providers. Telemedicine can be as simple as two doctors having a conference call via telephone to discuss the diagnosis of a patient or as sophisticated as a surgical procedure performed where the surgeon is in a different location than the patient.[254] Telemonitoring is a subset of telemedicine that uses electronic sensors and other digital devices to record physiological data, such as the weight, heart rhythm, and blood pressure, and transmit data to healthcare providers using telecommunications technology.[255]

I observed first hand an excellent example of telemonitoring in 2004 by visiting a woman named Joan. The local Visiting Nurses Association (VNA) was using technology to remotely monitor the condition of Joan in her home. The information technology industry has been doing remote monitoring of computers for decades. IBM mainframe computers had this capability in the 1970's. The computer would monitor key components and capabilities of the system. If a problem was detected requiring human intervention, the computer would automatically call IBM Service and tell them what replacement part the service engineer should bring. A variation on IBM's remote monitoring had been implemented by the VNA.

A VNA nurse and I arrived at Joan's house. We rang the doorbell, were beckoned to come in, and Joan turned her wheelchair around to greet us. The nurse explained I wanted to learn about her telemonitoring equipment. Joan was more than happy, actually I think she was proud, to show us. The telemonitoring system, which looked like a desktop PC, was setup to measure five different things. Joan pressed a button and the system said, "Good morning, Joan", then it stepped her through a sequence of activities. Prompted by the system, Joan climbed from her wheelchair onto the electronic digital scale. Her weight was displayed on a bright red LED panel. Next came the digital thermometer. Joan then inserted her arm into a blood pressure cuff and pressed the "BP Start" button. Seconds later her systolic and diastolic readings appeared. The final two measurements were taken when Joan was prompted to put her finger into an oximeter, which displayed the percentage of her hemoglobin saturated with oxygen. This is an important measurement, especially for elderly people because it is predictive of certain medical conditions which may require treatment. The device also measures the pulse.

After the measurements were completed, the system began to ask a range of questions programmed into it by one of the VNA nurses. "How are you feeling today? Have you had any discomfort? Have you been able to eat normally? Did you take your medications?"

At the completion of the measurements and questions, the system placed a phone call and transmitted the data to a central monitoring station. If anything was out of normal boundaries, or if Joan did not run the monitoring procedure on her normal schedule, she would receive a phone call and if she did not answer, her caregiver would be called. If any of the measurements were out of normal range, a VNA nurse would be dispatched to make a home visit.

The benefits to remote monitoring are significant. Doctors can see a graph showing trends — not just the measurements at today's office visit, but months of trend data. Trend data can show something may be developing, a nurse can be dispatched to check further, and if necessary a doctor visit can be arranged. Contrast this to a patient waiting until something goes wrong and having to call 911. Hospital and community costs can be reduced because of less emergency treatment.

What struck me about the visit to Joan was not the technology but the social aspects of the process. Joan was attached to the telemonitoring system — not technically, but emotionally. She was taking responsibility for her health. She had a health attitude. The data collected was Joan's data — she collected it — and she could see the impact of certain dietary choices or activities on the key measurements. People at the ER had previously called Joan a "frequent flier". Now she doesn't visit so often. Perhaps she fears being away from her system. The system had become her buddy. It was Facebook to Joan. Some studies have shown a person being monitored will fess up to having had a fall, which they would not have told a nurse about for fear of being told they would have to go to the ER to be checked.

The telemonitoring technology was expensive in 2004, but the cost has come down dramatically. As the technology continues to improve, the cost will continue to decline and the benefits for consumers and providers will be significant over time. Just like security-monitoring stations are watching thousands of homes for intrusions or freezing conditions in the home, healthcare telemonitoring will be watching thousands of people to monitor the health of chronically ill people. Over time, the data will be able to be consolidated and data mining will enable predictive treatments based on what has worked for others

The data collected by Joan's system was sent through a dial-up telephone connection to a monitoring center, much like an alarm center. The comparison between Joan's system and today's technology is dramatic. Instead of a big clunky PC based system, we now have the iPhone and a wide array of wireless sensors and devices.

The Apple Watch will move many functions from the smartphone to the wrist. The data can be transmitted continuously via broadband Internet service. Rather than the data going to an alarm center, it could be sent directly to a patient-centered medical home where a nurse or practitioner could review the data. Soon, the data will be examined by supercomputer analytics looking for patterns between weight, O2, blood pressure, and answers to various questions. The result might be a prediction a person is six days away from having a cardiac event. An algorithm might recommend increasing the person's intake of his or her diuretic drug by 50% for ten days to prevent a hospital admission.

The monitoring of a NASA spacecraft is highly sophisticated. The monitoring for CHF patients is archaic. Skeptics say there are too many clinical factors involved in diagnosing the condition of a CHF patient. They say only a cardiologist can make sense of the factors by seeing the patient in person. With a growing elderly population, there will not be enough healthcare funding or cardiologists to meet he demand unless we adopt different methods of providing care and treatments. I believe a few years from now we will be asking why it took so many years to realize complications of various chronic diseases are in fact related to collectible data.

Telemonitoring

Although there is no cure for CHF, I believe if patients and providers have health attitudes concerning telemonitoring, data collection can lead to a better quality of life for patients, and reduced cost of healthcare. It is possible home tele-monitoring can provide a useful supplement to heart-healthy diet, exercise, and medications, but the jury is out. Researchers, including myself, have performed many telemonitoring studies, and more are underway at distinguished medical centers around the country.

Most telemonitoring studies used multiple medical devices such as blood pressure cuffs, oxygenation sensors, and weight scales to gather data from the pa-tient. Such devices are often supplemented with interactive devices or telephone call center interaction to gather additional information from patients. Studies of this nature require significant involvement of the patient and can result in reduced compliance with the research protocol resulting in insufficient data to prove anything.

The study I conducted, "The Effect of CardioNet Home Telemonitoring For Congestive Heart Failure Patients: An Observational Research Study"[256], relied on technology from CardioNet, a Philadelphia-area healthcare technology compa-ny focused on cardiac monitoring for many years. The CardioNet approach was unique because it gathered data directly from the heart of the patient, sampling heartbeats 250 times per second. A study by Dr. Bharat Singh, "Update on Device Technologies for Monitoring Heart Failure" found blood pressure and weight are related to impending heart failure, but the warning comes too late to allow for an intervention that could prevent hospitalization.[257] He suggested the only way to gain accurate and timely information about an impending heart problem was to directly measure the activity of the heart. Dr. Singh's theory was a supporting reason for the CardioNet study.

The purpose of my study was to determine if the application of CardioNet telemonitoring could provide a warning sign to cardiologists. The hypothesis was telemonitored CHF patients would have reduced readmissions or helpful changes in care management. Using the CardioNet technology to monitor CHF patients was a groundbreaking study. The CardioNet technology was typically used to de-tect arrhythmia and had not been used to predict heart failure in CHF patients. The literature suggested implantable monitoring might be the best approach to predict impending heart failure, but the cost and complexity of such a study was prohibitive.

The CardioNet study offered the potential to use non-invasive mHealth technology with minimal patient participation in the monitoring. The theory of being able to predict impending heart failure based on heart activity data was unprecedented. It was of great interest to the Chief of Cardiology at the community hospital where the study was performed. Unfortunately, the study had a small sample size resulting from an unexpected large exclusion rate of patients who were too sick to participate in the study. Although the CardioNet study highlighted some important community-wide issues, the small sample size did not provide sufficient statistical results to make any judgments about the relationship between the use of CardioNet home telemonitoring and hospital readmissions.

A large study funded by the National Heart, Lung, and Blood Institute and supported by Yale University included 1,600 patients, and concluded telemonitoring had no significant effect on the readmission rates of the CHF patients.[258] However, other studies that combined telemonitoring with expanded home healthcare, hospital outreach, and other enhancements across the continuum of care showed statistically significant reduced readmissions.

In October 2014, The Centers imposed more than $200 million in fines on hospitals having excessive readmissions in 2013. They fined 2,610 hospitals The fines are complex and controversial, but they have caused an increased focus on patient safety and quality. Hospital leadership has put a laser focus on the root causes of readmissions. The recent expansion in the number of consumer mobile health devices for home telemonitoring opens a significant opportunity for new telemonitoring approaches. I am confident researchers and providers will find effective technology and protocols to predict impending events for CHF patients. This will allow time for interventions and reduce the high number of rehospitalization.

An emerging form of telehealth is the use of video chat. A survey of 2,061 young adults aged 18 to 34 in March 2014 showed 82% would prefer having a consultation with their physician via a mobile device.[259] These young people can easily adopt a health attitude because of their intimate familiarity with mobile phones and social media. They think a video chat from a smartphone is a very natural way to see a doctor. Google and numerous startups agree. *Forbes* reported Google is testing a feature offering a web searcher the option to set up a video chat session with a doctor who is able to provide help with a specific medical symptom searched.[260] For example, a user who searched for "knee pain" would find a blue "Talk with a doctor now" video icon. Google confirmed in October 2014 tests are underway in partnership with qualified physicians.

The Mayo Clinic has a pilot underway called the Mayo Clinic Health Connection, which it will offer through its HealthSpot technology platform.

MedCity News reported the offering includes cloud based software combined with a walk-in kiosk at places of employment.[261] The kiosks provide "high-definition videoconferencing enabling physicians, nurse practitioners, and physician assistants to see patients virtually face-to-face and prescribe treatments. Just like a bank ATM, patients will be able to walk up to a private kiosk without an appointment."[262] The concept will be best suited for minor, common health conditions such as colds, earaches, sore throat, sinus infections, upper respiratory infections, rashes and skin and eye conditions. As consumers learned to not expect all bank transactions to require a bank teller, they may change their attitudes about what is acceptable in healthcare. Convenient kiosks with virtual medical helpers may become acceptable or even expected.

Although great strides have been made in the understanding and treatment of heart disease, there is much more that can be done. As we all know, the heart is a pump. If NASA had a spacecraft pump experiencing difficulties it would put the pump in a lab, connect it to various sensors and test equipment and study it until the issue was resolved or the pump replaced. In some cases a similar regimen is followed with humans, but in most cases the analysis of a heart is done on a much more distributed basis. A primary care physician may look at a routine electrocardiogram (ECG) done in the office. If anything in the ECG looks suspicious, the physician would refer the patient to a cardiologist for further examination. It is likely the cardiologist would perform a second ECG, stress ECG, or other tests. The patient may be required to wear a holter monitor for a week or two. Some special testing may require a trip to the hospital. The patient then would go back to the cardiologist who does his or her best to integrate all the test results and determine what treatment plan would be appropriate.

The model I just described is not ideal. Part of the problem is the reimbursement model provides an incentive for more visits and more tests. Physicians are not paid to cure you, they are paid to see you, to test you, to see you again, and to re-test you. Part of the problem is the data is distributed among multiple technologies and locations. Beijing Goodwill Information and Technology Co., Ltd., a leading provider of electronic cardiogram systems in China, and IBM Corporation developed an inegrated telemonitoring system in China to address the problem by coordinating all tests and data through a central site.

The joint project is designed to be an all-in-one electronic cardiogram management system in China to achieve smarter healthcare by enabling physicians to analyze real-time ECG data coming from a stress test on a treadmill at the hospital or from a mobile health smartphone app used by the patient. The physicians are empowered with mobile apps to monitor heart patients rather than wait until a holter is returned and a report is created. All test results are stored in a single database in the cloud and are accessible from anywhere.

The combination of telemonitoring, the cloud, and mobile devices will enable physicians to retrieve patients' current and past ECG data, medical reports, and relevant scientific research. The integrated analytics tools will automate the examination and diagnosis of results in real time, helping physicians increase the speed and accuracy of their diagnosis. As a result of this high level of integration, systems soon will help hospitals diagnose more effectively, eliminate human errors, reduce cost, optimize resources, and enhance research and educational capabilities.

Medical Area Body Networks

The Federal Communications Commission periodically auctions spectrum, the airwaves used to transmit and receive cell phone, TV, and various radio signals. In May 2012, the United States became the first country in the world to allocate spectrum for medical area body networks (MBANs).[263] MBANs are low-power networks that include multiple lightweight disposable body-worn sensors that transmit a variety of patient data to a smartphone or a nursing station computer connected to a cloud based system, all without wires. I visited the critical care unit at a local hospital recently and saw a patient who was covered with wires from head to toe. The unit director told me that if there was an emergency, he might not be able to get to the head of the bed very easily to care for the patient. Wired connections carry risks, such as infection or being disconnected—intentionally or unintentionally—by patients.

MBANs could potentially provide a cost-effective way to monitor every patient in a hospital, so clinicians can receive real-time and accurate data, allowing them to intervene and save lives. MBAN sensors that look like Band-Aids can be used to actively monitor a patient's blood glucose, activity level, electrocardiogram readings, and other physiological data. MBANs will also make it easier to move patients to different parts of the healthcare facility for treatment and tests. Most importantly, MBANs will improve the quality of patient care by giving healthcare providers the data to identify life threatening problems or events before they reach critical levels. A nice byproduct will be an increase in patient comfort.

An exciting part of MBANs is the data will ultimately be transmitted from the home to a secure patient portal that can be monitored by specialists. An unexpected pattern of data can result in an email or text to a nurse to call or visit the patient. Home healthcare today is just 3% of what Medicare spends. MBANs may be just what Medicare needs to allow for more care for patients in their homes at a significantly lower cost. Telemonitoring reimbursements to providers from The Centers have been limited to use in rural communities without access to local healthcare providers, although the benefits of telemonitoring can be just as important in an urban environment. The Centers are beginning to change the rules so the cost of telemonitoring can be reimbursed to the providers regardless of where it takes place.

Big Data and Analytics

The storage capacities of laptops, desktops, and mobile devices have been growing rapidly, and the growth is needed to store the vast amounts of data being created. According to IBM, people create 2.5 quintillion bytes of data every day. Perhaps a quintillion bytes, 1 followed by 18 zeros, is not meaningful to most of us, but it is the growth rate that is even more staggering — 90% of all the data in the world has been created in the last two years.

Where does all the data come from? Data comes from everywhere: (1) sensors used to gather climate information, (2) physiological readings taken 1,000 times per second from a patient, (3) posts to social media sites, (4) digital pictures and videos posted online, (5) transaction records of online purchases, and (6) cell phone GPS coordinates. These are just a few examples.

Consider the CardioNet study with CHF patients. The patient wore pendant around his or her neck that had three sensors attached to the body. A wireless device read data from the sensors 250 times per second. Each sample of data included information about various characteristics of the heart of the patient. With thousands of patients being monitored simultaneously, it is easy to imagine that the amount of data collected is enormous.

Collectively, the information technology industry and consultants call the phenomenon of massive amounts of data from many sources big data. IBM describes big data as spanning three dimensions: variety, velocity, and volume.[264] Variety refers to the fact big data extends beyond structured data like we might find in a spreadsheet. It includes unstructured data such as text documents, email, audio and video recordings, social media postings on the web, log files that record financial and business transactions, and much more. Velocity of data refers to the fact data can be time-sensitive such as bid and ask data in a financial market or physiological data that affect the lives of patients. In these cases, historical data is interesting but real-time data is critical. The third parameter is volume. IBM says big data comes in one size: large. Organizations are flooded with data — terabytes, petabytes, or even yottabytes.

My first computer, a Radio Shack TRS-80 I purchased in 1977, had 80,000 bytes of storage on the hard drive. An average email back then was probably 1,000 bytes, so the TRS-80 hard drive could store eighty emails. The Apple iMac I used to write this book has a hard drive with a capacity of one trillion bytes — 12 and a 1/2 million times more storage than my first computer. The growth of storage is hard to imagine, until you think about the explosion of data underway. Fortunately, the availability of affordable and easy-to-use backup technologies is there too, and hopefully we will have the patience and discipline to use them. Losing a few emails is one thing but losing a video of a baby's first few steps is another.

Soon we will have a new word in our technical vocabulary, the yottabyte. How big is a yottabyte? Let's start with the basics. An alphabetic character such as an "a" is represented in most computers by a combination of eight zeroes and ones called a "byte", 1,024 bytes makes a kilobyte, 1,024 kilobytes makes a megabyte, 1,024 gigabytes makes a terabyte, 1,024 terabytes makes a petabyte, 1,024 petabytes makes an exabyte, 1,024 exabytes makes a zettabyte, and finally, or at least for now, 1,024 zettabytes makes a yottabyte. Other ways to consider a yottabyte are that it is 2 to the 80th power bytes, or 10 to the 24th power bytes, or 1,000,00 0,000,000,000,000,000 bytes.

Big data is a challenge in various technical ways, but more importantly, it is an opportunity to find insight in new and emerging types of data. Big data can answer questions not possible to analyze effectively in the past. Hidden data can be surfaced and acted upon. The result can be a more agile organization or in the case of healthcare, better outcomes for patients. Picture a hospital neonatal environment where a plethora of medical monitors connected to babies are used to alert hospital staff to potential health problems before a baby develops clinical signs of infection or other issues. There are breakthroughs on the horizon for how this will be done. Monitoring instrumentation generates huge amounts of information, up to 1,000 readings per second, summarized into one reading every 30 to 60 minutes. The information is stored for up to 72 hours and then is discarded. If the stream of data could be captured, stored and analyzed in real-time there could be an opportunity to improve the quality of care for special-care babies.

The Hospital for Sick Children in Ontario, Canada developed a vision based on using big data and acted on it. Dr. Carolyn McGregor, Canada Research Chair in Health Informatics at the University of Ontario Institute of Technology visited researchers at the IBM T. J. Watson Research Center, in Yorktown, NY who were working on a new stream-computing platform to support healthcare analytics. A three-way collaboration was established, with each group bringing a unique perspective — the hospital focus on patient care, the university's ideas for using the data stream, and IBM providing the advanced analysis software and information technology expertise needed to turn the vision into reality. The result of the collaboration was Project Artemis, which paired IBM scientists with clinicians and researchers to explore how emerging technologies could solve real-world healthcare problems. In this case, developing a highly flexible platform to help physicians make better, faster decisions regarding patient care for a wide range of conditions.

At the Children's Hospital the focus is real-time detection of the onset of nosocomial (acquired in the hospital) infections, which unfortunately, are common. Two infant beds were instrumented and connected to the system for data collection after the team had addressed regulatory, ethical, privacy, and safety issues. The team then created an algorithm that deciphered the streaming data emanating from the infants' beds. By analyzing the impact of moving a baby or changing its diaper, those things could be filtered out to help spot the telltale signs of nosocomial infection.

Dr. Andrew James, staff neonatologist, at the Hospital for Sick Children is optimistic. He believes as they learn more they will be able to account for variations in individual patients and eventually be able to integrate data inputs such as lab results and observational notes. In the future, any condition that can be detected through subtle changes in the underlying data streams can be used to enhance the system's early-warning capabilities. It is likely that sensors attached to, or even implanted in the body, will allow monitoring of important conditions from home or anywhere. Big data has the potential to improve the health of patients wherever they may be.

Watson

In a world of big data and analytics, following anecdotal evidence for diagnosis and treatment is no longer adequate. The new model relies on evidence based medicine where outcomes become part of the evidence. Evidence based medicine is practiced when the patient sees the doctor and the doctor consults with a database that contains anonymized (contains no personally identifiable information) information about similar patients and what treatments produced what outcomes. Evidence based medicine gives the doctor access to data about large numbers of patients and outcomes, not just the ones he or she has seen. This section will describe Watson in more detail.

When Watson, the IBM supercomputer, defeated Brad Rutter and Ken Jennings on the TV game show Jeopardy, it was the tip of the iceberg for future use of supercomputing. The Watson supercomputer is built with cognitive technology, a human brain-like capability, giving it mental abilities and processes related to knowledge that can process information more like a human than a computer. Watson can understand the meaning of words, generate hypotheses about a problem or question, and compare potential results against a vast amount of knowledge fed to it.

IBM is working with healthcare institutions such as the Cleveland Clinic and Memorial Sloan Kettering Cancer Center to use supercomputing to provide a personalized treatment recommendation based on the specific symptoms and status of an individual patient. The recommendation would take into account, based on DNA, how a certain medication would be assimilated by the patient and exactly how much of the drug to take and when to take it.

IBM describes how Watson can be applied for the benefit of healthcare at four levels. The basic level provides assistance to physicians by analyzing and presenting information which helps in diagnosis and treatment of patients. The second level supplements basic knowledge with analysis of patterns and conditions specific to a patient, based upon input from physicians. The third level provides potential diagnoses based on physician inputs plus a mapping of conditions and patterns of data about the patient. At the fourth capability tier is discovery where Watson can read hundreds of thousands of scholarly journal articles and other subject matter expert inputs related to research on the specific condition being studied.[265]

Medical futurist Dr. Bertalan Meskó said, "IBM's Watson is the stethoscope of the 21st century."[266] As the stethoscope enhanced the abilities of physicians by providing a new tool to listen to heart and lung sounds, Watson will provide a cognitive tool to enhance the diagnostic capabilities of physicians. Meskó said doctors, "may keep a few dozen study results and papers in mind, but IBM's Watson can process millions of pages in seconds." [267] Artificial intelligence does not have to lead to the loss of the human touch. In 1997, IBM's supercomputer Deep Blue beat Garry Kasparov, the reigning chess grand master. Kasparov later said that he could have performed better if he had access to the same databases as Deep Blue.[268] Physicians now will be able to perform better by leveraging their knowledge and compassion with the cognitive abilities of supercomputers and big data.

Algorithms

Muhammad ibn Musa al-Khwarizmi (780-850) was an Iranian mathematician, astronomer, astrologer, geographer, and scholar in the House of Wisdom in Baghdad. The word algorithm was transliterated from al-Khwarizmi's name. An algorithm is a procedure or formula used to solve a problem. A simple example would be an algorithm to calculate the area of a circle: area = pi times the square of the radius. The algorithms used by Watson are much more complex and sophisticated.

Today's smartphone personal supercomputers can perform millions of instructions per second and nearly instantaneously execute the calculations in an algorithm that previously required a room-sized supercomputer. Mobile health apps such as AliveCor use algorithms to diagnose diseases and healthcare conditions. The cameras in smartphones can take incredibly detailed pictures that can become the input to an algorithm. For example, using an attachment to take picture of the inside of a child's ear could be analyzed to determine if an ear infection is present.

Taking Advantage of Supercomputing

Entrepreneurial inventors have created attachments for the smartphone with a slot that can accommodate a paper test strip. The process begins by placing a drop of blood, saliva, urine, or other bodily fluid on the test strip and inserting the strip in the attachment on the smartphone. The next step is to take a picture of the strip. The personal supercomputer then performs a colorimetric analysis and uses algorithms to calculate a result and display it on the smartphone screen. A new smartphone app called Colorimetrix may enable consumers to monitor conditions such as kidney disease, diabetes, or urinary tract infections. Researchers at the University of Cambridge believe the technology will eventually be used to slow or limit the spread of pandemics in developing countries.[269]

There are the obvious risks of patients self diagnosing, self-prescribing, and possibly self-destructing discussed earlier, but the trend toward more consumer involvement in their diagnosis is clear. Algorithms will empower consumers to learn more about their condition. The implications for providers are not all positive. Many of the innovations will be transferring money away from doctors, hospitals, and laboratories into the consumer technology sector. Innovation is occurring at a level beyond consumer comprehension.

IBM has been collaborating with the Mayo Clinic for many years. A recent breakthrough by the two was an important advance in the early detection of brain aneurysms — a lethal condition that is not uncommon. The technique they devised combines the latest brain scan technology with analytics to identify a critical condition far sooner than previously possible. The joint project has examined more than 15 million images from thousands of patients.

Traditionally, a patient suspected of having a brain aneurysm due to a stroke or traumatic injury would undergo an invasive test using a catheter that injects dye into the body. The technique itself has risks. The new IBM/Mayo process uses non-invasive MRI angiography to create "automatic reads" running detection algorithms immediately following a scan. The instant the MRI images are acquired, they are automatically routed to powerful servers in the IBM/Mayo Medical Imaging Informatics Innovation Center where supercomputer algorithms analyze the images to locate and mark potential aneurysms so that specially trained radiologists can conduct a further and final analysis. The automated aneurysm detection can be done in three to five minutes, a potentially life saving difference from the traditional approach.

Blue Brain

The human brain is one of the many marvelous parts of humans. The complexity of the human body can appear overwhelming. IBM working, with a team of computational neuroscientists in Switzerland, is working on a project called Blue Brain to help make mysteries of the brain understandable. The goal of the project, being developed at the Brain Mind Institute at the Ecole Polytechnique Federale de Lausanne, is to create a digital model of the brain and use simulations from the model to develop cures for previously incurable conditions.

The concept behind Blue Brain is to create a detailed model of the circuitry in the neocortex, the largest and most complex part of the human brain. The project hopes to model other areas of the brain and eventually build an accurate, computer based model of the entire brain. The digital model creation process starts with wet chemistry. A dye is injected into each neuron to produce brain morphology, a kind of map of the brain's form and structure. After gaining a view of the neurons, it sets the groundwork to build a digital model in a supercomputer, called Blue Gene, which emulates a real human brain. The neocortex is organized into thousands of columns of neurons. Each column has a diameter of less than two one-hundredths of an inch and contains 10,000 neurons. Each neuron stands a little more than 1/16 inch high and receives over 10,000 inputs from other neurons. The brain is very complex. The Blue Brain study will enhance the understanding of how the human brain works. This knowledge could lead to curing brain cancer or other brain dysfunctions. A better understanding of the brain, the supercomputer of all supercomputers, will also help IBM develop even better supercomputers.

Simulation

The use of super computing creates the power to perform simulations. Simulation is a digital tool allowing a systems engineer or business analyst to imitate the operation of a real-world process or system over a period of time. A classic example is to simulate the flow of traffic by creating a digital model of the environment and then testing the effect of changing some of the variables. For example, a city planner could use simulation software to create a digital model of all the streets in a city. The variables would be the number of cars travelling on the streets during each second of each day. This data could be collected with traffic counters – the wire in the street that cars drive over or from sensors, cameras, or satellites that monitor traffic. The other variables would be the number of traffic lights and the time interval during which they are red, green, or yellow. By manipulating the number and timing of the traffic lights, the simulation software can calculate the average traffic flow and how long it takes to get from point A to point B. The advantage of simulation is that variables can be manipulated without having to install real traffic lights or changing the timing of those lights. The software can allow the planner to evaluate an unlimited number of possibilities, select the optimum case, and then make the physical changes to improve traffic flow.

Supermarkets have used simulation to experiment with the number of checkout lanes to operate during different times of the day to optimize the staffing and minimize the wait times for customers. The military uses simulation to determine the optimum number of battleships or airplanes to have in various locations at a given time. Manufacturing companies use simulation to optimize the flow of material and labor on the plant floor. Amazon uses simulation to determine the optimum number of robots to put to work in its warehouses. I did my master's thesis in Management Science in the 1970s using simulation software to create a digital model of the financial operations of a city in Florida. Systems engineering and simulation tools can also be applied in any industry, including healthcare.

The first step in simulation is to create a systems diagram of what it is the engineer or analyst wants to simulate. In a hospital, the inputs to the system would include human resources and capital for facilities and technology. The processes would include the movement of patients, delivery of supplies, and the performance of surgical or test procedures. The outputs would include patient care fulfillment and discharge from the hospital. This same concept of input-process-output can be applied from the top of the organization to the bottom.

A New England Hospital engaged a team of engineers and clinicians from IBM a few years ago to develop a systems model of the ER. Working with the hospital staff, the team developed a digital model of all ER processes including, most importantly, the triage process. Triage enables the ER to prioritize emergency care and identify patients who need immediate medical attention. After constructing the simulation model, it was possible to create possible scenarios and evaluate the simulated results. As a result of the simulations, the ER developed a plan to significantly increase ER capacity without adding any beds. Implementation of a new ER model based on the simulations resulted in improved utilization, fewer patients on gurneys in the hall, and postponement of significant capital expense.

Systems thinking and simulation can lead to a more efficient patient flow throughout the hospital, lower risk in deploying new processes, and improved efficiency. Simulation can enable healthcare leaders to develop plans to identify and mitigate impediments to efficient patient flow throughout the hospital. The rationale for the systems approach is that optimizing the flow and care of patients is essential to the prevention of patient crowding, a problem that can lead to lapses in patient safety and quality of care.

The University of South Florida in Tampa has taken simulation to a higher level. The Center for Advanced Medical Learning and Simulation is a state of the art training facility and medical simulation center providing health education and professional development in the medical field. The Center uses simulation to train surgeons, clinical teams, and residents. The Center's Surgical and Intervention Training Center enables healthcare professionals from around the world to hone their skills as individuals and teams. The training occurs working on digital human-like dummies full of electronic technology that makes them look, feel, and respond like real humans. Surgeons, interventionists, and residents can sharpen existing skills or develop new ones. There is no risk to human lives. The training leads to improved confidence and proficiency, fewer medical errors, and a better overall performance in patient care. Hands-on training of any type of surgery takes place in the 21 station Surgical Skills Lab. Each station is fully equipped with patient-grade anesthetic capabilities, clinical-grade operating room tables, and all the latest surgical instruments, including surgical robots.

Vaccines, Drugs, and the Microbiome

During my two years, six months, and 22 days in the United States Army from 1969 to 1971, I received many vaccinations. They were recorded on a yellow card, which decades later I replaced with the Microsoft HealthVault database on my iPhone. Vaccines were standard and effective, saving millions of lives. Vaccines for diphtheria, influenza, hepatitis B, measles, meningitis, mumps, pertussis, poliomyelitis, rubella, tetanus, tuberculosis, and yellow fever remain effective today, but there is a growing need for new vaccines for diseases such as dengue fever, Ebola, Alzheimer's disease, and possibly obesity.

The development and production of vaccines is slow and archaic, using an egg based manufacturing process that has been in existence for more than 70 years. The process begins with the Centers for Disease Control and Prevention (CDC) providing pharmaceutical manufacturers with vaccine viruses grown in chicken eggs. The viruses are then injected into fertilized eggs and incubated for several days to allow the viruses to replicate. The manufacturers then put doses into vials, syringes, or nasal sprayers.

Dr. Craig Venter, an American biochemist, geneticist, and entrepreneur known for being one of the first to sequence the human genome, is an advocate for a new and innovative approach for the development of vaccines. Venter said that the current process for developing the H1N1, otherwise known as swine flu, vaccine took many months and the supply was barely adequate to cover healthcare workers. He said that if the H1N1 virus had been as deadly and widespread as some had forecasted, we would have had a very bad situation.[270] Venter envisions vaccines can be developed using synthetic DNA instead of billions of eggs. He explained that data about the DNA of the virus to be protected against could be developed into a digital recipe and emailed to laboratories which could then begin production of the vaccine within 12 hours. Venter said FDA approval is imminent. As new viruses such as H7N9 and H3N2 emerge, and more predicted to be developed, the new approach to vaccine development could become extremely important.

Before measles vaccine became available in 1963, each year an estimated 3-4 million people were infected, 400-500 died, 48,000 were hospitalized, and another 4,000 developed chronic disability.[271] Following the introduction of measles vaccine, the number of measles cases declined dramatically. By 2000, after sustained vaccine coverage in children, measles was declared eliminated from this country. Jane Seward, Deputy Director in the Division of Viral Diseases, National Center for Immunizations and Respiratory Diseases, at the Centers for Disease Control and Prevention, said, "Unfortunately, elimination does not mean gone forever."[272]

Measles continues to be somewhat common in many other parts of the world, including Western Europe. Some U.S. residents have returned from travel and brought the measles virus with them. A record number of measles cases were reported in 2014, with 644 cases from 27 states.[273] From January 1 to February 13, 2015, 141 people from 17 states and Washington, DC were reported to have measles. Most of these cases are part of a large, ongoing multi-state outbreak linked to an amusement park in California.[274] The outbreaks began among children in CA who had not been vaccinated. Some parents apparently had fears, based on a 1998 paper by Dr. Andrew Wakefield, which claimed the vaccine for measles, mumps and rubella had caused autism in a dozen children.[275] The study was later proven fraudulent, but it fueled fears about the vaccine safety in Great Britain and the United States. The CDC maintains that the vaccine is proven safe and effective. It is time for a change in attitude where people can learn to trust vaccines which are effective.

Another example of changing attitudes in delivery of healthcare services is the trend to repurpose drugs. In past years, medicine has been qualitative in nature, relying on subjective feedback from patients and anecdotal prescriptions from physicians. Medicine today is becoming more and more quantitative in nature. The *Wall Street Journal* reported what they described as "high-tech recycling", where researchers have developed an innovative way to use already approved drugs used to treat a particular disease to work on diseases they were not intended to treat.[276]

Using a computer science technology called high-throughput computing, researchers were able to scan National Institutes of Health public databases containing the results of thousands of genomic studies. The focus was on 100 diseases and 164 drugs where normal and diseased tissue samples, drugged and not drugged, were compared. The program then looked for cases where a drug created a change in gene activity that was opposite to the gene activity caused by a disease, on the hunch this might indicate the drug could be an effective treatment.

A hypothetical example is, suppose a patient had a problem with his or her liver and the cause was an abnormality of the ABC gene. The XYZ drug used to treat heart problems happens to have an effect that corrects the abnormality of the ABC gene. Even though the XYZ drug was designed for heart problems, it may also be a cure for a liver problem. A real example is researchers found cimetidine, an ulcer drug, might be effective in treating lung cancer.[277] The bioinformatics merger of biology and computer science may change the practice of medicine more in the next decade than during all the changes of the past century.

We typically think of the human body as an entity, but our bodies are actually one part of something much more complex. Microbes, the oldest form of life on earth, are single-cell organisms so small that millions can fit onto the head of a pin, and millions upon millions of them live inside our bodies and on our skin. Some estimates suggest that microbes outnumber human cells by a factor of 10.[278]

Researchers are beginning to understand the implications of microbes. Each of us has a microbiome, the collection of trillions of microbes living on and in our bodies. The relationship between our microbes and us may not be random, and may actually play an important role in many of our basic life processes. A diverse collection of microbes interacts with each other and with the human cells that host them. Researchers are working hard to understand the mystery of these interactions and how they affect normal and abnormal processes occurring in our daily lives.

Significant research is focused on the microbiome because the potential could be enormous. By examining changes in our internal microbiome, some call it a gut check, clinicians may be able to predict impending disease. Just like physicians check our blood pressure as a clue for problems, research may develop standardized measures of our microbial species to gain a measurement of our risk for cardiovascular disease. It is possible markers based on microbiome readouts will be used like cholesterol measurements are used today. Our microbiome may play a role in treatment. Probiotics, organisms such as bacteria or yeast, may prove to be effective supplements to improve health. Prebiotics are carbohydrates that act as food for probiotics. When probiotics and prebiotics are combined, they form a symbiotic beneficial to the human host. More research is needed on this topic, but evidence is emerging demonstrating probiotics and prebiotics may help treat diarrhea, prevent and treat vaginal yeast infections and urinary tract infections, treat irritable bowel syndrome, provide enhanced treatment of intestinal infections, and possibly prevent or reduce the impact of colds and flu.

The most significant impact of a better understanding of our microbiome may be on the worldwide obesity epidemic. Differences in the microbiota, the collection of all the microbes in our gut, have been found between people who were obese and those who were not. Researchers have discovered the microbiota of an obese person has a greater capacity to absorb calories from the diet.[279] While some say the cause of obesity is simply eating too much, the reality may turn out to be complex. Hopefully, the rapidly evolving research into the human microbiome will offer new clues and ultimately a cure for obesity.

World Community Grid

The World Community Grid, a philanthropic initiative of IBM, brought hundreds of thousands of people and millions of computers together from across the globe to create the largest non-profit computing grid benefiting humanity. It does this by pooling surplus computer processing power from users' PCs. Although the PC will be the minority participant in the networked world compared to tablets and smartphones, there are millions of PCs out there. Most of them are utilized a very small percentage of the time. Rather than throwing any PC's away or leaving them idle, users can connect them to the World Community Grid, and let the spare computational capacity be deployed toward finding a cure for cancer and other diseases. Anyone can visit worldcommunitygrid.org and in a few minutes you will be helping the world. When your PC is idle, the unused computing capacity is used by the World Community Grid to work on difficult computational problems.

Grid computing has been around longer than cloud computing. It joins many individual computers using the Internet, creating a large system with massive computational power far surpassing the power of supercomputers. By splitting computational tasks into small pieces that can be processed simultaneously by a large number of distributed personal computers, research time is reduced from decades to months. More than 680,000 volunteers have joined the effort over the past decade and provided the computer power to work toward groundbreaking discoveries in cancer treatment, clean energy, tropical diseases, AIDS, and many other fields.

The Ebola virus is a significant global health threat. It is responsible for a growing humanitarian crisis in West Africa. Currently, there are no proven treatments or vaccines and the possibility exists the virus, rather than disappearing again, could become endemic - permanently persisting in human populations in one or more parts of the world. The World Community Grid is launching Outsmart Ebola Together to help researchers accelerate the search for a cure. Collaboration between The Scripps Research Institute and IBM's World Community Grid will facilitate screening of millions of chemical compounds, searching for ones that can disable the Ebola virus.

Dr. Erica Ollmann Saphire of The Scripps Research Institute said that as of December 2014, her team had already mapped nearly all of the critical proteins of the Ebola virus.[280] Saphire said, "The molecular images of the proteins are like enemy reconnaissance: they show where the virus is vulnerable and can be targeted to block key stages of its life cycle."[281] Outsmart Ebola Together is a crowdsourced effort to unleash the power of thousands of under-utilized PCs and smartphones to perform calculations. Calculations performed in hours instead of decades. The result is a determination of which chemical compounds have the potential to stop Ebola.

Summary

The pace of development of new tools and technology for healthcare providers is unprecedented. Smartphones, tablets, telehealth, big data and analytics, algorithms, and simulation offer the potential to boost physician productivity, perhaps to a level that will prevent the shortage of physicians. Assimilating the technological innovation will present healthcare leaders and clinicians with new challenges. Visionary leaders will capitalize on the trend for the benefit of patients. The largest challenge may turn out to be the rising expectations of consumers as they adopt a health attitude and seek new mobile health apps and devices enabling them to self diagnose. Two of the most exciting new technologies for healthcare are robots and 3-D printing.

CHAPTER 11

Robots and 3-D Printing

Two technologies which are emerging as major contributors to the advancement of healthcare are robots and 3-D printing. It is hard to say which is advancing more rapidly, but both are enabling cures not previously possible. I will discuss my personal experience with robotic surgery and image-guided radiation treatment. The 3-D printing examples I will describe continue to amaze me even as I read and write about them.

I have had an interest in robots and robotic devices for as long as I can remember. Robots can take many forms, but they all share some common features. Robots are mechanical devices, often but not always resembling a human or an animal which move and perform functions automatically under the control of software. Perhaps the most famous robot is R2-D2, the fictional character in the Star Wars universe created by George Lucas. Robotic devices do not always look like robots, but they perform in a similar manner. Robots are already playing a major role in healthcare. It will increase significantly in the near future.

The concept of a robot has a long history dating back more than 2,000 years when an ancient Greek engineer named Ctesibus made organs and water clocks with movable figures.[282] The most common robots today are those used in manufacturing facilities to assemble and paint automobiles or aircraft. Robots are very good at repetitive tasks. They can perform with precision and they do not need coffee breaks or vacations. They also can perform tasks too dangerous for humans such as inspecting and dismantling roadside bombs in war torn countries or handing hazardous materials such as after the Fukushima, Japan nuclear disaster.

In the retail sector, Amazon is using robots made by Kiva, a company it acquired in 2012. Rather than employees walking miles per day fulfilling web orders, the Kiva robots find the rack of shelves where an item is located, lift the rack from underneath, and move it to where the employee is standing. Humans cannot keep up with the hundreds of orders Amazon receives every second. The company has 15,000 Kiva robots spread across 10 warehouses with many more to come.

In August 2014, the Washington, DC based Pew Research Center published, "AI, Robotics, and the Future of Jobs. The report said the vast majority of respondents to a survey believe robotics and artificial intelligence will permeate wide segments of daily life by 2025.[283] The implications are especially significant in transportation and logistics, customer service, home maintenance, and healthcare. Some experts say robots will take over half of all human jobs within 10 to 20 years.[284] As with the Internet, which has created millions of jobs in companies that did not previously exist, robots may expand the need for new jobs in companies that design and build robots. The controversy over whether technology creates jobs or eliminates jobs will continue, but in the field of healthcare, robots are performing tasks humans either can't do or don't want to do.

Robots and robotic devices are playing an increasing role in healthcare performing tasks including: delivering meal trays in a hospital, interacting with chronically ill homebound patients, and assisting surgeons with complex surgical procedures. I had two personal experiences robots in 2014. and two months later with a radiation therapy robot-like system. Both experiences gave me a greater appreciation for the capabilities of robots.

Robotic Surgery

Approximately 15% to 20% of U.S. males will have a Prostate-Specific Antigen (PSA) test result triggering a prostate tissue biopsy. The PSA test and prostate biopsy are both controversial. The test is often inaccurate and the biopsy can be painful and result in significant side effects. Some men put off the biopsy with the chance a re-test of the PSA will show a more favorable reading. That was my hope because my PSA levels had vacillated over recent years. A further rationale for waiting was the PSA level is expected to increase with age. However, a spreadsheet and some basic analysis showed me the rate of increase in the PSA level was far greater than my increase in age. A study of thousands of men indicated, based on my PSA level, age, and a few other factors, if I were to have a biopsy there would be an 80% probability of it being positive.

I had the biopsy on May 2, 2014. On May 16, I received the predictable news the test was positive for prostate cancer. The pathology report from the biopsy yields a great deal of information about the stage and level of aggressiveness of cancer cells that may be present in each of the 12 cores sampled. Clinical researchers have collected large amounts of data useful in predicting the likely outcome for a person with prostate cancer. Despite controversy over the merits of the PSA, the results of the biopsy were irrefutable. I had cancer and was in a high-risk category. Wait and see was not an option. Action was required.

A bone scan and an MRI with a contrast medium looking for cancer cells elsewhere in my body were negative. With that good news, the remaining decision was what to do about the prostate gland. There are many treatment options for prostate cancer including: (1) watchful waiting with observation, physical examination, and palliative treatment of symptoms, (2) active surveillance with repeated biopsies, (3) radiation therapy, (4) cryotherapy, or (5) surgery. Many considerations go into making a treatment choice, but after evaluating a lot of data, research studies, and recommendations of respected physicians, I opted for surgery. The remaining question was what kind of surgery: traditional scalpel based surgery, referred to as "open" surgery, or a robot-assisted radical prostatectomy.

Surgical robotics was little more than a medical curiosity until 1999, when Intuitive Surgical, a Sunnyvale, California company now valued at nearly $20 billion, introduced the da Vinci® Surgical System. Intuitive Surgical is a leader in the rapidly emerging field of robotic-assisted minimally invasive surgery. The da Vinci® surgical robot combines 3-D visualization with enhanced dexterity, precision, and control in an intuitive, ergonomic interface that gives the surgeon enhanced surgical capabilities.

The results from thousands of surgery studies show no significant difference in the ultimate outcome between robotic or non-robotic surgery. However, if the surgeon is experienced in robotic surgery and has performed hundreds of procedures, the risks of complication, time of recovery, and levels of pain can be significantly enhanced with the robotic approach. A skilled surgeon with a scalpel can do almost anything, but an equally skilled surgeon with a robot can do it better.

Five small incisions of less than an inch allow for the insertion of a video camera with 3-D visualization and 10X magnification plus various tools used in the surgery. With more than two hands, a surgeon can hold one piece of tissue aside while using other hands to excise or manipulate tissues without damaging what is held aside. The 10X magnification enables the surgeon to be much more precise in dissection and excision of tissues and nerves. Blood loss is a fraction of that sustained during open surgery. A robot-assisted surgical patient goes home the next day, while an open surgery patient may be in the hospital three or four days or more. The levels of pain and recovery time with robotic surgery can be significantly less.

I arrived at the hospital early in the morning and the surgery took place a couple of hours later. The surgical team included two surgeons, an anesthesiologist, and two nurses. One surgeon made four incisions at the operating table and inserted the robot arms into my abdomen, which had been inflated with gas from a hose inserted through a fifth incision to ensure the maximum space for the operation. The robotic surgeon sat at the da Vinci® console, where he was able to view a high definition, 3-D image inside of my body. Somewhat like using a video game console, the surgeon was able to perform a complex surgery using a full range of instruments attached to the robot arms including forceps, extractors, clamps, and a cauterizer. The instruments have seven degrees of motion - a range of motion even greater than the human wrist. The system seamlessly translated the surgeon's hand, wrist, and finger movements into precise, real-time movements of the surgical instruments. The robotic surgeon removed the prostate gland, 16 lymph nodes, two seminal vesicle glands, and various other tissue samples. The surgeon and nurses at the operating table could watch the entire procedure on a vision system by the table. I was asleep throughout the two-hour procedure, arrived in the recovery room around noon, and was discharged at noon the next day. All surgery has risks, but I had no serious side effects, and the espoused benefits of robotic surgery turned out to be true for me. I attribute my successful surgery to the technology and the skill of the surgical team.

My Personal Robot

One week after the radical prostatectomy, the surgeon called me with bad news. The pathology of the various samples removed from my body indicated cancer cells were left behind. There were no further surgical options, but radiation has a good track record for producing a cure for 90% of patients. The manner in which radiation is applied is quite different than previously. In the past, when a cancer patient required radiation treatment, it was a one size fits all approach. A dosage of radiation would be aimed at a tumor or cancerous area of the body with the objective of stopping the growth of the cancer cells. The downside was the aiming was not precise, and the result was damage to healthy tissue and significant side effects.

I decided to pursue an aggressive strategy and start radiation as soon as I recovered from the surgery. The technology offered by the hospital was image guided, intensity modulated radiation treatment. This is a very advanced technology which produces good outcomes. Radiation oncologists use a computed tomography (CT) scan of the affected area as a digital model to create a treatment plan.

The treatment I pursued is called image guided, intensity modulated radiation treatment. I started out with a CT scan. A digital model was created of the cavity previously home to my prostate gland. The next step was dosimetry planning to calculate exactly how much radiation I would receive and exactly where I would receive it. After eight weeks of recovery from the surgery, I was ready to begin 38 days of radiation treatment.

Each weekday for eight weeks I made a trip to the radiation oncology department of the hospital. The robotic device I got to know quite well over the period of my treatments was a linear accelerator made by Varian Medical Systems, Inc., The company is a leading manufacturer of medical devices and software for treating cancer. Upon arrival I would lay on a narrow table technicians would raise to a height of approximately five feet above the floor. Then they would ensure I was perfectly aligned on the table. The exact placement was the same each day. That was accomplished by me putting my legs in a mold created during the prior planning visit and adjusting the rest of my body on the table by visually aligning me based on laser beams focused on three small tattoos on my body that became permanent parts of me during the planning day.

After the alignment, the technicians left the room, and the Varian robotic device began its automated actions. I got to know the whirring of the gears and motors by heart. The first step was a CT scan, performed by the same machine that would deliver the radiation treatment. The CT scanning head was the size of a chair, and it would rise from the left and pass over my body. As it reached my right side, I could see the image-capturing device, about two feet by three feet rise from beneath me. It was exactly opposite the image-capturing device, following it in a 360-degree arc around me. The scan took between two and three minutes. Then there was a pause for a few minutes while the technicians compared the digital

CT scan to the one taken during the planning. The technicians then adjusted the table from the remote control room to compensate for any differences that may have existed inside my body. Differences could occur because of an expansion or movement of some internal tissues from too much to eat the day before or other factors that can cause things to move around slightly inside your body.

After the pause, I would hear some gears move and the table would make a small jog. Then, after another brief pause, I could hear the CT scan device retract and get out of the way of the radiation delivery that was about to begin. The linear accelerator would then come to life and begin to create a powerful stream of photons that would then bombard the cancer cells during each of nine fields of radiation. The first application was directly under me and passed through the web-like table. After approximately 25 seconds, the robotic device would rotate toward my right side. I could then hear the multi-leaf collimator adjust its finger-like "leaves" to precisely focus the size of the radiation field to be applied. Field number 3 was parallel to my right side. After each field, the gears and motors would whirr and the collimator would make an adjustment, all under control of the robotic software. As the daily program continued, I got to know the exact sound and position of each of the nine fields of radiation. Numbers four to seven were at an angle to my stomach. Number eight was parallel to my left side. Number nine was at an angle below my left side. Then, the robot paused and the technicians returned to lower the table so that I could be on my way.

Once each week, I would meet with a radiation oncologist to discuss progress and side effects. At the final meeting I was told the cancer cells most likely were all killed. I won't know for certain none remain for years, but the odds are that I am cured. I never will forget the smiling faces of the compassionate technicians or the whirring of the motors and gears of the robot. The technicians go home to their families at the end of the day knowing they are helping save lives. The robot sleeps when it is not performing. It has no soul, but each of the thousands of robots saves lives every day. I always had a positive health attitude about robots, but being treated by them gave me even more confidence.

Challenges in Robotic Healthcare

A number of studies have challenged the cost and benefits of robotic surgery. For example, the *Wall Street Journal* reported in October 2014 researchers at Columbia University found the technology costs significantly higher. The results included more complications than regular laparoscopic surgery for removing ovaries and ovarian cysts.[285] All new technologies should be challenged and proponents should justify any added costs or risks. The surgeon who performed my robot assisted radical prostatectomy has done approximately 500 of the procedures and prostatectomy is his specialty. Some surgeons have performed thousands. A surgeon who has performed thousands of open surgeries and then begins to perform robot assisted surgeries may not get outcomes as good as a surgeon who specializes in robot assisted surgeries.

Studies show surgeons of equal experience get equal results, but from a patient perspective, the reduced time in the hospital and shorter recovery period also should be considered. My experience in more than 45 years watching new technologies emerging is new technologies have hidden costs and hidden benefits. Time will tell the true value. With the tremendous pressure on hospitals to lower their costs and improve their outcomes, medical technology companies will have to prove the value of what they propose.

Robots in Home Healthcare

Robots will take on a much wider and more significant role in home healthcare than in surgery. Giraff Plus is a European healthcare project aiming to combine social interaction and long-term monitoring to help people live independently. The Giraff is a home-resident robot specifically designed to take care of the elderly. The robot looks like a giraffe, with four wheels and a long neck with a camera and video display. It enables a caregiver to provide a remote online consultation with a person in his or her home and record the results in the person's EHR.

Giraff Plus is a complex system that can monitor activities in the home using a network of sensors in and around the home as well as on the body. The sensors can measure blood pressure, weight, heart rate, and oxygenation of the blood. Sensors can tell if a refrigerator door has not opened or has remained open for a protracted time. Motion and activity sensors can detect if someone falls down. Different services, depending on the individual's needs, can be pre-selected and tailored to the requirements of both the older adults and healthcare professionals. At the heart of the system is the Giraff, a unique telepresence robot that uses a Skype-like interface to allow caregivers or relatives to virtually visit an elderly person in the home from thousands of miles away. The video capabilities enable care providers to see and converse with the patient, providing him or her advice and answering questions.

Conventional wisdom points to a shortage of nurses in healthcare. The number of elderly is climbing and so is the number of retiring nurses. An even larger shortage may develop for home healthcare aides. The demand is growing since one percent of chronically ill patients consume 22% of healthcare expenditures.[286] Elderly patients get shuttled back and forth to multiple providers often resulting in a poor quality of life for them and their families. Telehealth shows promise as a method to provide a larger share of the care in the patients' home or residence, potentially reducing the demand for nurses and aides. The European Union has 15 trials of Giraff Plus underway in Sweden, Italy, and Spain, and is hopeful that the technology will result in fewer hospital admissions and readmissions.

In theory, robots could take on a much greater role in home healthcare. They also could also help people recovering from a stroke to re-learn how to perform basic functions. Therapists and aides can perform the task, but such therapy can be expensive and not pleasant to administer. Robots, on the other hand can work around the clock, and they never get bored with repetitive tasks. The question about robots is whether people will accept them and not be intimidated by them. A reason to be hopeful is that while the technology is gaining more and more capabilities, it is also becoming more human-like. Health attitudes will adapt and robots will become allies in our healthcare.

Researchers at the Personal Robots Group at MIT's Media Lab have developed a robot with a baby face with a round head, small chin, and wide eyes that appears more capable of feeling than robots of other designs.[287] The MIT Group found people prefer baby-faced robots for medical advice and for tasks that depend on emotion such as from a therapist. The research also showed child-faced robots are less likely to threaten the autonomy of elderly individuals. The Robot Group at MIT has built a robot named Nexi that exhibits many of the characteristics which may be critical to the long-term future of robots in healthcare.

Dr. Adam Waytz, Assistant Professor at Northwestern University's Kellogg School of Management, and Dr. Michael Norton, Professor at Harvard Business School have developed a list of five human-like characteristics they believe will be most important in the acceptance of robots. Faces and voices may be the most obvious. The ability to express empathy is a close third. More surprising but important characteristics Waytz and Norton believe will be important are the ability to provide mimicry and unpredictability.[288] The latter two characteristics pique the interest of humans and result in more acceptance and trust. The reason is these two characteristics are more like humans.

3-D Printing

MecklerMedia Inc., a New York tradeshow company, sees 3-D printing becoming as ubiquitous as robots. It was clear from the enthusiasm I witnessed at the Inside 3-D Printing Conference and Expo at the Javits Convention Center in New York in April 2014 the technology is garnering a lot of attention. Four thousand people attended the conference. The keynote speaker, Carl Bass, President and Chief Executive Officer of Autodesk, a leader in 3-D design, engineering, and entertainment software, said that 40% of Americans sampled had never heard of 3-D printing.[289] Not only is 3-D printing enabling manufacturers and consumers to create new products, it is also changing business processes that have been part of manufacturing for decades. One speaker called it an industrial renaissance. Another said that the design-to-manufacturing value chain market opportunity is $35 billion. I think of 3-D printing as an industrial revolution, which will equal the impact of the Internet across all industries, including healthcare.

Some people have difficulty imagining how 3-D printing works. Perhaps a few examples will help. Imagine a paper and ink matrix printer with a movable print head. The print head would go back and forth over the paper and deposit ink to create characters and images. A typical 3-D printer also has a movable print head. Instead of ink, it uses acrylonitrile butadiene styrene, a plastic called ABS. The ABS comes in a reel of filament, just like a reel of wire. The 3-D printer feeds the ABS filament into the print head, which heats the filament to a very high temperature. Instead of printing on paper, the 3-D printer prints on a horizontal platform, typically six inches by six inches. It prints one layer of material at a time.

Imagine printing a cube of ABS one inch by one inch by one inch. A digital model of the object to be printed can be downloaded from various websites and loaded into the 3-D printer. The printer would then print a physical model of the object. For the cube, the printer would print 250 layers of ABS. The job might take a few hours or more depending on the printer. Now imagine printing a plastic coin that looks like a U.S. quarter. In this case, all the layers printed would not be the same. The layers at the bottom and top would need less ABS to account for the raised surface of the Alaskan bear, the date, and the bust of Thomas Jefferson. Finally, to really understand the concept, imagine printing plastic Japanese Yen. Since the Yen has a hole in the center, the printer will not print at all during some of the passes back and forth. The place where it does not print creates the hole.

The range and variety of 3-D printed objects on display at the conference was amazing. A ring with rotating gears was printed as one item. Imagine all the spaces between the gears as the spaces not printed. One vendor showed custom eye-glasses printed based on the width of your nose bridge and distance between your temples. Prior to printing, a digital camera takes a picture of a person's head and creates a digital model of the appropriate glasses. The model is downloaded and printed to produce the glasses. Imagine the possibilities to create printed dental and hearing implants, the doorknob that doesn't seem to be available anywhere, and parts for a 1953 Chevy. GE is printing jet engine parts. A ChefJet product prints chocolate candies and offers personalized nutrition to print your food. Other printed items shown at the conference included games, dollhouse furniture, fashion accessories, shoes, jewelry, belts, and even garments. One presenter showed off his colorful 3-D printed shoes as he walked on stage. The conference had a Ford Torino with a multi-surfaced 3-D printed car body.

In the late 1980s, 3-D printing used bland-colored resin to print small objects one item at a time and one layer at a time. The printers cost many thousands of dollars and were not accessible to consumers. At the conference in New York, a Chinese company, XYZprinting Inc., introduced a 3-D printer available online for $499. It supports 12 different colors. The printing capabilities of a 3-D printer appear to be limitless. If you can imagine it, you can print it. Shapeways, a Dutch founded, New York based 3-D printing marketplace and service, allows users to design and upload 3-D printable files. Shapeways prints the objects for the designer or others. As of June 2012, Shapeways had printed and sold more than one million user-created objects.

3-D printing is an exponential technology introducing change in how many things are made. The low-cost technology has enabled democratization of making things, anybody can make things by printing them. Very little expertise is required, and the software tools make the complex shapes a non-issue. Material science may be the most important aspect of 3-D printing. Even printing with metal is now possible, but continued development is needed to get the strength, cost, and speed where it needs to be.

As I listened to speakers and walked the expo floor and talked to demonstrators, I became excited about the many possibilities. I thought of one of my motorcycles, a 1977 Honda Trail Bike, for which it is hard to get parts. I thought of various gadgets, knobs, brackets, and things around the house that are not available. They are now. If you can take a picture or draw it, you can print it. Before this conference, I thought of 3-D printing as being limited to a prototyping tool. Now I can see fabrication-grade direct metal printing, where thousands of parts can be printed per printer per day. The printed parts will be lighter and more effective than parts of the past. There are tremendous possibilities to apply 3-D printing in the field of medicine and the potential for patient specific body part replacement.

One of the e-newsletters I look forward to every week is from MedicalAutomation.org. The site describes its mission as filling the need for unbiased information about processes and technologies that can make healthcare more effective, efficient, and equitable. One of the topics appearing more frequently in the weekly newsletter is 3-D printing.[290] A recent story was about a man who lost half of his face to cancer, but now can eat and speak again thanks to a 3-D printed implant.

Following is an example of the extraordinary promise of healthcare innovation using 3-D printing technology. A 60 year old British man suffered from chondrosarcoma of the pelvis, a rare form of untreatable cancer. The only option was to replace the diseased half of his pelvis. Such surgery would have been unheard of in the recent past, but with the advent of 3-D scanners and printers, there was a chance of success. A United Kingdom implant maker used a 3-D scan and then printed a custom model of the half pelvis. The 3-D printing process used a laser to fuse multiple layers of titanium powder to create the new pelvis part. The part then was coated with a mineral that would be receptive to the growth of new bone. The surgical team used a surgical robot to assist in the 12 hour procedure. The final step was to perform a hip replacement to fit into a socket of the new pelvis part. British newspapers reported three years after the complex procedure, the man is able to walk with the help of a cane. A few years from now, the complex set of steps for 3-D printing of a pelvis or other human parts may seem primitive. More fully automated processes leading from diagnosis to treatment will seem commonplace.

Peking University doctors successfully have implanted a 3-D printed vertebra in a 12 year old boy who had a malignant spinal cord tumor.[291] A digital model was created from which the vertebra was printed. Most 3-D printing uses polymers or metals but, in this case, the University used titanium powder, which is typically used for orthopedic implants. What was atypical was the implant did not require cement or screws because the implant was made to precisely fit. Normally, implants come in pre-determined sizes and may not fit exactly, hence requiring cement or screws. The 3-D printed implant included holes in it which could allow bone tissue to grow into the implant and hold it in place.

The U.S. Centers for Disease Control and Prevention reported four in 10,000 children are born with some congenital hand loss. There is a need for 1,500 child hand prosthetics each year.[292] A prosthetic can cost up to $40,000, and insurance has usually not covered them. As children grow, they can have trouble adapting to a prosthetic. The need for pediatric prosthetics spawned a network of volunteer medical workers, engineers, designers, parents, and 3-D printing enthusiasts who have been designing, printing, and outfitting children with prosthetics.

Meredith Cohn at *The Baltimore Sun* wrote about how Albert Chi, a trauma surgeon at Johns Hopkins, was able to print a hand for a two year old. Chi said, "We thought the child was too young, but we weren't even able to finish strapping it on, and the kid was picking an object up."[293] A network of thousands of volunteers and the non-profit e-NABLE are using 3-D printing technology to create free printed hands and arms for those in need.[294] Cohn reported the organization has provided more than 400 kids with printed prosthetics during the past year. With free designs available online and the advent of sub-$1,000 printers, families may be printing hands at home with free designs on e-NABLE's website. With prosthetics below $20, it is practical to print new ones every few months as children grow.[295] They can also pick their favorite color.

Another example of successful 3-D printing is in human tissues work. One of the challenges in using artificial tissue has been it lacks blood vessels. Harvard researchers say they have created tissue interlaced with blood vessels.[296] Professor Jennifer Lewis at MIT and a team of researchers, using a new 3-D printing technique, have created a patch of tissue containing skin cells with an interwoven biological structural resulting in blood-vessel-like structures. Lewis's group created hollow, tube-like structures within a mesh of 3-D printed cells using ink that liquefies as it cools. The gelatin based ink is printed in layers and acts as a structural mix of proteins and other biological molecules surrounding cells in the body. Other inks contain either human or mouse skin cells. All three inks are viscous enough to maintain their structure after being printed. The potential of this 3-D printing breakthrough is it could create an architecture for blood vessels in artificial tissue. The researchers believe small blood vessels will develop and grow on the tissue. This accomplishment represents a partnership between biology and 3-D printing. Creative developments such as this will lead to cures previously thought impossible.

3-D printing of tissues and organs will continue to become refined and expanded in scope. Another powerful use of the technology is for printing models to aid in surgery. A recent case at Morgan Stanley Children's Hospital in New York represents a touching story which demonstrated the potential. A two-week-old baby suffering from a congenital heart defect was in urgent need of surgery. The baby's heart was riddled with holes and presented a highly complex surgical challenge. Rather than stop the heart and examine its interior to determine a surgical strategy, as would have been the only option in the past, 3-D printing was used to create a model of the baby's heart using data from an MRI.[297] The model served as a guide both for planning and during the surgery. Thanks to 3-D printing and the skill of a Columbia Presbyterian Hospital surgeon, the baby should lead a normal life. Thirty-five thousand babies are born each year with congenital heart defects. 3-D printing has the potential to improve the outcomes for those needing surgery.

Regenerative Medicine

The breakthroughs are not just 3-D printed body parts. Regenerative medicine involves making parts of parts to accommodate growth of new tissue or bone into the replaced parts. At the 3-D Printing Conference in New York, I listened to an inspiring speech by Dr. Anthony Atala, Director of the Wake Forest Institute for Regenerative Medicine. The U.S. Department of Health and Human Services called regenerative medicine the "next evolution of medical treatments".[298] The Wake Forest laboratory has already created 22 different human tissues, including muscles that can expand and contract. Dr. Atala said that regenerative medicine would not only improve the quality of life for many people, but save lives. With the potential to heal, Dr. Atala believes regenerative medicine will revolutionize healthcare.

Patients with diseased or injured organs can be treated with transplanted organs. However, there is a severe shortage of donor organs, more than 75,000 actively waiting for transplants, that is worsening yearly due to the aging population. Regenerative medicine and tissue engineering may solve the problem. By applying the principles of cell transplantation, material sciences, and bioengineering, teams such as Dr. Atala's, are able to construct biological substitutes that may restore and maintain normal function in diseased and injured tissues. 3-D printing is playing a critical role. Living tissue can be printed using cells, instead of ink, from the patient. Rather than replacing an entire organ, regenerative medicine uses a replacement technique that supplements a failing tissue or organ. Cells can be extracted from a functioning part of an organ, enhanced and grown outside of the body, and then printed on a lattice structure. The result is then implanted in the patient. Since the cells came from the patient's body, there is no rejection. We can expect to see major advances in the technology in the future. Dr. Atala said, "regenerative medicine promises to be one of the most pervasive influences on public health in the modern era".[299] HHS said, "We can make tissue and organ failure a relic of the past by 2020."[300]

Summary

There are critics of healthcare technology who believe a lot of money is wasted on unproven technologies and technology providing excess capacity. While these may be valid concerns, the overarching aspect of healthcare technology is it saves lives every day. Robotics and 3-D printing can be major game changers in many areas. Much as the web has proved since its inception 20 years ago, these new technologies are disruptive to the healthcare system of today, but essential for the future.

The United States Census Bureau reported in 2012 nearly 1 in 5 people have some form of disability. Humans getting more like robots and robots getting more like humans opens non-trivial ethical issues. However, it is possible brain implants, advanced prosthetics, and 3-D printed tissues and organs will be able to compensate for physical, emotional, and intellectual shortcomings. Continued breakthroughs in 3-D printing technologies may lead to the end of many disabilities.

CHAPTER 12

Breakthrough Technology, Education, and Research

Technology breakthroughs are occurring at a rapid pace. I will introduce some technologies I believe are on the leading edge. Medical education is changing to adapt to new technologies. I will discuss the need to focus education in needed areas and suggest improvements to the research grant process. Research must continue to look for innovative cures.

Healthcare innovations are occurring at a fast pace. Advances in healthcare during the next 10 years may surpass what has occurred during the past 100 years. The pace is accelerating because healthcare is beginning to adopt new technology, not just from within the industry, but from other industries. Robotics has come from the manufacturing plant floor to the operating room. 3-D printing has moved from prototyping mechanical parts to printing biological tissues and prosthetics. Big data and analytics have emerged from optimizing Internet company operations to focusing on genomics for healthcare.

Bioengineering has become a structured curriculum for students interested in the intersection between engineering and biological sciences. Previously, most of the focus of engineering was on electronic circuits, chemical interactions, and structural designs. Mechanical engineers can measure the tensile strength of steel girders. Biomechanical engineers are measuring the stiffness of a single living cell. Engineers still design bridges and circuits. Now, bio-engineers are working at the molecular level to improve the quality of life by redesigning parts of the human being, and designing new components to take the place of worn body parts.

It nearly is impossible to keep current on all the developments in healthcare, but Dr. Robin A. Felder, Professor and Associate Director of Clinical Chemistry and Toxicology at the University of Virginia, comes pretty close. Dr. Felder is Chair of MedicalAutomation.org, a website that champions effective, efficient and equitable healthcare, and promotes the intersection of parallel revolutions in biomedicine, informatics, nano-technologies, and process management. He believes individualized medicine, through the integration of these technologies with healthcare can make better health a more achievable goal. I look forward to reading the MedicalAutomation.org e-newsletter each week and learning of the exciting developments underway.

Artificial Cartilage

Many baby boomers will need joint replacements. The number of hip and knee replacements is approaching one million per year. Projections indicate there may not be enough surgeons to handle the rapidly growing demand. In many cases, the need for the replacement comes from overuse, injury, or osteoarthritis leading to destruction of cartilage, the flexible connective tissue in hip, shoulder, and knee joints. The common phrase uttered by those facing the joint replacement is "I'm down to bone on bone". Researchers at Duke University found a way to create artificial replacement tissue that mimics both the strength and suppleness of native cartilage.[301]

Native cartilage is smooth and cushiony, yet strong and load bearing. The idea of artificial cartilage is not new, but being able to match the features of real cartilage has proven extremely challenging. The concept of artificial cartilage begins with a scaffold made from a three-dimensional fabric. The fabric is constructed from minuscule woven fibers, with each of the scaffold's seven layers being about the thickness of a human hair. Stem cells are injected into the scaffold and then they grow into articular (joint) cartilage tissue.

The toughest challenge has been to develop a material to fill the spaces in between the stem cells — not too hard, not too soft. Xuanhe Zhao, Assistant Professor of Mechanical Engineering and Materials Science at Duke University developed the idea of a water based polymer gel (hydrogel), and collaborated with a team from Harvard University to develop the advanced material.[302] Zhao said, "It's extremely tough, flexible and formable, yet highly lubricating. It has all the mechanical properties of native cartilage and can withstand wear and tear without fracturing."[303]

Hopefully, the new material will be available soon. Engineering previously centered on designing and building bridges and other large structures. Today, electrical, mechanical, and bio engineers are working with physicians to bring nano-sized structures to our wearing joints.

Bionic Eyes

Monash University was established in Melbourne, Australia in 1958. The University considers itself to be a youthful, enthusiastic, optimistic, and accessible organization. It believes quality education and research can change the world for the better. Researchers at the University have developed the Monash Vision System to combine state of the art digital and biomedical technology with consumer-friendly glasses.[304] A digital camera embedded in the glasses will capture images of what you are "looking" at. Digital processors will modify the images captured by the camera and a wireless transmitter will then present the image you are "looking at" to a chip that has been implanted at the back of the brain. The brain chip will stimulate the visual cortex of the brain with electrical signals using an array of electrodes, and the brain will learn to interpret these signals as sight.

This vision research is in the early stages. Monash is developing the direct-to-brain bionic eye for people with vision impairment caused by specific conditions, including glaucoma and macular degeneration. It may also help people who have damage to their optic nerves or eyes resulting from trauma or disease. It is not hard to imagine the technology evolving to the point the blind will be able to see.

Nano Sponges

Nanotechnology is one of the most exciting areas of technological advancement in healthcare. I remember attending a conference 15 years ago where a presenter said that the day would come when we would be able to drink a nanobot cocktail, and nanorobots would then traverse our bodies and make corrections or replacements to things they found wrong. To most attendees, it seemed unbelievable. Fast-forward to now and the announcement that engineers at the University of California, San Diego have invented a nanosponge capable of safely removing dangerous toxins from the bloodstream – including toxins produced by the difficult to treat MRSA infections in humans, E.coli, and even poisonous snakes and bees.[305]

The nanosponges have already been studied in mice and have been found to neutralize poor-forming toxins, which destroy cells by poking holes in their cell membranes. The nanosponges look like red blood cells, and therefore serve as red blood cell decoys, which can collect the toxins. The nanosponges absorb damaging toxins and divert them away from their cellular targets. Researchers have a goal to translate their work into approved therapies. This would be a welcomed breakthrough in the treatment of MRSA, a dangerous and antibiotic-resistant bacterium that has been prevalent in hospitals.

Stem Viruses

The potential spread of infectious diseases such as avian influenza (bird flu), dengue fever, Ebola, and other dangerous viruses is frightening. The challenge has always been to try to gain an understanding of how they spread — what they will do next. Will the virus mutate? Will it jump across continents? Where are the greatest vulnerabilities? Can the path be predicted in time to get vaccine to the next area?

IBM has developed software it says can answer these questions. The company said that it is donating the software to scientists and public health officials to enable them to build digital models of infectious diseases to help understand and plan more efficient responses to potential health crises. The software is known as Spatiotemporal Epidemiological Modeler (STEM), and is one of the key technologies being used in the Global Pandemic Initiative, a collaborative effort of IBM and more than twenty major worldwide public health institutions. It includes the Center for Disease Control and the World Health Organization to help prevent the spread of infectious diseases.[306]

The STEM tool is designed to help scientists and public health officials not only aid in understanding diseases, but also potentially prevent them. The software creates a graphical representation of the spread of a disease based on a variety of parameters such as population, geographic and macro-economic data, roadmaps, airport locations, travel patterns, and bird migratory routes around the world. STEM also facilitates collaboration between governments, scientific researchers, and the public health community who can share the epidemiological models STEM creates.

Policymakers responsible for creating strategies to contain diseases and prevent epidemics need an accurate understanding of disease dynamics and the likely outcomes of preventive actions. In an increasingly connected world with extremely efficient global transportation links, the patterns of infection can be quite complex. STEM may be a breakthrough which could save large numbers of lives in the years ahead.

Strawberries

For years I have had a personal objective to gain an understanding of genomics. I asked several experts what book would enlighten me. They unanimously recommended *Genome: The Autobiography of a Species in 23 Chapters* by Matt Ridley.[307] The human genome, encompassing the complete set of human genes, comes packaged in twenty-three separate pairs of chromosomes. Twenty-two pairs are numbered according to their size, from the largest to the smallest. The 23rd pair consists of the sex chromosomes: two large X chromosomes in women, one X and one small Y in men. Ridley explains the human genome chromosome by chromosome, selecting a gene from each chromosome as an example to tell the overall story of genomics. After reading the book, I was convinced the amount I did not know was more than I thought, but the book convinced me genomics is going to have a major impact on healthcare in the years ahead.

An early indicator of what lies ahead in the field of genomics may have been revealed by Elizabeth Weise, Science Writer at *USA Today*, who summarized the latest genomic innovation by comparing it to strawberries. Her article, "Woodland Strawberry Genome Sequenced", is about the genome of the woodland strawberry, a cousin to today's cultivated strawberry, which has now been sequenced by an international research consortium.[308]

The strawberry, with just 14 chromosomes, is the second smallest plant ge-nome to be sequenced. Sequencing a strawberry means constructing a "parts list" of the strawberry. Weise reported, as a result of the sequencing, that breeders might be able to create tastier and hardier varieties of the popular berry and other crops in its family, including almonds, apples, peaches, cherries, and raspberries. The researchers are optimistic they will also find new parts that will provide resis-tance to strawberry wilt, a common, soil-borne pathogen that spoils cultivated strawberries.

The consequences of human gene sequencing are mind-boggling. Gene hunt-ers are finding more genes and linking them to diseases and predispositions to diseases. The next phase will be developing methods of prevention and cures. A genetic revolution of innovations is unfolding. Dr. Reid Robison, from Tute Genomics, a Utah software company specializing in biomarker and gene discov-ery, said, "Eventually, everyone will have their genome sequenced. Imagine a world in which your medical care is 100% unique. Every diagnosis, every medication, every dietary guideline can be tailored to you and only you."[309]

New Kind of X-Ray

Another area of innovation is x-rays – a technology that hasn't changed much for decades. The current technology is fine when taking a look at your knee or shoulder, but when the internal organs need to be examined, a patient needs to swallow a contrast agent like iodine or barium that will bind to a tumor or other structure. The problem is these agents can be hard on the kidneys and in some cases result in mortality. CT scans are overused and potentially dangerous after the accumulation of multiple scans.

A new technique, called x-ray phase-contrast imaging (XPCI), works by measuring the change in an x-ray's phase. X-rays move more slowly when they pass through muscle mass than through blood. For example, as an x-ray passes through your lungs, which is mostly air and blood vessels, the wave will arrive sooner than a wave that passes through the heart. As a result, specialists can ex-amine internal organs and tumors using the new technique. The phase contrast technique can differentiate images, and provide physicians with a non-invasive diagnostic ability not previously available.[310] For example, an XPCI image could differentiate between premalignant and malignant breast lesions. XPCI involves no toxic agents, and works with a substantially lower dosage than CT scans. A recent conference in London addressed steps needed to bring XPCI into mainstream imaging.

The technologies described in this chapter are a small sample of many under development. Technology is not the complete solution to making healthcare better. When combined with medical research, new technologies have the potential to help reduce costs and improve outcomes.

Role of Research

The National Institutes of Health (NIH) said improvements in the health of Americans can be attributed in large part to medical research.[311] Americans today are healthier and living longer. Life expectancy has increased from 47 years in 1900 to 78.8 years as reported for 2012. Disabilities in people over age 65 continue to drop, and the death rate from cancer has fallen 20% from its peak in 1991.[312]

The NIH is the nation's medical research agency, and includes 27 Institutes and Centers for conducting and supporting medical research to find causes, treatments, and cures for both common and rare diseases. The scope of NIH research is vast. With an annual budget for 2015 of $31 billion, the NIH makes almost 50,000 grants to more than 300,000 researchers at more than 2,500 universities, medical schools, and other research institutions in every state and around the world. Three billion dollars of the budget supports projects conducted by nearly 6,000 scientists in its own laboratories, most of which are on the NIH campus in Bethesda, MD.

The NIH has accomplished a lot, but as taxpayers we should expect even more from such a large budget and staff. There are still disabling and chronic diseases. More vaccines are needed. Although life expectancy has increased, America still lags other developed countries.

There has been criticism of the NIH for not having more breakthroughs because it doesn't take enough risk in the projects in backs. The grant process is competitive, and researchers write proposals they estimate to have the best odds of winning a grant which often means conforming to past norms. Stanford researcher Dr. John Ioannidis, and a colleague, Joshua Nicholson from Virginia Tech, analyzed the NIH grant funding process and concluded it is "totally broken".[313] Research applications go through a peer-review process that utilizes groups of reviewers called study sections that review and rank submissions by their colleagues. Ionannidis and Nicholson believe the review process is inherently flawed and "encourages conformity, if not mediocrity." If innovation is the goal, the NIH process may actually ensure there will not be any. The researchers said, "A truly innovative idea cannot be judged by peers: if it is truly innovative, no peer has any clue about it; if peers already know about it, it is not innovative."

Beginning in 2015, the NIH is will begin to respond to the criticism by making 85 grants to scientists proposing highly innovative approaches to major contemporary challenges in biomedical research. The High Risk-High Reward program seeks scientific leaps, new scientific paradigms, and revolutionizing of entire fields. Francis S. Collins, the NIH Director, said, "Supporting innovative investigators with the potential to transform scientific fields is a critical element of our mission."[314] He said that the new program would allow for more creativity and risk taking, but have the potential to lead to dramatic breakthroughs.

Dr. Collins is making positive changes. For example, a new Early Independence Award provides an opportunity for exceptional junior scientists who have recently received their doctoral degree or finished medical residency to skip traditional post-doctoral training and move immediately into independent research positions. The current system requires a medical researcher to be 47 before they can become an independent researcher. The changes will lower the age and should inject fresh thinking into the research program. However, the total budget for the new high risk, high reward program is $141 million, less than a half-percent of the total budget. As new technology and research introduce new ways to provide healthcare, changes will be needed in medical education.

Education in Healthcare

Forbes reported on a 2014 survey of 20,000 physicians, and said, "Fifty-six percent of physicians describe their morale as negative."[315] The article also said, "The requirements of the Affordable Care Act are being incorporated into medical practices, and almost one-half of physicians grade the new healthcare act with a D or F." As a result of these and other factors, some believe there will be a large shortage of physicians to care for the impending addition of tens of millions of uninsured people. One key dependency is the pipeline of medical students and graduate medical education they will need to practice medicine.

Students are applying to medical school in record numbers. In 2013, 48,014 students applied to U.S. medical schools, a 6.1% increase from the previous year and 20,055.[316] More students enrolled in medical school in 2012-2013 than the previous year despite not being guaranteed a residency position after graduation and the prospect of having enormous debt of an average of $170,000 at graduation. The medical students take on the debt with no assurance they will be able to earn a sufficient living to pay it off while providing for their families. The real issue is not how many uninsured will get coverage or whether or not there will be a shortage of physicians. The real issue is whether there will be enough primary care physicians to coordinate care for those in need.

Congress has passed much legislation and then failed to provide the funding for implementation. Medical residency training is an example. The Balanced Budget Act of 1997 froze funding of graduate medical education at 1996 levels for most teaching hospitals. Teaching hospitals are facing restrictions on their ability to develop or expand new programs, according to the Association of American Medical Colleges. The CEO, Darrell Kirch, MD, said that if Congress does not address the funding issue there could be a serious shortage of physicians to serve the population.

Funding is only part of the problem in medical education. Despite the 1997 freeze on any increases in funding, the government is spending billions of dollars for graduate medical education for the training of physicians at hundreds of hospitals in America. Dr. Ramin Ahmadi, Chair of Medical Education, Research, and Global Health for Western Connecticut Health Network, said, "The problem is that there is no accountability in medical education funding to ensure the training addresses the critical need for primary care physicians."[317] The Obama Administration has set a goal of bringing nine million more Americans onto the rolls of those with healthcare insurance. The addition will increase the need for PCPs, but the training programs at hospitals give a priority to training more subspecialists. The total number of physicians being trained may be adequate, but the number of PCPs will fall short. The Institute of Medicine is proposing a 20% holdback of the funding to hospitals for graduate medical education. The 80% will enable hospitals to continue to operate training programs, but to get the additional 20% of the funding, teaching hospitals must demonstrate they are addressing the specific need for primary care.

The number of patients will increase by millions. The practice of medicine will change to focus more on preventive medicine and coordination of care. Adoption of new technology will increase physician productivity, but the demand for primary care will still increase. Graduate medical education must change to ensure the right training is in place to meet the needs. Other shifts in education are occurring in the field of engineering that will be relevant to the future of healthcare.

In 1963 there were two tracks an electrical engineering student at Lehigh University could choose from, electronics or power. Electronics was about solid-state devices such as transistors. The Intel 4004, a microprocessor now four decades old, was not invented until 1971. The "power" track was mostly about electric motors and power generation. There was no computer science program until the University acquired a GE 225 computer that occupied a good part of the basement floor of one of the College of Engineering buildings. Nearly every department at Lehigh began to include computer programming as part of their curricula. Although computer science and computer engineering continued their own educational programs in the electrical engineering department, every department across the university integrated computer science as part of their curricula.

Fast forward forty years and you can see a very similar evolution occurring with bioengineering. Initially "bio" was a special interest area with deep roots in the biology department, but the roots began to spread into various engineering disciplines. Bioengineering has now become a structured curriculum for students interested in the intersection between engineering and biological sciences. The bioengineering faculty at Lehigh is drawn from several departments in the College of Engineering and Applied Science and the College of Arts and Sciences. Students can choose from three tracks of study: (1) biopharmaceutical engineering encompassing biochemistry and chemical engineering, (2) bioelectronics and biophotonics focusing on applications of electrical engineering and physics in bioengineering using signal processing, biosensors, and biochips, and (3) cell and tissue engineering straddling the fields of molecular and cell biology, materials science, mechanical and electrical engineering, and encompassing biomaterials and biomechanics. Studies range from cells and tissue to organs and systems. The vocabulary is hardly reminiscent of transistors and electric motors.

Three articles in a recent issue of *Resolve*, the Lehigh College of Engineering quarterly magazine, highlight the type of projects in bioengineering. The first article was "Measuring the Stiffness of a Single Living Cell", an article about how changes in the mechanical properties of biological cells may be a major contributing factor to the development of bone, kidney, and vascular disease. The second article was "Mending a Wounded Heart", a story about how heart attacks can cause extensive scarring of the cardiac muscle tissue and how inadequate structural remodeling can be supplemented with an implanted cardiac patch composed of heart muscle cells grown on a porous polymer scaffold. A third article describes the mechanics of proteins — how protein molecules are made from a linear chain of amino acids that fold into a 3-D globular form.

The exciting part of all this is engineering students with bio in their pedigree have a much broadened career potential including healthcare, biomedical, pharmaceutical, biomaterials, and medicine. Bioengineering will supplement the clinical efforts of medical doctors. A new professional master's degree program in healthcare systems engineering will prepare graduate students for engineering and management careers in healthcare and health related products and services companies. The increasing complexity of delivering healthcare with high quality and positive patient outcomes requires professionals who are trained to think in terms of systems. The Institute of Medicine and the National Academy of Engineering have urged the healthcare field to embrace systems engineering as a way to deliver safe, effective, timely, patient-centered, and efficient healthcare. Engineering schools are forging partnerships with pharmaceutical companies and hospital systems to develop collaborative programs. Engineering students with medical education and medical students with computer science and engineering education will bring new talent to healthcare.

Even more exciting than the educational shift is the possibility for those with aging bodies that some day soon they will benefit from bio-engineered components. The implantable pacemaker was just the beginning. Bioengineering graduates will be developing pacemakers for the brain, cochlear implants for hearing deficiencies, artificial cartilage for our knees, devices to enable people who are blind to see, and cures for today's incurable diseases. Soon, the nanotechnology cocktail will bring nanobots to our internal systems to replace faulty cells with newly engineered ones. Just like computers have become ubiquitous, it is clear that bio-everything has become part of engineering and applied science education. As the line between humans and robots blends, bioethics will emerge as an important area of study and policy development.

Summary

New technologies such as artificial cartilage, bionic eyes, nanosponges, STEM models of viruses, and personalized medicine offer great promise. Each can provide capabilities which would have been a dream not many years ago. In a few years we will likely take these breakthroughs for granted and have expectations for further innovations.

The National Institutes of Health is expending billions of dollars to fund research programs to find cures for new and old diseases. Medical research has contributed to a longer life expectancy and improved quality of life. I believe the funding model needs to change to inject more risk-taking with the goal of achieving more breakthroughs.

Dr. Eric Topol, noted healthcare author, in a February, 2015 NPR On Your Health radio interview said, "It is the beginning of a new era in medicine. Medicine in 2020 will be unrecognizable from the medicine we have today."[318] Education is changing to fuel continued advances in medicine. Engineering, in particular, is morphing into bioengineering, creating new solutions which were previously thought to be impossible. Providing education and training for primary care will be essential for the coming era. To ensure continued investment in new technology, the cost of existing healthcare must be reduced.

CHAPTER 13

Reducing the Cost

T his chapter assesses the potential to capitalize on new tools and technologies. It describes approaches to eliminate waste and reduce the cost of healthcare. The Health Care Cost Institute (HCCI) was established in 2011 as a non-profit, independent, non-partisan research institute to develop a comprehensive source of information on healthcare activity in the United States. The HCCI staff believes rising healthcare costs are stifling economic growth, consuming increasing portions of the nation's gross domestic product, and putting added burdens on businesses, the public sector, individuals, and families.[319]

The root causes driving healthcare spending are unclear because of many variables. For example, the cost of healthcare for those privately insured grew a modest 3.9% in 2013, but the prices for healthcare services rose significantly because the use of costly services fell.[320] An analogy would be in dining out. If you stopped going to five-star restaurants, but used more three-star restaurants than previously, your total dining expense may decline while the price you pay for your meals rises. Three examples may further clarify what happened with healthcare spending in 2013. Inpatient hospital services fell 2.3% while prices for those services rose 6.7%. Outpatient services declined by 0.8% while prices rose 6.4. The use of brand name prescriptions dropped by 15.5% while the average price of prescriptions rose 21.2%.

One reason why utilization of healthcare services declined is the significant increase in health insurance deductibles. When out of pocket cost rises, consumers tend to be more careful about what services they use. People are more likely to comparison shop for the services they need. Nevertheless, with rising prices for services and millions of previously uninsured joining the ranks of the insured, the total spending on healthcare will rise. Although there is room for differing opinions, two certainties are healthcare cost is too high compared to other developed countries in the world, and it is not affordable for many in America.

This chapter will describe a variety of actions to help reduce the cost of American healthcare. It is by no means comprehensive. Chapter 3 highlighted some of the most significant cost problems. This chapter will highlight some significant areas for cost reduction. Most researchers agree every aspect of healthcare delivery could be more efficient and cost effective.

Measuring Cost to Reduce Cost

The first step in reducing cost is to understand the details underlying all costs. Cost accounting dates back to the 1920s, and is rigorously pursued in most industries. The reason for its use is simple. By understanding exactly what it costs to design, produce, deliver, and support a product, you can devise successful pricing strategies to maximize profitability. The motivation to manage costs in healthcare has been different. Historically, healthcare providers had no incentive to control costs because providers with high costs got high reimbursements. Seeing a patient twice would produce twice the revenue. Healthcare reform is beginning to change how reimbursements work, but the pace of change needs to accelerate to not just slow the rate of healthcare spending, but reduce it. Healthcare leaders will need to adopt a new attitude about costs.

Robert Kaplan, a Baker Foundation Professor at Harvard Business School, and Michael E. Porter, the Bishop William Lawrence University Professor at Harvard, collaborated on a study of hospital costs. They concluded the biggest problem with healthcare is not with insurance or politics. Kaplan said, "It's that we're measuring the wrong things the wrong way."[321] In "The Big Idea: How to Solve the Cost Crisis in Health Care" published in the *Harvard Business Review*, the authors describe the importance of understanding the cost associated with producing an outcome, in the case of a hospital, the cost to treat and cure a patient. Kaplan said that hospitals measure cost based on what they hope to get paid, and have no idea what the real cost of care is. Some have argued measuring the actual cost in a hospital setting is too complicated. Kaplan says that is because hospitals make it complicated, and if the costs are not measured properly, you can't manage or reduce them.

Hospital care tends to be organized around the specialties of care, not around the patient's condition. A patient going in for surgery gets sent to a primary care physician for a pre-op examination; to an imaging center for X-rays, CT or MRI scans; and to the lab for blood tests. Administrative aids call the patient before surgery to review profile information, which probably had not changed since the last visit. Upon entering the hospital, a nurse requests some of the same information. Then, the anesthesiologist interviews the patient, again asking for much of the same information. A physician's assistant may conduct the same interview. The multiple handoffs, duplicate procedures and data entry, all add to the cost of care.

Kaplan and Porter worked with four hospitals to develop methods to analyze every step of selected healthcare procedures in great detail. They discovered many of the processes were not needed and in some cases introduced the possibility of errors. They concluded significant cost reduction is possible without reducing the quality of outcomes, and cost reduction is essential to achieve affordability. Hospitals are under great external pressure from public and private payers to reduce their cost and increase their quality. Kaplan and Porter suggested rather than trying to convince the payers why the hospital should be reimbursed for all the procedures, they should suggest a reimbursement model that includes incentives to reduce cost and share in the savings.[322]

The concept of cost reduction has many parts. Kaplan et al said that these include: (1) more effective purchasing of supplies and medical equipment, (2) more streamlined and efficient processes, (3) automation of manual processes, (4) better scheduling and reduction of overtime, and (5) outsourcing of processes that can be performed less expensively by others. Unfortunately, many cost reductions result in reductions in the headcount of healthcare provider organizations. In some cases the reductions will mean layoffs, but hopefully the reductions can be accomplished through normal attrition. Staff reductions may be painful, but necessary to achieve affordability. Efficiencies will need to be identified to maintain the level of services provided with less staff headcount. The healthcare sector accounts for a disproportionate share of the American economy. Healthcare cost reductions may produce a resilience in other sectors that leads to job growth for the overall economy.

Reduce Administrative Costs

The Commonwealth Fund, a private foundation promoting a high-performing healthcare system with better access, improved quality, and greater efficiency, funded a research study to compare hospital administrative costs with those in Canada, England, Scotland, Wales, France, Germany, and the Netherlands. The study used data from 2010 and 2011. Administrative costs include coding, billing, accounting, contract administration, payroll, human resource management, and other administrative activities. The conclusion of the study was administrative costs accounted for 25% of hospital spending in the United States, more than double the cost in Scotland and Canada.[323] The second highest among the eight countries studied was the Netherlands at 20%. During the period from 2000 to 2011, the cost of hospital administration rose from .98% to 1.43% of the entire American economy. Had U.S. administrative cost on a per capita basis been equal to that of Canada, the savings for 2011 would have been $158 billion. The researchers found no correlation between higher administrative costs and higher quality healthcare.

Part of the solution to reduce administrative cost is more widely adopted use of EHRs, which could reduce the number of administrative tasks by automating and accelerating information transfers. Today, much of the tasks remain either manual or handled by independent systems that are not integrated with other systems. Integration of data transfers into all the relevant systems could reduce repetitive tasks and paperwork used to find unavailable or misplaced records. The lack of integration and use of EHRs results in more people doing more things, thereby adding more cost. The U.S. Department of Labor's Bureau of Labor Statistics reported that in 2011, healthcare providers employed more billing and posting clerks than any other industry.[324]

The Center for American Progress, a nonpartisan research and educational institute, published "Paper Cuts: Reducing Health Care Administrative Costs" in June 2012. The study is dated but presents a relevant methodology to examine administrative cost. The authors were Elizabeth Wikler, a doctoral candidate in health policy at Harvard University; Peter Basch, a practicing physician and Medical Director for Electronic Health Records and Senior Fellow at the Center for American Progress; and David Cutler, Professor of Applied Economics at Harvard University and Senior Fellow at the Center for American Progress. The authors dug deep into the nuts and bolts of healthcare administration looking for answers to why the cost was so high and so far out of line with other countries.

To find the root causes of the high cost, the authors looked at each of eight administrative stages including a range of activities beginning with providers negotiating with health insurance companies to establish what services the providers are qualified to deliver and for what reimbursement, to the final payment and reporting. Table 6, from "Paper Cuts: Reducing Health Care Administrative Costs", shows the eight administrative stages.[325]

Table 6: Healthcare Provider Administrative Stages

1	Providers negotiate with insurers on contracting/credentialing
2	Patient schedules appointment and eligibility verification
3	Patient visits and treatment
4	Billing and claims submission
5	Claims inquiries, collections, remittance, and payment posting
6	Denials and reconciling overpayments and underpayments
7	Appeals
8	Reporting

In each step, the authors discovered a range of factors for adding unnecessary cost. They described the set of activities as "Our way too complex healthcare payment process".[326] Some of the key cost-adding factors included: (1) redundant forms, (2) lengthy approval processes, (3) retroactive additions and changes, (4) complex payment processes, (5) confusion, (6) time-consuming prior authorizations, (7) inconsistencies from one payer to another, (8) variations in claims requirements, (9) lack of standardized codes and variations in use of codes, (10) nonstandard verification processes, (11) outdated systems, (12) costly and time-consuming manual processes, (13) inconsistent requirements among insurers and hospitals, and (14) uneven adoption of electronic capabilities.[327]

The list is staggering, but even more so is the amount of time providers spend because of these cost-adding factors. The author's report, "Paper Cuts: Reducing Health Care Administrative Costs", said, "Physicians spend an average of 43 minutes per day, or three weeks per year, interacting with healthcare plans. This is in addition to the 21 hours of nursing staff and 53 hours of clerical staff spent per physician per week on administrative transactions, particularly claims and prior authorizations."[328] A more recent study by Harvard Medical School research-ers found the average doctor spends 16.6 percent of his or her working hours on non-patient-related paperwork. Based on a nine-hour day, 16.6% translates into 90 minutes, double what was found in 2012.[329] The researchers attributed the in-creased paperwork burden in part to healthcare reforms driven by the Affordable Care Act.

Wikler, Basch, and Cutler concluded that administrative complexity exists at all levels of the healthcare system, and they developed a three-part strategy to address the problems. First and foremost, they recommended all administrative transactions be electronic and integrated into all health information technology systems to enable stakeholders to communicate electronically and in real-time. Second, they recommended, "reporting and enrollment systems be coordinated across national, state, and local regulatory bodies to reduce redundant tasks that take away from patient care."[330] Finally, they said policymakers should, "exert lead-ership on administrative simplification reforms to ensure timely and innovative results."[331] The authors said if all three recommendations were followed, adminis-trative costs would be reduced by 25 percent and save $40 billion annually.[332]

Paper Blizzard

There are certain aspects of the annual physical exam not pleasant for any-one, but the thing I enjoy the least is filling out the paperwork. Step one at the doctor's office is the presentation of a clipboard and forms with data fields that are too small and questions I don't know the answer to, like the address of my healthcare provider. I once said to a receptionist I had been a patient of the doctor for years and nothing had changed since the last time I filled out the paperwork. "Yes, but we have a new billing service and they require all patients fill out the pa-perwork every six months." It seems like at every visit there is some reason I have to print my name, address, phone number, and date of birth multiple times. After I printed the health insurance information from my insurance cards, the office as-sistant asked for the cards, and then made a photocopy of the front and back of them to put in a manila folder. Every aspect of healthcare is burdened with paper. Why do we have so much paper? I believe one source is from legal efforts.

Ralph Losey is a practicing attorney in a national law firm with 50+ offices and more than 800 lawyers. He leads the firm's Electronic Discovery Practice Group, and is an expert in the search and review of electronic evidence using artificial intelligence. Losey says lawyers love paper because it is all they have ever known. Following is an abbreviated version of what he wrote in his blog:

> They grow up in a paper world. They learn how to read on paper. They study paper books. They surround themselves with great piles of paper literature and paper case law. When taking evidence and trial classes, law students are taught with paper documents, shown how to test the authenticity of paper records and how to have paper admitted into evidence. They are shown how to generate papers, copy papers, pile papers, file papers, notarize papers, shuffle papers, staple papers, clip papers, highlight papers, redact papers, watermark papers, and even add paper stickums to paper.[333]

When I finished my law degree in 1971, there was no Internet or World Wide Web. Now that we have the web, some lawyers embrace it as a productivity aid, but some do not. It may correlate to age, but I know older lawyers who are quite high-tech, and some young ones who are techno-phobic. My daughter is a legal nurse consultant. When she was about to review her first case for a law firm, she asked for access to the EHR of the patient. The firm printed it out and shipped her a box with 18 inches of paper. The hourly charge to create all the paper and ship it was marked up and billed to the client.

Is it possible for an organization to go paperless? Yes it is, if the organization is motivated to do so. If producing and handling paper takes more time and you are paid by the hour, the motivation may not be there. But, if you are a hospital, there is motivation, and it is coming from the government. The Health Information Technology for Economic and Clinical Health Act has paid out nearly 10 billion dollars in incentives for healthcare providers to implement electronic health records. Beginning in 2015, a penalty will be imposed on hospitals that have not developed a full implementation, referred to as stage seven meaningful use. There are approximately 5,000 hospitals in the United States, and approximately 100 are essentially paperless as of 2013.[334]

Paperless does not mean all documents must be spreadsheets or Word documents. For the foreseeable future, many documents will be scanned and saved in the portable data format (PDF). Although not optimum, PDF files can be searched for, searched in, archived, combined, and shared. Dave Sparks is a 46 year old business attorney and self-described geek in Irvine, California. His "*The*

MacSparky Paperless Field Guide" describes in great detail a methodology for scanning, naming documents, and saving them in a manner making them easy to find later. I have followed his advice, and as a result I have nothing in my file drawers. Healthcare providers can apply more sophisticated and automated processes to become paperless. If healthcare leaders adopt Sparks' attitude about the benefits of going paperless, their organizations could streamline their operations and save money.

Coupon Book

It isn't just lawyers who love paper. Health insurance companies have been slow to adopt paperless technology. During the open enrollment period for 2014 healthcare insurance, my wife and I chose a plan from the largest of insurance companies available to us. Three months after enrolling in the plan, I received their coupon payment book, a physical paper payment book with printed coupons in it, along with 12 envelopes in which to return checks for my monthly premium payments. The last coupon book I can recall was when I bought my first car in 1967 and took out my first bank loan. I cannot remember the last time I wrote a check. My wife received the same set of coupons and envelopes. Sending 12 envelopes and a book of coupons to millions of consumers is yet another cost that flows through the healthcare system and is ultimately absorbed by consumers.

This is the digital 21st century, but a multi-billion-dollar health insurance company is using coupon books. They do offer the option of automated deductions of the monthly payments from either the social security payment or by a deduction directly from a checking account, but the default is the coupon book, checks, and envelopes. If you choose the automatic deduction option, you have to fill out a paper form and mail it with a check --more paperwork, more cost. The company said it could take up to three months for the payments to become automatic, and I should continue to mail checks and coupons until I receive a letter from them.

Fax Machine

Coupon Chile, a website that lists and publishes valid coupon codes, voucher codes, and online discount deals, did some research about fax machines and found there are 46.3 million of them around the world, 17.4 million in the United

States. The estimated total number of faxes sent each year is 16.9 billion, representing 853 miles high of paper, which equates to 2 million trees cut down every year. The fax machine and the Internet have something in common. They both provide integration for incompatible data. Anybody with a fax machine can send anybody a fax and know the recipient will be able to read it or have it translated. The Internet allows anyone with a browser to be able to connect to any server and retrieve information, regardless of what kind of server contains the information. In effect the World Wide Web provides integration and removes any incompatibilities. If the Internet had arrived sooner, there would have been no need for fax machines, which have since seen a steady decline in usage throughout the business community, but not in healthcare.

Jeff Tangney is the founder of Epocrates, a smartphone app which replaced the 3,250 page Physician Desk Reference, and is used by one million Epocrates subscribers. He is now CEO of Doximity, a social media company networking service used by more than 50% of U.S. physicians. Tangney said, "Fax machines are the lingua franca of healthcare."[335] Faxing is ingrained in the workflow of physicians. Tangney added, "It's still an industry that runs by and large by the fax machine."[336] It is not that doctors like paper or faxes, but I believe many feel they are chained to the eco-system of which they are a part.

Healthcare is making progress toward paperless in some areas. For example, e-prescribing is improving patient safety and streamlining the process of getting a prescription from the doctor to medication in your hands. However, it doesn't always work that way. Millions of prescriptions are handled by specialty pharmacies operated by all the major pharmacy companies. They handle medications needing refrigeration or some form of special preparation or handling. When a physician completes an online e-script to a specialty pharmacy, the e-script is converted to a fax. When the specialty pharmacy receives the fax, someone manually keys it into his or her system. It usually takes an extra day for an e-script to be filled in this manner, and the extra steps add cost to the fulfillment. While the healthcare industry is making great strides in adopting the Internet, it has a long way to go. Without the fax machine, healthcare would come to a screeching halt.

Standards

There are numerous reasons why our healthcare is so expensive. In my opinion, costs are high because the healthcare industry has been slow to adopt progressive information and communications technology to reduce waste through improved administration. In Sweden, all drug prescriptions are electronic. E-prescribing is rolling out in the United States, and the pace is picking up because standards are in place to handle the prescriptions in a uniform manner. The result is a reduction in medical errors and the costs associated with correcting the errors or settling legal claims.

Hospitals and other providers are struggling to reach a full implementation of EHRs in part because of the lack of standards. Hospitals and doctors must adhere to uniform accounting standards to report their financial performance, but they can use whatever EHR system they choose. There are 250+ EHR vendors, and there is not sufficient adoption of standards to ensure they are fully compatible. Germany has 300+ healthcare insurance companies, but they all must comply with certain standards established by the government. Although some would argue to reduce government involvement in healthcare, the setting of national standards for exchanging data between EHR systems could help accelerate the adoption and lead to lower cost.

Blueprint For Innovation

Innovation can play an important role in driving down cost. In April 2014, I attended Blueprint Health's fifth annual Demo Day. Blueprint Health is a mentorship-driven startup accelerator program in NYC, supporting entrepreneurs who are building innovative companies at the intersection of health and technology. Blueprint runs a three month program that provides healthcare technology startup companies with access to capital, clients, and mentors. The concept behind an accelerator is it can help a startup company reach critical mass and become a successful business more quickly. The mentors include nearly 200 healthcare entrepreneurs, investors, and industry executives who are committed to helping the startups grow and prosper. Blueprint's 12,000 square foot loft in SoHo is home to 45 healthcare tech startups, thought leaders, and funders, and forms the center of gravity within the healthcare ecosystem.

A thriving entrepreneurial ecosystem in the healthcare industry can play a significant role in spurring innovation leading to improved efficiency and lower cost for providers. Most of the startups focus on opportunities in hospitals, where administrators are interested in improving efficiency, delivering safer and more effective care, and reducing costs. Doug Hayes, Executive Director at Blueprint Health said,

> The healthcare industry represents nearly 20% of the American economy, and investors see it as one of the top investment opportunities. We are working hard to bring investors, entrepreneurs, and early adopters together to innovate and help the industry lower its cost structure.[337]

After a networking lunch with more than 500 investors, analysts, and members of the press, Blueprint introduced seven startup companies, who each gave a 10 minute presentation about their strategy, financial model, and financing plans. See Table 7: Demo Day Presentations for an abbreviated summary about the companies and how they plan to help the industry increase revenues and reduce costs.[338]

Table 7: Demo Day Presentations

BoardRounds	Helps hospitals transition patients from the hospital to in-network physicians, improving patient care, and generating additional revenue. BoardRounds schedules follow-up appointments for patients with providers to ensure proper follow-up occurs. A typical hospital can generate over $1M in additional in-network services and improve its quality scores. BoardRounds is in use at Mount Sinai Hospital and is negotiating with five hospital systems.
Decisive Health	Enables specialists to see more patients by improving the quality and efficiency of patient consultations. Decisive Health educates patients about recommended treatment options, predicts patient treatment preferences, and qualifies patients for procedures sooner. Clients include physicians at the Hospital for Special Surgery and Virginia Hospital Center.
ProofPilot	Makes it easy to design, launch, and manage complex research studies and clinical trials. With the ProofPilot platform, researchers launch studies four times faster and cut over 50% of costs. Current clients include NYU Langone, Saatchi & Saatchi Wellness, and the Huffington Post.
MediQuire	Helps hospitals measure and improve clinician performance. Their platform takes EHR data and compares clinicians to peers based on the quality of care they deliver. MediQuire then reduces performance gaps by delivering personalized education in the areas where clinicians need to improve most. Their platform allows hospitals to efficiently manage hundreds of new performance requirements, thereby avoiding penalties and reducing waste.

PulseBeat	Is all about home healthcare for the 21st century. PulseBeat offers family members peace of mind by remotely monitoring and caring for their aging family member. They provide caregivers with real-time notifications and daily health report cards that provide a holistic view of their loved one's health. Through partnerships with home healthcare companies, PulseBeat offers 24/7 access to a home care nurse or aide. They are working with the Visiting Nurse Association of Orange County, CA opening the door to thousands of potential customers in southern California.
RubiconMD	Helps primary care providers earn an additional $45k per year, by treating more specialty related cases. Over 40% of specialist referrals are unnecessary and could be treated by primary care providers. RubiconMD connects primary care providers with specialists for remote opinions. Provider networks see considerable cost savings. RubiconMD has three clients including Doctors Express Urgent Care Clinic, the largest urgent care network in the U.S.
Twiage	A mobile and web-based platform that provides secure, realtime transfer of information and rich media from the ambulance to the ER. They improve pre-hospital communication between the ambulance and the ER, saving the average ER over $350k annually in false service activations alone. South Shore Hospital, in South Weymouth, MA, began using Twiage for their EMTs and Emergency Room in 2014.

Summary

Reducing the cost of healthcare is not easy, but it can be done. All fifty states issue electronic cards for users of the Supplemental Nutrition Assistance Program, formerly called the Food Stamp Program. The new program is an automated paperless process. Tens of millions of people use food benefits, and now they are able to do so without having to wave coupons. Food stores are seeing dramatically less cost for processing, and reduced delays in receiving payments. State governments will see less fraud and lower overall cost. Amazon, eBay, the Assistance Program, and thousands of online retailers operate without paper. With government assistance on standards, innovation from startups, health attitude, and leadership from healthcare providers and health insurance companies, the cost of healthcare can be reduced significantly. To accomplish this, we need forward thinking healthcare policy, agile healthcare management, and new health attitude.

Part Four

Healthcare Policy and Management Techniques

CHAPTER 14

Access and Equity

E quity of the access and quality of care varies greatly from patient to patient. Millions of people have no access to healthcare except for emergency care. Some have access but cannot afford the care they should get. Others get care, but it is not equal to what they would get if they could afford better care. In this chapter, I will focus on cost, high deductibles, and the myths of free emergency care.

Family Health Insurance

In 2014, the Patient Protection and Affordable Care Act (ACA) enabled seven million people to get coverage through healthcare.gov or state-run exchanges.[339] It is not yet clear how many of those who signed up under the new plans were actually newly insured. An estimated five million people had received cancellation notices of prior plans because those plans did not conform to ACA requirements, and a significant number of those who lost prior coverage may have been among the seven million.

Even if all seven million were insured for the first time, it still would leave 16% of the population uninsured. Survey results released by the CDC in September 2014, showed the uninsured to be at 15.2%. The only good news is the number of uninsured adults dropped from 18.2% in 2010 to 15.2% for 2014.[340] And that is the problem – 15% or nearly 48 million people are not insured. Another problem is disparity with the uninsured being 9.7% white, 13.5 % black, and 25.3% Hispanic.[341]

The United States is the wealthiest country in the world, and yet the only developed country that does not have health insurance coverage of some kind for the entire population.

The high cost of American healthcare is a major inhibitor of expanding care for the uninsured. Experts do not agree, but the waste in our current healthcare system is at least $500 billion and perhaps as much as $1.5 trillion. The cost of healthcare per capita is approximately $8,900. Multiply the per capita cost times the 48 million uninsured, and it would cost roughly one-third of the higher estimate of waste. If we could eliminate all the waste, we could cover everyone and still reduce our per capita spending significantly. The dollars are there; the political consensus to maximize the savings opportunities is not.

Another factor adding to the cost of health insurance for individuals and families is the deductible. In 2009, 22.5% of those surveyed had private coverage with a deductible of $1,250 per individual or $2,500 for a family. As of early 2014, the number with a large deductible had grown to 36%.[342] A family at an income level of $25,000 may get a subsidized health insurance plan they can afford by accepting the high deductible. Some young people get a high-deductible plan so that they can have well-baby coverage for their children, but paying $2,500 for their healthcare cost is not a reality for them.

Unfortunately, in 2014, deductibles are much larger. The situation for a young couple in the Northeast puts this point in perspective. The husband is 38 and the wife is 37. Their income is $70,000, but their children qualify for health insurance through a state-funded program. The parents are healthy, but feel the need to have coverage, "just in case". They visited the state-run health exchange and entered their profiles and various documents the site requested. The site responded with 38 policy choices from four health insurers. The monthly premiums ranged from just under $500 per month to just over $1,000. A tax credit available to the couple would provide approximately $100 per month.

Comparing the various plans is difficult unless you know exactly how often you may need medical care and how much it would cost because the premiums are established based on actuarial data, and the complexity of analyzing the pros and cons of the various plans is overwhelming. One policy document the couple considered was 145 pages and listed 58 things not covered. The policy for $500 per month may sound affordable until you consider the family deductible, $12,000. There is no co-pay for a doctor visit, but not until each had spent $6,000. The deductible is a two-edged sword. A larger deduction results in a more affordable premium, but on the other hand it creates the potential of having to spend far more than is in the family budget.

Some young people might decide they cannot afford any plan, and are willing to face the possibility of a penalty from the IRS. When a person is in their 20's, they may feel they do not need health insurance. They have not yet embraced a health attitude. The main motivation for younger people to buy health insurance is if they have a pre-existing condition or need coverage for a spouse or children.

I think there are three reasons why a family should try to find a way to afford health insurance. First, having a health insurance policy provides favorable prices from providers compared to what the price would be without the insurance. Second, the policy would provide catastrophic coverage in the event medical spending exceeded the deductible. Third, the health insurance companies evaluate the providers, and the insured can be confident they will receive quality healthcare.

A positive feature of a handful of policies a young couple could choose from included a health savings account (HSA). The HSA allows the insured to put up to $6,000 into the HSA either directly, through pre-tax payroll deduction, or via a transfer from an IRA account. The HSA account can earn interest and is tied to a debit card to be used to pay for health services. In addition to the tax benefit, any funds not spent during the year are rolled over to the following year, thereby creating a long-term investment and an incentive to choose only the healthcare needed. The HSA is a good plan if you can afford it. If the couple could afford $1,000 per month, they could get the $500 per month policy and put the other $500 per month into the HSA. In many situations, a family cannot afford to spend $1,000 per month no matter how appealing the HSA may be.

Role of Deductibles

The number of people with a high deductible in their health insurance policy is increasing. The deductible has some hidden benefits to the insured and to the healthcare system at large. The downside is consumers with a high deductible face the risk of needing to spend a substantial amount of their income for doctor fees, hospital visits, surgeries, and drugs. The upside of the high deductible is significant to the healthcare system at large.

Consider a person with a sore back who goes to his or her primary care physician who provides a referral to an orthopedic surgeon who subsequently suggests an MRI. A person with a low deductible will readily accept the suggestion to go down the hall or across the street to an imaging facility affiliated with the surgeon who recommended it, and which may share a portion of profit with affiliated physicians. A person with a large deductible will likely ask two questions. First, do I really need the MRI, and what are the consequences if I do not get it? If the person is convinced he or she needs the MRI, then the second question is whether it is ok to get the MRI elsewhere. The physician may highlight the convenience of the nearby imaging center, but will probably say yes. The person then may do some research and comparison-shopping, and may find an imaging center across town can perform the MRI study for half the price.

The transparency of the price of various healthcare services is a major emerging issue. In France, getting the price for various medical tests and procedures is easy; when you go to the doctor, the standard fee schedule for the various treatments offered is posted on the wall, showing exactly what the charges will be and how much of it the national insurance plan will cover.[343]

Such transparency has not been available in the United States, but things are changing. Over 30 states are currently considering legislation to require increased price transparency. There is no debate that more price transparency causes prices to go down in most industries, but healthcare is much more complex. Some research suggests patients at times base treatment decisions on the experiences of friends and family members, or the immediacy of the need, than on cost.

A 47 page analysis of the transparency topic by Muir, Alessi, and King published in the UC Hastings College of the Law Legal Studies Research Paper Series, concluded the most important aspect of any price transparency initiative is the education provided to employers and consumers.[344] The price and quality information can help each group make better-informed decisions and gain the best possible price for healthcare. Some experts estimate the potential savings from improved transparency could be as much as $100 billion during the next decade.[345]

New mobile health (mHealth) apps can help consumers compare healthcare services, providers, available treatments, and treatment facility selection. The availability of quality and cost information for local care providers through mHealth apps will help consumers manage their healthcare expenses. For example, the Health4Me app from UnitedHealth Group allows you to pick from 635 medical services, find local healthcare providers by specialty type, and get cost information for various tests and procedures. I gave it a test drive and found it comprehensive, although cost estimates are based on actual contracted rates UnitedHealth has with providers and facilities in their network. Using a Florida zip code, I found the cost for a lumbar spine MRI is $506 and an X-Ray is $30. Using a New England zip code, the same tests cost $682 and $41.

Many insured or uninsured are confused about the cost of medications. A smartphone app called GoodRX opens up transparency on the cost of drugs. Simply entering a zip code and the medication, dosage, and number of pills you need, the app will display all pharmacies that have the medication and what the cost is. The differences in price are staggering. In some cases the cost of a drug at Walmart or Target or other retailer can be less than the deductible on an insured plan. In other words, in some cases, it is cheaper to go to Walmart as an uninsured to purchase a medication than to go to the pharmacy that is part of your plan and pay the deductible.

Consumers with large deductibles will want to get all the information possible. Judy Mottl, a journalist at *InformationWeek*, reported four out of five smartphone users worldwide are interested in mHealth technology as a way to interact with healthcare providers and evaluate treatment options.[346] Healthcare interactions can be done with a Mac or PC using a browser, but users are shifting to smartphone apps as a preferred method of retrieving information. Web pages can get cluttered and tedious to use. New mHealth apps are created from scratch and designed to include what you need at your fingertips.

Businesses Avoiding Health Insurance Cost

Howard Schultz, CEO at Starbucks acknowledged the Affordable Care Act might increase company-provided health insurance cost, but said the company's benefits for all employees, including part-time employees, will continue.[347] Schultz told CNN, "It's not about the law. It's about responsibility we have to the people who do work and who represent us."[348] In 2010, Starbucks spent $300 million on benefits, more than it paid for coffee.

Other companies do not agree. Many businesses struggle with the costs of health care. Some companies have cut staff or benefits, dropped health coverage, or increased employee cost sharing to compensate for the cost. The ACA specifies that if an employer has 50 or more employees, the company must provide options for health insurance. Some 50 person companies are considering splitting into two 25 person companies to avoid having to provide healthcare to their employees. Some full-time employees, who may want to earn overtime, are being asked to cut their hours, again to avoid having to be provided with healthcare. I believe these actions are understandable, but they do more harm than good for the health of Americans. The implementation of the ACA is designed to force the economics to work. The Administration is being challenged about healthcare provisions from every direction, even including labor unions and some Democrats who voted for the ACA.

Myths About Emergency Care

Many Americans believe people without health insurance get access to the care they need by going to the hospital ER. It is true that no person with a legitimate medical condition can be turned away from the ER. Congress created the Emergency Medical Treatment and Active Labor Act in 1985 out of concern patients were being denied emergency medical treatment because of their inability to pay.[349] The Act contains two basic requirements: first, hospitals must provide an appropriate medical screening examination to determine whether or not an emergency medical condition exists and, if the screening examination reveals an emergency medical condition, it must stabilize the medical condition before transferring or discharging the patient. Stabilize and transfer or discharge is not necessarily a cure, and they do not provide any preventive care such as counseling to avoid problems in the future.

The Institute of Medicine's Committee on the Consequences of Uninsurance studied the outcomes for the uninsured and reported its findings in "Care Without Coverage: Too Little, Too Late" in 2002.[350] The study primarily focused on uninsured adults with cancer, diabetes, HIV infection and AIDS, heart and kidney disease, mental illness, traumatic injuries, and heart attacks. They found for one in six working-age Americans without health insurance suffering from those diseases, there are often dire consequences. According to a study published by the American Journal of Public Health, nearly 45,000 people die each year because they do not have health insurance.[351] A person with a serious cancer not diagnosed until the pain was significant enough to go to the ER can get emergency treatment. They may go home with painkillers, ultimately to die. Researchers also found working-age Americans with no health insurance are more likely to receive too little medical care and receive it too late. They may be sicker and die sooner and receive poorer care when they are in the hospital, even for acute situations like a motor vehicle crash."[352]

The myth the uninsured get healthcare through the ER is commonly held. If an uninsured person presents herself to the ER when in labor or facing death from an acute ailment, then yes, such a person gets care. But the list of what they don't get is much longer. The ER does not provide preventive care. There is no screening for a multitude of ailments. There is no treatment for depression or any of the numerous chronic mental diseases. There is no help for children's autism, developmental issues, or attention deficit hyperactivity disorder.

The other part of the myth about ER care for the uninsured is that it is free. Community hospitals do not pay income tax, and part of the justification for this is the hospitals offer millions of dollars in charity care. However, it does not mean people who visit the ER do not get billed for the services they receive. They get billed, and hospitals pursue collection of the amount due just like any business would. Some hospitals retain collection agencies to pursue those with unpaid bills. In some cases, wages are garnished. In other cases, low wage earners make weekly payments to the hospital. Credit ratings can be damaged and in some cases financial ruin follows. *Health Affairs* reported medical bills are a contributing factor in 17 percent of personal bankruptcies.[353] A joint study by Harvard Law School and Harvard Medical School estimated such bankruptcies at 700,000 per year.[354]

Equity in Healthcare

The word equity has several meanings. If you are a homeowner, the equity in your home is equal to the market value of the home minus any mortgages or home equity loans. If you are an investor in a company, your equity is related to the number of shares you own compared to the total number of shares. Financial equity is relatively easy to understand. It can be calculated with numbers and validated to assure the equity is correct.

When it comes to healthcare, equity has a different meaning relating to fairness or justice in the way people are treated. Healthcare equity is difficult to reconcile because it means different things to different people. It is even more difficult to calculate. Instead of numbers, the determinants of healthcare equity include subjective factors such as the effectiveness of patient/provider communications, stereotyping, and patient mistrust.

An equitable healthcare system would provide equal access to all, regardless of race, ethnicity, gender, age, or socioeconomic status. If healthcare providers mirrored the population it serves, patients would trust their providers. Health outcomes would be the same for all. There would be no differences in morbidity, mortality, or life expectancy. Unfortunately, our system is not even close to health-care equity.

The Institute of Medicine recommended increasing the proportion of under-represented minorities in the healthcare workforce. The authors of "Improving Quality, Achieving Equity, and Increasing Diversity in Healthcare: The Future is Now" said that minorities represent almost 35% of the population, but represent 5% of dentists, 14% of nurses, and 17% of city and county public health officials.[355] A study by the Association of American Medical Colleges showed race and ethnic-ity for 40% of physicians is unknown, but, for the 60% reporting, Latinos make up 5.5%, African-Americans 6.3%, and American Indian and Alaskan Natives less than 0.6%. Two years later, the Association revealed the racial/ethnic composition of medical school faculty showed disparity with minorities representing only 21.5% nationally. Only 12.3% of medical school graduates are non-white so the problem of achieving increased diversity of physicians does not have a short-term solution.

Summary

The principle of equity in the access and quality of care should not vary from patient to patient. However, numerous studies have confirmed disparities exist not only in access to care but also other areas such as patient safety and avoidance of adverse clinical consequences. The problem of mismatch between patients and providers will get worse because minorities will comprise almost half of the 32 mil-lion newly insured under the ACA.[356] Having a healthcare workforce reflecting our increasingly diverse population is vital if we are to achieve healthcare reform and deliver high quality care to the entire population. In the next chapter I will discuss the reform I propose.

CHAPTER 15

Healthcare – A Right or A Privilege?

There are countless academic studies arguing for and against various provisions of healthcare policy. This chapter, although informed by research, contains mostly my own point of view. My viewpoint comes from careful reflection and study. It is also influenced from nine years of service on a hospital board.

The most important policy question to address is whether healthcare is a right or a privilege. This question is hard to answer without considering cultural, value based, and political considerations. Prior to studying the subject, I may have said healthcare is a privilege. Today, I do not equivocate – I believe it is a right. A review of the literature produces many diverse opinions from both extremes and many in between.

The World Health Organization said that health is a state of complete physical, mental, and social well-being, and not merely the absence of disease or infirmity. To formulate my position on the question of right or privilege, I start with the belief America will be more productive if everyone can meet the World Health Organization definition of health. A population that is sick cannot be productive and contribute to the economy. I cannot prove this, but I believe taxpayers will end up paying more in the end if they don't provide healthcare for all.

If I have to choose between the two words – privilege or right – I choose right, but it is a right with responsibility. The responsibility would include two elements. First is the responsibility to contribute financially to the cost of healthcare in relation to one's means. Second is the responsibility to be prudent with regard to one's lifestyle. I believe federal, state, and local governments and communities have a responsibility to promote healthy lifestyles and provide appropriate clinics and educational opportunities. If individuals refuse these opportunities, the safety net should still be in place for all. There are multiple "what if" questions associated with my answer to the question of right or privilege, but healthcare as a right represents the core of my belief.

The basic unit of society in most countries is the individual, and basic rights for individuals have typically been related to life, liberty, and the pursuit of happiness. Some philosophers have suggested the basic rights for individuals come from nature or from God. The Founders believed individual rights included freedom of speech, press, religion, and freedom from unreasonable searches. Some believe there are no further rights needed. This may have been true in the early days of our country, but I believe we have moved beyond that premise. Thomas J. Papadimos, Associate Professor of Anesthesiology at The University of Toledo in Ohio, has studied the subject in depth. Starting with the irrefutable fact that tens of millions are lacking healthcare for many different reasons, he attempted to answer the question as to whether the intervention necessary to provide access to the uninsured should be considered a privilege or a right.

Papadimos examined the question of privilege or right from the perspective of Western thought. He examined the works of theorists and philosophers such as Aristotle, Immanuel Kant, Thomas Hobbes, Thomas Paine, Hannah Arendt, James Rawls, and Norman Daniels. He published his findings and conclusions in "Healthcare Access as a Right, Not a Privilege: A Construct of Western Thought" published in 2007 in *Philosophy, Ethics, and Humanities in Medicine*.[357] The eight page article concludes, "Based on the natural rights we maintain as individuals and those we collectively surrender to the common good, it has been determined by nature, natural laws, and natural rights that human beings have the right, not the privilege, to healthcare access."[358] Papadimos acknowledges once healthcare access becomes a right, numerous complexities arise. He posed many questions:

> Do the elderly receive liver transplants? Can a morbidly obese person receive a reoperation for coronary artery bypass grafting? Can a diabetic receive a second kidney transplant? How much is enough healthcare access? Will healthcare delivery become a tiered process? Are we wise

enough to make the necessary and correct decisions? Who will be society's proxy to make such decisions? There are no clear answers.[359]

Rights of Americans

As Americans, we are fortunate to have many rights. We can vote for or against our political leaders, and be confident the process we use to vote is auditable and fair. We can sleep at night knowing we have the right to be protected from crimes at the federal, state, and local levels. If we have the misfortune to encounter flood, epidemic, or fire, we have the right to expect public resources will come to our aid. If there is a public school near where we live, we have a right for our children to attend without paying tuition.

One of the great resources we have in America is the public library. There are some exceptions, but generally, if you are a resident of a location having a public library, you have a right to use it. Public libraries provide Internet access and trained professionals to help us find information. During recessions, public libraries are a resource for finding a job. At tax time, people go to the library to find forms and documentation online. Libraries provide a wide range of services and programs. These include: public space for meetings, seminars for authors to discuss their books, literacy classes, career help, teen centers, story times for young children, computers and computer classes, art galleries, and community gathering spaces. Seminars put experts in front of the community. Many people who can't afford a computer in their home use the library for their online access. The bottom line is an American, whether he or she makes $2 million dollars or $20,000, has access to a wide range of rights and public services, except for one, healthcare.

Political leaders and policymakers should stay laser focused on driving down the cost of healthcare. I believe they should support new organizational models such as the patient-centered medical home and the Accountable Care Organization. Accountable care may have the most potential to move us closer to universal coverage. For example, if payers such as Aetna, Blue Cross, UnitedHealthcare, Medicare, and Medicaid enter into contracts with health systems to cover the entire population of a city or zip code, that health system will be highly motivated to understand the population they are responsible for at a very detailed level. They will utilize big data and analytics to determine what diseases are prominent in that population, and will develop preventive care and clinics to address those diseases.

The shift to population based healthcare is just beginning and it will take years before it becomes the dominant form of care. In the meantime, millions of Americans have no health insurance coverage, and thousands die every year as a result. We can do better. A review of comments made by Presidents Carter, G. W. Bush, and Clinton, reveal they all in different words, agreed healthcare should be available to all who need it.

Presidential Points of View

President Jimmy Carter was a crusader for universal healthcare. He addressed parts of American healthcare as a moral issue. In a 1977 speech he said, "We have an abominable system in this country for the delivery of healthcare, with gross inequities toward the poor, particularly the working poor, and profiteering by many hospitals of the ill."[360] He fought hospital and medical lobbyists, and tried to implement cost containment measures for hospitals, while insuring adequate healthcare at a reasonable cost. In a 1976 speech on public health, President Carter outlined his healthcare goals: a comprehensive program of national health insurance, government reorganization to remove bureaucratic fragmentation, alternative delivery systems such as HMOs, and clean up disgraceful Medicaid scandals.[361]

The Clinton Administration tried to make healthcare universal, affordable, more competitive, and of a higher quality. President Bill Clinton believed if different insurance companies had to offer the same benefits and compete on quality, the result would be better, cheaper healthcare. In his book, *My Life*, President Clinton said, "The bureaucratic costs imposed by insurance companies were a big reason Americans paid more for healthcare, but still didn't have the universal coverage that citizens in other developed countries have."[362] President Clinton rejected the single-payer and Medicare models, preferring a quasi-private system called "managed competition" that relied on private market forces to drive down costs through competition. He thought the government should have a smaller role overall, but it should set standards for benefit packages, and help organize purchasing cooperatives so hospitals could reduce costs.

In the 2000 State of the Union Address, President George W. Bush said he believed every American should have access to quality, affordable healthcare by giving consumers better information about healthcare plans, providing more choices such as medical savings accounts, and changing tax laws to help more people, such as the uninsured and the self-employed, afford health insurance.[363] He also believed keeping America competitive required affordable healthcare. He argued government should confront the rising cost of care, strengthen the doctor-patient relationship, and help people afford the insurance coverage they need. The Bush administration initiated the wider use of electronic records and other health information technology to help control costs and reduce dangerous medical errors. President Bush was a consistent supporter of strengthening health savings accounts and making the coverage portable so workers could switch jobs without having to worry about losing their health insurance.

I believe if you made a list of all the comments and goals from the prior paragraphs about Presidents Carter, Clinton, and Bush points of view, and removed the names, it would be very difficult to correctly attribute who said what. In the past, both political parties would like to achieve many of the same goals. It is the methods, programs, and financing that cause political gridlock. Most of the principles described in the following sections of the chapter could be implemented if our political leaders of both parties would negotiate and compromise in good faith.

Key Questions About Healthcare Policy

Healthcare policy is a complicated topic. Politicians are divided about it. In this section I try to simplify the subject by asking a handful of basic questions. I started with a discussion of whether healthcare is a right. The follow up questions are: (1) who provides the healthcare, (2) who pays for healthcare insurance, (3) where does the funding come from, and (4) who provides the health insurance.

If you believe healthcare is a right, then this is an easy question to answer. In my opinion, all citizens should be able to obtain some form of healthcare insurance regardless of their ability to pay. The only requirement is to have a valid identity, so providers can create an EHR. The EHR can facilitate follow-up on needed care, allow epidemiologists to track diseases, and enable healthcare planners to develop preventive healthcare programs and clinics. Some politicians argue requiring a traceable identity is an invasion of privacy or a hardship for the poor to travel or pay to get an identity card.[364] I reject that argument. There are various ways to obtain an identity at little or no cost, and the Health Insurance Portability and Accountability Act (HIPAA) provides strong protections of privacy.

Healthcare providers can be public or private, for profit or not for profit. The only operating limitation is there must be no conflicts of interest. For example, if a physician is an investor in the laboratory or imaging facility or receives a share of the profit from them, it must be publicly disclosed, and should be clearly stated in the office. A patient should always be offered a choice of where to go for imaging studies, lab work, prescription medicine, or specialist care, unless his or her health insurance requires the use of certain providers.

I advocate the principle everybody pays something according to their means. All citizens should have health insurance. It can be provided by either private health insurance companies, government, or both. Means testing should be used for government provided health insurance. For example, in 2015 the nearly 50 million people enrolled in Medicare Part B, which covers physicians' services, outpatient hospital services, certain home health services, durable medical equipment, and other items, will require premiums. For individuals making less than $85,000, the premium in 2015 will be $104.90. For individuals making more than $214,000, the premium will be $335.70. The premium is graduated in between.

Medicaid and the Children's Health Insurance Program (CHIP) provide health coverage for nearly 60 million Americans. The Affordable Care Act created a national Medicaid minimum eligibility level of 133% of the federal poverty level ($29,700 for a family of four in 2011) for nearly all Americans under age 65. Each state has its own rules about who qualifies for Medicaid and CHIP. Persons who qualify for these programs pay no premium.

I would suggest two changes to current policy. First, all citizens must have health insurance – no exceptions. The states can and should run their healthcare programs, but no citizen can be excluded. Second, every citizen should pay something. For those below the poverty level, it may be $10 per month. For the most indigent, it may be a pledge to pay some small amount when they get on their feet. The principle is every citizen pays something.

Habitat for Humanity, which has built or repaired more than one million houses since 1976 with people in need of decent, affordable housing, believes homeowners who invest something take pride in their homes and feel good about themselves. Today, more than 4 million people are living in Habitat homes. The homes were built with the resident, not for the resident. Habitat uses the term "sweat equity" to refer to the hours of labor homeowners invest in building their homes. Habitat homeowners typically complete a minimum of 400 hours before they can move into their homes and begin making no interest mortgage payments. Habitat has eligibility requirements to ensure the homeowner is able to make the monthly payments.

In round numbers, the cost of healthcare for 50 million people would be $500 billion. Eliminating the waste in the current system would more than cover the needs. Some of the sources of cost reduction already discussed include: tort reform; reductions in defensive medicine, fraud and abuse, and duplicative services; electronic health records and e-prescribing; Medicare negotiations with Big Pharma for lower drug cost; and Six Sigma quality improvements. If the level of spending in the current system could be brought in line with other developed countries, there would be enough funding left to get the entire American population in the healthcare system.

A common plea from many people who are dissatisfied with the overall healthcare system is a call for a single payer system. Germany has universal healthcare coverage and excellent healthcare outcomes – better than in America. They have 200+ payers. Canada has universal health operated by 10 provinces and three territories. The United Kingdom has a single-payer system. There is controversy in both Canada and the U.K. about what the right model is. Some believe components of their healthcare system should move from public to private.

The United States health insurance industry is very specialized because of the complexity of providing coverage for tens of millions of consumers in 50 states. The industry is comprised of approximately 35 companies with better known names including CIGNA, Blue Cross Blue Shield, AETNA, Health Net, Humana, Kaiser Permanente, UnitedHealth Group, and WellPoint. In my opinion, replacing the health insurance industry with a single government payer is not practical because of the size and complexity of being the single-payer for 50 states. There is an opportunity, however, to change how health insurance is managed and regulated. Priority should be given to setting payment standards so processes can be simplified and administrative costs can be lowered. Another area of opportunity to lower healthcare cost is with Medicare and Medicaid.

Medicare and Medicaid

In July 1965, President Lyndon B. Johnson signed amendments to the Social Security Act creating Medicare and Medicaid, two governmental programs that provide medical and health-related services to more than 100 million people in the United States. The two programs are quite different, but both are managed by the Centers, which is a division of the HHS. Medicare is a social insurance program for people who have contributed to it and can start collecting benefits at age 65. There are more than 52 million enrollees at a Federal cost of $586 billion.[365] Medicaid is a social welfare program that serves more than 60 million people at a cost of $449 billion.[366] Combined, the two programs represented 35% of national healthcare spending in 2013.

Medicare and Medicaid are similar in size but very different in how they operate. Medicare is managed and funded at the Federal level. Medicaid is managed by the states, although the Federal government has rules that must be followed. As part of the ACA, the Federal government has offered incentives to the states with the goal of boosting the rolls of Medicaid, thereby reducing the number of uninsured. Medicaid has typically been funded 50% by the states and 50% with Federal funds. The ACA provides 100% funding through 2017 and then 90% thereafter if a state agrees to open up the Medicaid plan to more enrollees. A boost to physician reimbursement was put in place under the ACA for 2013 and 2014. The $1.1 trillion budget passed in late 2014 excluded the boost, in effect reducing reimbursements to doctors who see Medicaid patients. In other words, Congress passed legislation to boost state funding of Medicaid while reducing the funding for the doctors who will take care of the increased number of Medicaid enrollees.

The numbers vary widely by state and by type of physician specialty, but an example using typical numbers may help shine a light on the issue of equity for Americans. A doctor may charge $100 for an office visit for the management of congestive heart failure. If the patient had private insurance, the doctor might receive $80 for the visit from the insurance company and a $20 copay from the patient, for a total of $100. If the patient was on Medicare, the doctor might get $45 from Medicare, possibly $20 from a secondary insurance plan of the patient, and an additional $20 copay from the patient, for a total of $85. If the patient was on Medicaid, the doctor would receive $27 from Medicaid and nothing else. In effect, a doctor receiving $27 for the visit would be subsidizing the care of the patient, because the cost of the visit to the doctor likely exceeds $27, perhaps double the reimbursement. It is not surprising less than half of doctors accept Medicaid patients. The bottom line is the ACA is driving millions of uninsured to the Medicaid rolls, but as with many government programs passed by congress, there are funding gaps. The funding is secure for the next two years, but depends on new fees and taxes to fund it after 2017.

The issue of equity arises in all dimensions of healthcare. It has been discussed in several chapters in different contexts. In the example described above, a doctor seeing a patient with Medicare or private health insurance is compensated $85 to

$100. A doctor seeing a patient on Medicaid receives $27. Another way to say it is the American healthcare system values the health of a non-poor person three times that of a poor person. This is what Jimmy Carter meant when he said, "We have an abominable system in this country for the delivery of health care, with gross inequities toward the poor."[367] Every president since Lyndon Johnson, democrat and republican, has in one way or another said every American should have access to quality, affordable healthcare. But, they do not.

The government runs many healthcare programs. The majority of the spending occurs in Medicare, Medicaid, CHIP, and the Veterans Health Administration. The largest health insurance plans are Medicare and Medicaid: one for those over 65 and one for those who are poor. Both plans involve establishing eligibility, determining what coverage is provided, providing reimbursement to the providers, and measuring the outcomes from the healthcare provided. In essence, both plans do the same thing. Merging the two into one program is not a new idea, but it is an idea that could work and save billions of dollars if properly managed.

Managing Government Healthcare Plans

One can argue for or against a single national healthcare system. The argument for the single system, often called a single-payer system, is having one payer would provide more consistency and less complexity than having the 35 health insurance companies and their many divisions and subsidiaries we have today. Some argue for state control of healthcare on the basis of states rights; the federal government should be smaller, not larger, and the states know best how to take care of their population. My argument for a transition to giving more autonomy to the states is not political, but rather is based on the concept bigger is not necessarily better.

In theory, it would be possible to merge Medicare and Medicaid, expand the consolidated plan to cover the entire population, and have a single payer. This is an unproven theory. I believe Healthcare.gov showed us a single national healthcare website may not have been the best approach. Connecticut, one of the smaller states, has been regarded as one of the more successful health insurance exchanges. In "Organizational Diseconomies of Scale", published in the *Journal of Economics & Management Strategy*, R. Preston McAfee and John McMillan explained there is a cost of operating a large hierarchy, and cost increases as the hierarchical distance between the information source and the decision maker increases.[368] Consolidating a large number of insurance companies into one could have unintended consequences from a diseconomy of scale.

I have witnessed the disadvantage of consolidation. A large company like IBM or GE has many divisions and departments around the world. Company chief financial officers are always looking for ways to get economy of scale. If a division has 20 departments, a consolidation to 10 departments can save 10 department managers and 10 of numerous categories of expense. The savings invite further consolidations. Five departments instead of 10 can save more money. Now that divisions only have five departments, consolidating divisions into groups, and then consolidating groups can realize even more savings. With fewer executives running departments, divisions, and groups, the chief financial officer can impose across-the-board budget cuts. The rationale is every organizational unit can cut 5% of their spending. Yes, they can, but is that good? Perhaps some units should be increasing their spending by 25% to address growth opportunities while others should be cut 50% because of stagnation of its market.

While consolidation can provide many benefits to an organization, it can have unintended consequences in human resources. The human resources leader can impose rules determining every unit must rate and rank its employees following a company-wide guideline. For example, IBM and GE required every division must have five or 10% of its employees ranked in the bottom category and consequently those in that category would receive lower salary increases and be under pressure to resign. The top down approach for a big company makes sense from the top, but when the rule gets to the department level, it may damage the organization. Just as in the budget allocations, cutting 5% of the staff in a highly innovative unit may slow or even stop innovation, while other poorly performing units should possibly get a 50% cut. Although government is different than for-profit enterprises, I believe there are many similarities from an organizational point of view. In 2013, the United States government imposed a sequester that resulted in 5% across the board budget cuts. There was no consideration given to where more spending may have been needed or where much larger cuts could be made.

Another example related to economy of scale to consider is the size of hospitals. A small community hospital with 50 beds can no longer survive on its own because it does not have sufficient economy of scale. The benefit of hospital mergers has been demonstrated in many parts of the country, although there is a valid concern in some cases where the mergers have resulted in higher prices. At the other extreme from the 50-bed hospital is the Veterans Affairs hospital system with 1,700 hospitals, clinics, and other facilities. The giant healthcare system has more than 280,000 employees and a budget of more than $150 billion. Although the VA information system is more advanced than many hospitals, and the VA system outcomes are impressive, numerous other problems have emerged including excessive wait times for veterans needing medical attention. The newly appointed VA Secretary, Robert McDonald, said that the VA has taken disciplinary action against 5,600 employees in the last year, and more firings will follow. This is where the diseconomy of scale comes in. Such massive human resource actions, appeals, backfilling of positions, and making organizational changes will consume inordinate amounts of management time.

Size of a Health Insurance System

Canada and Germany administer their healthcare plans efficiently by enforcing standards for information management. Denmark has a single national system, but the country's population is two-thirds the size of New York City. I believe the logical size to run a large healthcare system is a state. California, Florida, New York, Ohio, and Texas are truly different, and they are each large enough (all are larger than Denmark) to fund and develop efficient information technology systems. The states should be the primary managers, and there is evidence they can do a good job.

Medicaid has a program called Section 1115 that provides states waivers to test experimental, pilot, or demonstration projects that do not meet federal program rules. Thirty states have requested waivers tailored to specific needs of the states. Such requests are typically proposed to achieve more effective coverage, improved quality, or cost savings by doing things a different way instead of the Federal way. The Centers agreed and approved the requests.

Getting from where we are to a consolidated model with implementation by the states will take years to accomplish, but it could begin by expanding the Medicaid waivers and opening up the waiver process to include Medicare. Some states can move faster than others, but as the states come forward for waivers, the current model could gradually shift to the combined model I propose.

Role of the Federal Government

The role of government in healthcare is important — not to implement big ideas but rather to provide funding and establish a framework for healthcare that would be implemented by the states. The framework would set broad goals to assure healthcare is available to all those in need. For example, delegation to the states does not mean a state having budget problems could decide to drop coverage for the unemployed or orphaned children. However, within the boundary of all citizens having healthcare coverage, the states could decide how best to provide the care based on their own demographics and available healthcare resources.

A major role for the Federal government should be to foster the creation of standards among IT companies, healthcare providers, and the health insurance companies to make billing, claims, and reimbursements more efficient. Likewise, standards should be enforced for electronic health record systems so they could be interoperable across all healthcare organizations and with federal, state, and local governments. It is critical to our health that all participants in the continuum of care can reliably and securely exchange healthcare data. I am not an advocate of government control, but when it comes to standardizing formats and protocols for EHR systems, there is a role the government should take assertively. Population health depends on big data and analytics, which in turn depend on reliable and consistent healthcare data.

An additional role for the Federal government is to set targets, collect data, and report the results about patient safety and quality. This is done today, but The Centers apply incentives and penalties based on averages. The government should suggest targets for various quality metrics and share the data with the states. The states should decide the incentives and penalties based on their unique situations. The effectiveness of their programs will be visible to the public. Finally, the Federal government should continue to fund and manage medical research and fund residency programs for graduating medical students.

Patient Protection and Affordable Care Act

The news media, many politicians, and even President Obama call it ObamaCare, but the ACA, which the President signed into law in March 2010, is much more than meets the eye. According to a survey of 1,000 likely voters conducted in May 2014 by Rasmussen Reports, 42% of likely U.S. voters view the healthcare law somewhat favorably, while 53% hold an unfavorable opinion of "it". Is it possible that a significant percentage of voters, including members of Congress, don't know what "it" is?

Along with a companion bill called the Health Care and Education Reconciliation Act, the ACA represents the most significant regulatory overhaul of the U.S. healthcare system since Medicare and Medicaid went into effect in July 1965. News reports tend to focus on healthcare insurance issues and the cost of healthcare. Both of these are important, but the ACA encompasses multiple goals including improved affordability of health insurance, expanded public and private insurance coverage resulting in fewer uninsured, increased quality and patient safety, availability of preventive care, and reduced costs of healthcare for individuals and the government.

After four years, political leaders and the people cannot agree on whether any of these goals have been met or if healthcare is on the right path. Thousands of people die each year because of medical errors, yet we hear very little about arguably the most important goal of the ACA – improved quality and patient safety. Is the ACA part of the problem or part of the solution?

In "ACA Implementation: How's It Going?", John McDonough, Professor of Practice, Department of Health Policy and Management at the Harvard School of Public Health, explained the 10 titles of the ACA that make up the law.[369] They include: (1) reform of private health insurance including the individual mandate, (2) expansion of Medicaid to all low-income Americans, (3) reform of the U.S. medical care delivery system and changes to Medicare, (4) prevention, wellness, and public health initiatives, (5) health workforce initiatives, (6) fraud and abuse prevention, transparency and comparative effectiveness research, (7) creation of a regulatory pathway for marketing and sale of biosimilar drugs, (8) Community Living Assistance Services (CLASS) (repealed by Congress on January 1, 2013), (9) revenue measures to pay for about one half the cost of the ACA, and (10) amendments to Medicaid and the Indian Health Care Improvement Act.

McDonough said that each title description could have ended with the words "and a lot more". I am not suggesting all of the ACA titles are free of error or questionable concepts. No doubt, all of them can and should be improved, but when a politician says we should repeal "it", I am not sure he or she knows what the "it" is.

Victor R. Fuchs, Henry J. Kaiser Jr. Professor at Stanford University, Emeritus, was called "the dean of health economists" by The New York Times. He has spent decades studying the economics of healthcare. His approach to reform is to start with the essentials—coverage, cost control, coordinated care, and choice. Fuchs believes if policymakers could agree on the essentials, it would be easy to make refinements along the way.[370]

Some states have done a better job managing healthcare than others, but making the results public can help all to improve. The Commonwealth Fund's Scorecard on State Health System Performance, 2014, assessed states on 42 indicators of healthcare access, quality, costs, and outcomes from 2007 to 2012.[371] The scorecard showed Minnesota, Massachusetts, New Hampshire, Vermont, and Hawaii as the top performers. They have lead the country in most dimensions of care, and have done so over time. The Commonwealth Fund suggested their "Consistently high performance may be the result of their willingness and wherewithal to address health system change with focused initiatives spanning the public and private sectors."[372]

While there is plenty of room for improvement, there are some excellent ACA programs underway and improving patient safety and quality and reducing the rate of cost growth of healthcare. Do we want to repeal the programs that have led to those improvements? Repealing "it" may be throwing out the baby with the bath water. Lets fix the ACA: replace some provisions, fine tune others, and add some new programs to fill the gaps. A healthier population can lead to a healthier economy for all.

Summary

As Americans we are fortunate to have many rights. Some people do not have the opportunity to take advantage of them. Tens of thousands of people die each year because they have no healthcare coverage. We spend more than enough money on healthcare to change this. The opportunities to save hundreds of billions of dollars to pay for healthcare for all are available. Our current system of Medicare and Medicaid can be improved. The two systems should be combined and delegated to the states to implement in a way that could turn diseconomies of scale into more effective and efficient healthcare. The ACA has strengths and weaknesses. The patient safety and quality areas are improving. The cost curve is beginning to bend. However, there are improvements which should be made as quickly as possible, especially to reduce the complexity of the health insurance provisions. To make these things happen will require healthcare administrators with health attitude and net attitude.

CHAPTER 16

Health Attitude and Net Attitude

T he final chapter of *Health Attitude* is directed mainly to healthcare administrators, CEOs and senior leaders who are charged with managing in these complex and demanding times. I was fortunate to be deeply involved in the early days of the web as Vice President for Internet Technology at IBM. I learned a lot about the culture of early pioneers of the Net, and I learned how to get things done from them. I hope some of the principles I learned from four decades in the technology industry during those early days of the Internet will be valuable to healthcare administrators and policymakers. Many ideas here are adapted from my book about the Internet, *Net Attitude*.[373]

The pressure on healthcare leaders is intense. You are facing declining reimbursements, competition from other providers, and the need to deliver efficient, safe, and high quality services to patients. At the same time, you need to innovate to take advantage of the rapidly expanding array of new technology, excel at communications, stay on top of social media, and listen to empowered consumers.

A good place to start to bring a net attitude to your workplace is to evaluate your website. The level of customer satisfaction with websites varies widely. Some sites are extremely easy to use, while others are nearly impossible. Some sites still have links saying "click here to buy", and when you click the page says, "Print this form, fill it out, and fax or mail it to us." Some web pages ask for a phone number, and after you key it in, the page says it was an error because you did not put dashes between the parts of the number. Other websites give an error if you do include dashes. More than a few websites give you the impression the purpose of the site is to make things easy for the company or organization, not for you. The list goes on. These are not technical problems – they are attitude problems and very easy to solve technically. Computers are quite able to insert dashes or remove dashes to change what you enter into what the site's database needs. *Net Attitude* describes a way of thinking – walking in the customer's shoes, adopting the culture of the Internet, and learning how to think like startup companies.

Many of the problems in the healthcare system have to do with a lack of health attitude. *Health Attitude* offers a progressive way of thinking about healthcare. Consumers need to take more responsibility for their health. Physicians need to embrace the attitude that puts keeping patients healthy ahead of ordering tests and procedures that may not be needed. Hospitals need to develop an attitude that discharging a patient from the hospital is not the end of the patient's treatment. The attitude needs to include reaching across the entire continuum of care in the community. Providers need to develop the attitude that their mission is to understand and care for the population for which they are accountable. Providers need to develop an attitude to develop easy to use information systems for employees and patients. Political leaders and policymakers need to develop an attitude all American citizens should have some form of health insurance.

Other problems have to do with a lack of net attitude. These include not having an effective web presence, lack of innovation, and focusing inwardly instead of outwardly. *Health Attitude* and *Net Attitude* have a lot in common. This section includes a series of management principles I learned during many years of working with young technology innovators who believed anything was possible if you had the right attitude. These principles can help you develop a net attitude and a positive health attitude.

Think Big, Act Bold, Start Simple, Iterate Fast

The most important ingredients to accomplishing great things in a rapidly changing environment are to find, attract, recruit, hire, motivate, and retain really great people.[374] The crop of students gets better every year, so you have to continually raise the bar of expectations. Look at every change of staff and ask yourself if you are improving your hand.

At least annually, my senior managers and I would have a planning retreat. One principle we followed was the "parking lot exercise". For each department, we would envision all the employees going out to the parking lot. We would then pick the ones we would bring back inside to be part of the team. "If you could only have one person on your team, who would it be?" You then picked a second person, and so on until you reached an agreed to team size. The prioritization of the exercise was input to which employees should get retention bonuses, and which should be counseled to look elsewhere.

Everyone has to bring skills for specific tasks but also bring unique value to the overall organization. When things are working right, the whole organization breeds and feeds on itself. If the caliber of your team is high, there's a much greater likelihood of being able to attract additional high caliber people. Once you have them, it is critical to nurture, recognize, and support them.

A lot of knowledgeable experts are weighing in with their points of view about went wrong with the launch of healthcare.gov. There are net attitude lessons to be learned from what happened. A project as massive as healthcare.gov can have many possible points of failure. When I first heard about the upcoming October 1, 2013 launch, it reminded me of the website my team at IBM built for the Atlanta Olympics of 1996.

In 1995, there were not many people who knew a lot about how to build really large websites. The Olympic website was the largest in the world at that time. We learned a lot building it. We were humble about our expectations. We didn't know how many people would come to the site, when they could come, or what they might do when they got there. We learned many lessons, but I can summarize it in a simple mantra: Think big, act bold, start simple, iterate fast. Another way to say it is to take a lot of baby steps. It appears that the direction for healthcare.gov was think big, start big, avoid failure.

Clay Shirky, author of "*Here Comes Everybody: The Power of Organizing Without Organizations*", analyzed the planning behind the site, the management system that influenced it, and the interactions of various constituents.[375] Shirky said that there was a gulf between planning and reality. Instead of baby steps, they built what they thought was the final site, and instead of testing with one state or one function, and then adding another state and another function, they put it all out there close to when it had to go into production. It was just the opposite of a net attitude. Shirky said the reason they did it that way was because they didn't want politicians to be able to see it early, criticize it, and then try to stop it from being launched.

Skunk Works

Many CEOs have asked how to make innovation projects go faster. More than a few CIOs I have met worried about innovation projects going too fast. The CIO has spent decades getting information technology under control and making it reliable. Innovative technology projects can disrupt the status quo and are sometimes in conflict with the stability and security goals. The solution to the dilemma is multifaceted, but one key element is to utilize a "Skunk Works" where rapid prototyping is the modus operandi.

The origin of the term Skunk Works was at the Lockheed Corporation in 1943. The name came from the "Skonk Works" of Al Capp's L'il Abner comic strip, where they had a hidden still in a secluded hollow. The name still fits, because exciting things continue to "brew" there.[376] For over a half century, the Skunk Works team built a reputation unique in the world. Almost routinely, this elite group created breakthrough technologies and landmark aircraft redefining the possibilities of flight. The Skunk Works designed the P-80 Shooting Star, America's first production jet aircraft. Since then they have created a string of firsts. In the 1950's it was the U-2, which to this day defines the possibilities of high-altitude jet aircraft. Then there was the SR-71 Blackbird which, with its titanium airframe, is still the fastest jet aircraft in the world. The F-117A Stealth Fighter, which incorporated low-observable technology into an operational attack aircraft, created a revolution in military warfare. Its capabilities were demonstrated dramatically in combat during the Gulf War.

The company, now Lockheed Martin, said the key has been to "identify the best individual talents in aviation, blend and equip them with every tool needed, then provide complete creative freedom so they may arrive at an optimum solution in short order."[377] This simple formula is highly effective not only for creating state of the art aviation but also for any kind of corporate or healthcare endeavor.

The Lockheed Martin Skunk Works continues to serve as a wellspring of innovation for the entire organization as they continue to build advanced aerospace prototypes and a string of innovations in the areas of data analytics, nanotechnology, robotics, energy, advanced aeronautics, and scientific discovery. Lockheed Martin says this happens because they are not big on titles or protocol. They focus on just getting the job done, regularly meeting schedules on time and under budget.

Small Independent Teams

Product and services development is typically managed in a very structured organization with multiple levels of management and a lot of controls. This can be effective in many cases and is probably necessary for extraordinarily complex projects like putting a man on the moon. In most cases this approach likely will not bring many breakthroughs. The Skunk Works uses a different model. Small teams with maximum freedom of action, very flat management structure, and minimal controls can lead to breakthrough ideas, if the people are allowed to work below the radar tracking level of the larger bureaucracy. Small teams of creative people are also more productive and have more fun than a significantly larger team.

Skunk Works are also good at figuring out what key problems there are in existing systems. Skunk Works members have no vested interest in the success or failure of those systems. They can often solve problems the larger organization can't solve because the larger organization is too close to the origins of the problem. It is usually best to let the Skunk Works figure out what things they should work on as opposed to assigning problems or projects to them. Problems the organization thinks are most important may not be optimal ones for the Skunk.

The formal requirements processes typically used to determine what should be developed don't always anticipate some of the most profound issues and problems. The Skunk Works often just stumbles into profound things if you trust them and give them freedom of action. The instant messaging system used by hundreds of thousands of employees at IBM did not come about because somebody asked for it or because a strategic plan or requirements process called it out. A few Internet software engineers stumbled into it, tried it out, built a prototype, and then nurtured it. In a couple of years it became an indispensable application for the company.

A Skunk Works does not have to be and should not be large. It can be a fraction of the total development resources. A subtle but critically important element in a successful Skunk Works is executive support, or "air cover". There needs to be a well respected and highly placed executive, preferably the CEO, who trusts the "lunatics" who are out on the edge. At times the executive will be scared to death a project the Skunk Works is pursuing will fail, but has to have the nerve to place a bet on it and trust the team to come through. Visiting the team late at night or on a weekend, bringing pizza and soda, showing you care and have a clue about what the team is working on, even if you don't really understand the details, are critical ingredients. The little touches motivate the team beyond belief.

Principles of Net Attitude

One of the biggest challenges with a Skunk Works is figuring out how to take the prototypes developed by a small team and integrate it with a more disciplined development process of the larger organization. In effect, you have a tiny gear spinning at high speed trying to synchronize with a much larger and slower turning gear. One approach to solving this dilemma is to use an impedance matcher. The impedance matcher is an organizational concept I developed to facilitate integration of new innovations with existing processes. Think of impedance matching as placing an in-between-sized gear between the small one and the large one. Rather than a gear, of course, it is a small group of people whose mission is to adapt the prototype to the standards of the larger organization. Their focus is not developing but rather adapting, smoothing over the rough edges, and getting it into good enough condition the larger organization will look at it and say it is good enough to be adopted and taken to market or put into production. The result is a speed to market that is a little slower than pure prototype but much faster than the full-blown process. Without the impedance matcher the larger organization is more likely to view the prototype as a virus and seek to eradicate it.

A successful organization has to be willing to have projects that are going to fail. A process designed to keep failures from happening is antithetical to a net attitude for innovation. But, you need to be able to declare a failure, move on, and not punish the participants for being assigned to or even creating the failure. A good process encourages people to submit ideas as quickly and as often as possible and allow others downstream to figure out which ideas are worth pursuing further. There should be no penalty for submitting an idea the organization rejects.

Just enough is good enough does not mean to do sloppy work or throw something against the wall and hope it sticks. Many new technologies which have been introduced on the Internet including eBay, Amazon, YouTube, Facebook, Twitter, and even the protocols of the Internet itself were arguably inferior to alternate approaches that already existed. However, just enough turned out to be good enough to get the idea out there and enable people to start to benefit from it. Early adopters are happy to try new things and are willing to spend hours providing their feedback on bugs and suggested improvements. The principles from *Net Attitude* can be applied to projects of all kinds in any size organization.

For some e-health applications the "quick and dirty" approach of the early web days is still adequate. One of the concepts integral to having a net attitude is to avoid a "one size fits all" approach. A payroll application that allows an employee to set up deductions on the web needs all possible rigors. An application to enable an employee to signup for next weeks blood drive doesn't. The risk of harm to the organization or to the customer needs to be weighed against the time and effort to apply all the processes to creating the application.

Making things easy is a key principle from *Net Attitude*. It doesn't come naturally; you have to plan for it, test it, and refine it. Some of the hardest things are subtle. Most people do simple things on the web, schedule an appointment, make a payment, check for lab results, and other basic transactions. It is important to make those things easy to do. One simple idea is to make URLs easy to remember and type. For example, it would be nice if xyzhospital.org/paybill worked, but likely it does not. Some URLs are hundreds of characters long. Making URLs intuitive and simple leads to happier patients. Making things easier applies to employees, too. Part of a net attitude is treating your own people's time as valuable -- time they spend struggling with a hard-to-use intranet is time they can't spend working on healthcare issues.

Planning and Over Planning

There are four phases of building an e-health organization on the principles of health attitude and net attitude: (1) planning, (2) building, (3) operating, and (4) using the e-health organization. It starts with sorting out your business strategy, figuring out what your value proposition and business model are, committing yourself to meeting the expectations of people who visit your e-health organization and finally, establishing a framework that provides for an e-health organization which is scalable, manageable, available, reliable, and secure.

In a world where so much is possible, it is really important to think big. The challenge is to think big, but start with a simple implementation, and grow it fast toward the big idea. Many organizations have planners. Planners like to plan -- that is their job. New ideas require a plan before they can be implemented, but the problem is the plan can expand so much it can't be implemented, or by the time it is, the whole world changed, and the plans have to be scrapped, and things go back to square one.

Prior to the Internet becoming commercialized, the model for creating new IT applications was Plan, Build, Deliver on an eighteen-month cycle. With technologies and markets now changing at Internet speed, the new model has to be based on the principles of *Net Attitude*, sense and respond, an 18 hour cycle. Sense what is happening with the project or your website and respond to it immediately. Seek feedback, listen to it hard, and act on it. Iterate with baby steps, but on a fast cycle. Evolve as fast as possible toward the big thought. The traditional model yields a second release of a new system a year or two after the initial release. A net attitude takes you down a different path. Deliver a .1 release. A month or less later, deliver a release .2 product. After a year you are at Release 1.0. Chances are good your Release 1.0 after one year is way ahead of where a traditional Release 2.0 would be after two years.

Expectations

During the early days of the web, I had lunch with the CEO of a major insurance company. I described to him how the only thing standing between me and being really satisfied with his insurance company was his agent. I explained when I want to do business, the insurance agent is not working. When he is working I don't have time to focus on insurance. I described how I would like to see a web page where I could check off all of my needs for coverage; car, motorcycle, boat, house, and liability. Then I would like to iterate on various coverage options until I find what I wanted. I then described how I had a home in one state and a vacation cottage in another state. I had to have two different agents and I couldn't understand why I couldn't just deal with one. He said, "You aren't normal."

An increasingly large number of consumers are "not normal". They expect to have digital information about all aspects of their health available in real-time and on any device. They expect it to be synchronized and secured in the cloud. There are regulatory, security, and privacy issues for sure, but the real problem is lack of a net attitude. There is fear and misunderstanding and a lack of leadership to make it happen. Major institutions have been dealing with regulatory issues for decades. They have found ways to educate and influence regulators to enable them to do business in developing countries, break into new markets, get approval for new products, and get investment tax credits. A combination of the principles from *Health Attitude* and *Net Attitude* can fulfill needs across the continuum of care, organizing to get things done in the fast paced world of the consumer-led healthcare technology revolution. Health attitude and net attitude are new ways of thinking. Moving out a bit closer to the edge – where things are somewhat uncertain; where you don't have the control you would like to have, but where innovation is happening continuously

Attitude and Culture

There is so much we can learn from kids. They represent the way e-health is going to be. Hire summer interns, listen to them, and ask for their suggestions. They think about things differently, like most of your customers are beginning to think. The way kids use the web is the way e-health will develop.

Talk to your kids or your neighbor's kids. Look over their shoulder, and ask them what they do with their smartphones. Talk to them about their values. What do they think of intellectual property rights? What do they like most about the Internet? What do they like least? What sites are really with it? Which are brain-dead? What do they think the Internet will be like in five years? How do they expect they will use it after they get a job? If what they tell you makes sense, think about how you can incorporate some of their ideas into your business or institutional planning. If what they say doesn't make sense, or you don't agree with what they say, talk to the kids some more. If you don't have any kids, borrow one! If you can't find any kids to talk to, then talk to some adults! Consumers who were in their twenties during the early days of the Internet are now in their forties. As they begin to make more use of the healthcare system, they are going to have high expectations, because they have been using the web for two decades.

Path to Adopting a Health Attitude

When you become infused with health attitude and net attitude, and have a firm grasp on the coming changes in healthcare, what do you do now? Following are some suggestions to help you expand your healthcare net attitude:

❖ Use social media as an electronic town hall meeting. You can learn first hand what your patients like and dislike. Having a Facebook page and Twitter feed, and urging people to like you, is not enough. Be proactive. Monitor and participate in the dialog; use the dialogues to deliver key messages about your organizational philosophies, the principles you are dedicated to, and the plans you have for the future. Be brief, candid, and friendly.

❖ Make your website a comprehensive information resource for patients and your employees. Include press releases, healthcare guides, journal articles, technical and customer support, information about your services, videos from docs, and patient testimonials. Put someone in charge of keeping the site and links current and managing the archives.

❖ Provide external links related to your healthcare services. Include links to leading universities and hospitals doing medical research, to relevant healthcare related social media sites such as patientslikeme.com. Don't make your constituencies have to find these places on their own. If you provide plenty of links away from your site, people will remember it and they will return often.

❖ Examine how you have linked your brand to your web presence. Make sure the policies and actions on your website are consistent with the values and principles of your organization.

❖ Include an organizational directory to enable people to find departmental email addresses and other content easily. Accept the principle of opening up your organization and allowing outsiders to easily send you e-mail. Become the easiest organization in the world to communicate with. Insure all emails are answered within a maximum of 24 hours.

❖ Make sure key people are well connected outside of the organization. Encourage clinical and staff executives to attend conferences where they can learn what thought leaders and key influencers in healthcare have on their minds. Encourage your senior team to network outside of the organization. Make trip reports widely available on the intranet.

❖ Use the Internet as the world's largest focus group. Analyze incoming email and social media in detail and take it seriously. Realize that extreme or even insulting views may be directed at your organization from the Internet, and accept that these messages often represent the leading edge of opinion. People on the Internet are passionate about their areas of interest. Listen really hard to what people are saying. You may save a lot of time and money and be able to anticipate problems that the masses would experience later.

❖ Investigate setting up a Skunk Works somewhere in the organization where it can't get snuffed out or attacked by the white corpuscles of the organization. It doesn't have to be large. It can be as small as one innovative, creative, and skillful person. Give it top-level support.

❖ Use incentives, recognition, and communications to encourage knowledge sharing. Consider appointing a Chief Knowledge Officer with responsibility to facilitate broad and deep sharing of knowledge across the organization.

❖ Build an information technology infrastructure to enable you to have a scalable, manageable, highly available, reliable, and secure e-health presence on the Internet and the intranet.

❖ Seek feedback from visitors and constantly improve the site based on what visitors tell you. Upgrade the site often, but in small increments. Make your web interface at least as easy for the customer as talking to a real live, experienced, and well-informed representative.

❖ Include multimedia capabilities in your infrastructure featuring audio, video, and animation, to provide constituencies with demonstrations, infomercials, and tutorials on how to be healthy.

❖ Put as much energy into creating a powerful intranet for your employees as you do for your external customer website. Identify all processes from signing up for the blood drive or healthcare benefits, to ordering business cards, to using e-meetings for more effective collaboration. Encourage the formation of communities within your organization

❖ Look at all the functions a patient can do with your organization. Evaluate how many of these functions are available on your e-health site, prioritize the ones that aren't, and develop plans to get them in place.

❖ Create a culture with a healthy component of net attitude and health attitude. Let people know you care about *attitude*. Show leadership from the top, but encourage participation from the grass roots.

❖ Setup an Advisory Council composed of some of your new, young employees in the organization and a couple of sixteen year old high school interns. Meet with them monthly. Give them assignments to look at key business or organizational problems and have them come back with ideas on what solutions they would apply. Take their suggestions seriously.

❖ Show strong commitment to your communications programs. Electronic communications has the effect of flattening the organizational structure, thereby potentially threatening some middle management groups. The commitment from the top is critical to keep the grassroots teams energized and to avoid bureaucratic resistance to the implementation of new ideas.

❖ Pick a time of the week, Saturday morning, Tuesday night, or sometime that can be reasonably consistent and spend an hour on the web reading websites of competitors and research institutions looking for new ideas and learning what others are doing.

Summary

Embracing the principles in *Health Attitude* will energize your organization. Adopting a positive health attitude allows you to transform your vision and expectations of affordable, quality healthcare services in the future. I believe affordable and universal healthcare is achievable. I challenge you to join me in being part of the solution.

In *Health Attitude*, I unraveled some of the complexities of our healthcare system and offered solutions. Every day, new technologies and policy issues emerge changing the healthcare landscape. I invite you to participate in an ongoing dialog and receive periodic updates by visiting healthattitude.org/keepmeposted

See also facebook.com/healthattitude

Acknowledgements

T here are a number of people I would like to thank for helping me with *Health Attitude*. First and foremost is Kathleen Imhoff. Her editing skills are unparalleled. Every day over a period of months, Kathleen offered countless suggestions which crystallized the story I want to tell. I am grateful for the time and interest of the following who read and commented on early drafts: Gene Bolton, Jon Bolton, Bob Greenberg, Peg Grimm, Brock Hamilton, Bob Langley, Ron LaPorte, Eric Lutker, Cary Passik, Bob Patrick, Joanne Patrick, Fernand Sarrat, Harold Spratt, and Dempsey Springfield. My thanks go to John Murphy for his thoughtful preface. Finally, I would like to thank my wife, Joanne, for her patience during my studies, research, and writing.

List of Abbreviations

ACA - Patient Protection and Affordable Care Act
ACO - Affordable Care Organization
AI - Artificial Intelligence
APRN - Advanced Practice Registered Nurse
ATM - Automated Teller Machine
BI - Business Intelligence
CDC - Center for Disease Control and Prevention
CER - Comparative Effectiveness Research
CHIP - Children's Health Insurance Program
CHF - Congestive Heart Failure
CIO - Chief Information Officer
CNS - Clinical Nurse Specialist
CPT - Current Procedural Terminology
CT - Computed Tomography
DNP - Doctor of Nursing Practice
DPH - Department of Public Health
ECG or EKG - Electrocardiogram
EHR - Electronic Health Record
EOB - Explanation of Benefits
ER - Emergency Room
FDA - U.S. Food and Drug Administration
HCCI - Health Care Cost Institute
HCV - Hepatitis C
HHS - U.S. Department of Health and Human Services

HIE - Health Information Exchange

HIPAA - Health Insurance Portability and Accountability Act

HSA - Health Savings Account

ICU - Intensive Care Unit

IOM - Institute of Medicine

IP - Internet Protocol

MBAN - Medical Area Body Networks

MRI - Magnetic resonance imaging

NIH - National Institutes of Health

NP - Nurse Practitioner

OECD - Organization for Economic Cooperation and Development

OR - Operating Room

PA - Physician Assistant

PCMH - Patient-centered Medical Home

PCP - Primary Care Physician

PDF - Portable Data Format

PHO - Physician Hospital Organization

PSA - Prostate-Specific Antigen

PSC - Personal Super Computer

STEM - Spatiotemporal Epidemiological Modeler

The Centers - Centers for Medicare & Medicaid Services

UPC - Universal Product Code

USHC - United States Healthcare System

USPS - United States Postal Service

VA - United States Department of Veterans Affairs

VNA - Visiting Nurses Association

XPCI - X-ray Phase-contrast Imaging

Index

About the Author

Dr. John R. Patrick is President of Attitude LLC and former Vice President of Internet Technology at IBM, where he worked for thirty-eight years. John was a founding member of the World Wide Web Consortium at MIT in 1994, a founding member and past chairman of the Global Internet Project, a member of the Internet Society and the American College of Healthcare Executives, a senior member of the Association for Computing Machinery, and a Fellow of the Institute of Electrical and Electronics Engineers. John is a board member at MecklerMedia Inc. and OCLC, and is a member of the Western Connecticut Health Network Biomedical Research Institute Advisory Council. John was a member of the board of Danbury Hospital from 2003 to 2013. He served on the Governance and Technology Committees of the board and was Chair of the Planning and Quality Committees. John holds a Doctor of Health Administration (DHA) from University of Phoenix, an MS in Management from the University of South Florida, an LLB in Law from LaSalle Extension University, and a BS in Electrical Engineering from Lehigh University. He is the author of *Net Attitude* published by Perseus Publishing. John lives in Ridgefield, CT with his wife Joanne. His website is at healthattitude.org and you can contact him at john@healthattitude. org. See also facebook.com/healthattitude.

Notes

1   "Health Expenditure, Total (% of Gdp)," The World Bank, http://data.world-bank.org/indicator/SH.XPD.TOTL.ZS.

2   Malcolm Gladwell, *The Tipping Point : How Little Things Can Make a Big Difference* (Boston: Little, Brown, 2000).

3   James A. Johnson and Carleen H. Stoskopf, *Comparative Health Systems: Global Perspectives* (Sudbury, Mass.: Jones and Bartlett Publishers, 2010).

4   Ibid.

5   Goran Ridic, Suzanne Gleason, and Ognjen Ridic, "Comparisons of Health Care Systems in the United States, Germany and Canada," *Materia Socio Medica* 24, no. 2 (2012).

6   Jason M. Sutherland, Elliott S. Fisher, and Jonathan S. Skinner, "Getting Past Denial--the High Cost of Health Care in the United States," *The New England Journal Of Medicine* 361, no. 13 (2009).

7   "Healthcare Market Profile: Miami-Fort Lauderdale-Pompano Beach," review of http://www.modernhealthcare.com/article/20110725/SUPPLE-MENT/307249988, *Modern Healthcare* 2011.

8   "Facts & Stats ", review of http://www.fha.org/facts.html, *Florida Hospital Association*.

9   "Beds Per 1,000 People," *American Hospital Association*, http://aha.org/research.

10   Arnold Milstein and Helen Darling, "Better U.S. Health Care at Lower Cost," review of http://www.issues.org, *Issues in Science & Technology* 26, no. 2 (2010).

11   S. Ward Casscells et al., "How to Achieve a High-Performance Health Care System in the United States," review of http://www.acponline.org/journals/, *Annals of Internal Medicine* 148 (2008).

12   Ibid.

13   Ronen Avraham and Max Schanzenbach, "The Impact of Tort Reform on Private Health Insurance Coverage, February 2010," *American Law and Economics Review* 12, no. 2 (2010).

14   Kevin Fiscella, "Health Care Reform and Equity: Promise, Pitfalls, and Prescriptions," *Annals Of Family Medicine* 9, no. 1 (2011).

15   Ibid.

16   George D. Lundberg, "The Us Healthcare System Vs the Us Postal Service," *Meds Multispecialty* (2014), http://www.medscape.com/viewarticle/823721?nlid=55704_1521&src=wnl_edit_medp_wir&uac=165842DT&spon=17.

17   Ibid.

18   Milstein and Darling, "Better U.S. Health Care at Lower Cost."

19   D. Eric Schansberg, "Envisioning a Free Market in Health Care," review of http://www.cato.org/pubs/journal/index.html, *Cato Journal* 31, no. 1 (2011).

20   Gretchen Gavett, "24-Year-Old Dad Dies of Tooth Infection," review of http://www.pbs.org/wgbh/pages/frontline/health-science-technology/dollars-and-dentists/tragic-results-when-dental-care-is-out-of-reach/, *Frontline* 2012.

21   Rachel Nardin et al. to Health Affairs Blog2013, http://healthaffairs.org/blog/2013/06/06/the-uninsured-after-implementation-of-the-affordable-care-act-a-demographic-and-geographic-analysis/.

22   Karen Garloch and John Murawski to CharlotteObserver.com2013.

23   "Consumer Reports Poll: Strapped Americans Foregoing Prescription Meds, Skipping Doctor Visits, Putting Off Medical Procedures," *Consumer Reports National Research Center*2012.

24   Mathew Herper, "Grading Pharma in 2013: 16 Drug Companies Ranked," *Forbes* (2013), http://www.forbes.com/sites/matthewherper/2013/12/31/grading-pharma-in-2013-16-drug-companies-ranked/.

25   Caroline Humer, "Unitedhealth: New Hepatitis C Drug Costs Far More Than Forecast," review of http://www.reuters.com/article/2014/04/17/us-united-heal-grp-results-idUSBREA3G0KN20140417, *Reuters* 2014.

26   Maria Seyrig, "The Economic Cost of Advanced Liver Disease," review of http://www.henryford.com/body.cfm?id=46335&action=detail&ref=1465, *Henry Ford Health System*2011.

27   "Hepatitis C," World Health Organization, http://www.who.int/mediacentre/factsheets/fs164/en/.

28   Alessandro Donati, "World Traffic in Doping Substances," (http://www.wada-ama.org/Documents/World_Anti-Doping_Program/Governments/WADA_Donati_Report_On_Trafficking_2007.pdf2007).

29   "Wyden and Grassley Seek Details on Solvaldi Pricing," The United States Senate Committee on Finance, http://www.finance.senate.gov/newsroom/chairman/release/?id=e1639d08-74d8-4f0a-88dc-532875ccc706.

30 Cynthia Geppert and Sanjeev Arora, "Ethical Issues in the Treatment of Hepatitis C," *Clinical Gastroenterology and Hepatology* 3, no. 10 (2005).

31 Peter Loftus, "Lucrative Drug Niche Sparks Legal Scramble," review of http://online.wsj.com/articles/lucrative-drug-niche-sparks-legalscramble-1405898259?mod=djem10point, *Wall Street Journal* 2014.

32 to $93,000 Cancer Drug: How Much Is a Life Worth? 2010, http://www.freere-public.com/focus/f-news/2596744/posts.

33 Hester Plumridge, "U.K. Health Service Panel Rejects Roche Cancer Drug on Price Grounds," *Wall Street Journal* (2014), http://online.wsj.com/articles/u-k-health-service-panel-rejects-roche-cancer-drug-on-price-grounds-1407497976?KEYWORDS=europe+health+care.

34 Ibid.

35 "S&P 500," *S&P Dow Jones Indices* (2014), http://us.spindices.com/indices/equity/sp-500.

36 "Let Medicare Negotiate Drug Prices: Our View," *USA Today* (2014), http://www.usatoday.com/story/opinion/2014/04/20/medicare-part-d-prescrip-tion-drug-prices-negotiate-editorials-debates/7943745/.

37 Gagnon, M-A, and Joel Lexchin. "The Cost of Pushing Pills: A New Estimate of Pharmaceutical Promotion Expenditures in the United States." PLoS Med 5, no. 1 (2008): e1.

38 "Let Medicare Negotiate Drug Prices: Our View".

39 Eric Lipton and Kevin Sack, "Fiscal Footnote: Big Senate Gift to Drug Maker," *The New York Times* 2013, January 19.

40   Matt Canham, "Hatch Is under Fire for Helping Drugmaker," *The Salt Lake Tribune* (2013), http://www.sltrib.com/sltrib/politics/55686984-90/amgen-hatch-bill-legislation.html.csp.

41   "Influence & Lobbying," The Center for Responsive Politics, http://www.opensecrets.org.

42   "Open Payments," *Centers for Medicare & Medicaid Services* (2014), http://cms.gov/openpayments/.

43   Peter Loftus, "Doctors Net Billions from Drug Firms," *The Wall Street Journal* (2014), http://online.wsj.com/articles/u-s-agency-reveals-drug-makers-pay-ments-to-doctors-1412100323?cb=logged0.8188743414357305.

44   Ibid.

45   "Maine's Prescription for Drug Savings: Go Foreign," review of http://www.pbs.org/newshour/bb/health-july-dec13-mainerx_11-09/, *PBS NewsHour* 2013.

46   Ibid.

47   "New England Compounding Center (Necc) Potentially Contaminated Medication: Fungal Meningitis Outbreak," U.S. Food and Drug Administration, http://www.fda.gov/safety/medwatch/safetyinformation/safetyalertsforhu-manmedicalproducts/ucm322849.htm.

48   Christopher S. Girod et al., "2014 Milliman Medical Index," review of http://www.milliman.com/mmi/, *Milliman* 2014.

49   "Health at a Glance 2013: OECD Indicators," OECD, http://www.oecd.org/els/health-systems/Health-at-a-Glance-2013.pdf.

50   Ibid.

51   Patrick A. Rivers, Myron D. Fottler, and Jemima A. Frimpong, "The Effects of Certificate of Need Regulation on Hospital Costs," *Journal of Health Care Finance* 36, no. 4 (2010).

52   Francette Koechlin, Luca Lorenzoni, and Paul Schreyer, "Comparing Price Levels of Hospital Services across Countries: Results of Pilot Study," (Paris: Organisation for Economic Cooperation and Development (OECD), 2010).

53   Beth Howard, "Should You Have Surgery Abroad?," *AARP The Magazine* (2014), http://www.aarp.org/health/conditions-treatments/info-2014/medical-tourism-surgery-abroad.html.

54   Panos Kanavos and Sotiris Vandoros, "Drugs Us: Are Prices Too High?," *Significance* 8, no. 1 (2011).

55   Nancy Shute, "Imagining a Future When the Doctor's Office Is in Your Home," *npr shots* (2015), http://www.npr.org/blogs/health/2015/01/12/376741693/imagining-a-future-when-the-doctors-office-is-in-your-home.

56   "Connecticut's "Unprecedented" Number of Hospital Mergers ", *AHIP Coverage* (2014), http://www.ahipcoverage.com/2014/03/26/connecticuts-unprecedented-number-of-hospital-mergers/#sthash.wBcp3dLC.dpuf.

57   Roni Caryn Rabin, "Wide Range of Hospital Charges for Blood Tests Called 'Irrational'," *Shots Health News From NPR* (2014).

58   Steven Brill, "Bitter Pill: Why Medical Bills Are Killing Us," *Time* 2013.

59   David Whelan and Robert Langreth, "The $150 Million Zapper," *Forbes* (2009), http://www.forbes.com/forbes/2009/0316/062_150mil_zapper.html.

60 Andre Konski et al., "Is Proton Beam Therapy Cost Effective in the Treatment of Adenocarcinoma of the Prostate?," *Journal of Clinical Oncology* 25, no. 24 (2007).

61 Whelan and Langreth, "The $150 Million Zapper".

62 Robert Kocher and Nikhil R. Sahni, "Rethinking Health Care Labor," *New England Journal of Medicine* 365, no. 15 (2011).

63 "Supporting Better Primary Care," *RubiconMD* (2014), https://rubiconmd. com/learn_more.html.

64 Ibid.

65 Ibid.

66 "Birth Defects," *Centers for Disease Control and Prevention* (2014), http:// www.cdc.gov/ncbddd/birthdefects/data.html.

67 L. D. Hermer and H. Brody, "Defensive Medicine, Cost Containment, and Reform," *Journal of General Internal Medicine* 25, no. 5 (2010).

68 Ibid.

69 David M. Studdert, Michelle M. Mello, and Troyen A. Brennan, "Defensive Medicine and Tort Reform: A Wide View," *JGIM: Journal of General Internal Medicine* 25 (2010).

70 Atul Gawande, "The Cost Conundrum: What a Texas Town Can Teach Us About Health Care." *The New Yorker Annals of Medicine* (2009), http://www. newyorker.com/magazine/2009/06/01/the-cost-conundrum.

71 David A. Pratt, "Focus On... Waste in the Health Care System," *Journal of Pension Benefits* 18, no. 1 (2010).

72   Ibid.

73   Ibid.

74   Christopher S. Stewart, "How Agents Hunt for Fraud in Trove of Medicare Data," *Wall Street Journal* (2014), http://online.wsj.com/articles/how-agents-hunt-for-fraud-in-trove-of-medicare-data-1408069802.

75   Ibid.

76   Ibid.

77   Editors, "Why Can't the Pentagon Stop Smoking?," *BloombergView* (2014), http://www.bloombergview.com/articles/2014-08-19/why-can-t-the-pentagon-stop-smoking.

78   Ibid.

79   David C. Dugdale, "Hypertension," review of http://www.nlm.nih.gov/medlineplus/ency/article/000468.htm, *MedlinePlus* 2011.

80   CDC, "High Blood Pressure Facts," Centers for Disease Control, http://www.cdc.gov/bloodpressure/facts.htm.

81   Lora E. Burke and Jing Wang, "Treatment Strategies for Overweight and Obesity," *Journal of Nursing Scholarship* 43, no. 4 (2011).

82   Marcia Frellick, "AMA Declares Obesity a Disease," *Medscape* (2013), http://www.medscape.com/viewarticle/806566.

83   "Calculate Your Body Mass Index," *National Heart, Lung, and Blood Institute* (2014), http://www.nhlbi.nih.gov/health/educational/lose_wt/BMI/bmi-calc.htm.

84   Raj S. Padwal and Arya M. Sharma, "Treating Severe Obesity: Morbid Weights and Morbid Waits," *CMAJ: Canadian Medical Association Journal* 181, no. 11 (2009).

85   Odelia Rosin, "The Economic Causes of Obesity: A Survey," review of http://www.blackwellpublishing.com/journal.asp?ref=0950-0804, *Journal of Economic Surveys* 22, no. 4 (2008).

86   Burke and Wang, "Treatment Strategies for Overweight and Obesity."

87   N. L. De Groot et al., "Systematic Review: The Effects of Conservative and Surgical Treatment for Obesity on Gastro-Oesophageal Reflux Disease," *Alimentary Pharmacology & Therapeutics* 30, no. 11/12 (2009).

88   Andrew J. Boyle, "Bariatric Surgery Reduces Mi, Stroke, and Death," review of http://www.ahcmedia.com/public/pages/Clinical-Cardiology-Alert.html#top, *Clinical Cardiology Alert* 31, no. 2 (2012).

89   Frankie Phillips, "Bariatric Surgery Drastic Measures?," review of http://www.practicenursing.com/, *Practice Nurse* 41, no. 9 (2011).

90   Burke and Wang, "Treatment Strategies for Overweight and Obesity."

91   B. Hofmann, "Stuck in the Middle: The Many Moral Challenges with Bariatric Surgery," *American Journal of Bioethics* 10, no. 12 (2010).

92   Phillips, "Bariatric Surgery Drastic Measures?."

93   Boyle, "Bariatric Surgery Reduces Mi, Stroke, and Death."

94   Edward G. Goetz, "Comment: Public Housing Demolition and the Benefits to Low-Income Families," review of http://www.planning.org/japa/, *Journal of the American Planning Association* 71, no. 4 (2005).

95   Hofmann, "Stuck in the Middle: The Many Moral Challenges with Bariatric Surgery."

96   "Mortality in the United States, 2012," *Centers for Disease Control and Prevention* (2014), http://www.cdc.gov/nchs/data/databriefs/db168.htm.

97   "Chronic Disease Prevention and Health Promotion," Centers for Disease Control and Prevention, http://www.cdc.gov/chronicdisease/overview/.

98   Brandon Hemmings, Joshua Fangmeier, and Marianne Udow-Phillips, "The Impact of ACA Taxes and Fees," *Center for Healthcare Research & Transformation* (2013), http://www.chrt.org/publications/price-of-care/the-impact-of-aca-taxes-and-fees/.

99   Ibid.

100 Aetna, "Understanding How the Health Insurance Providers Fee and Transitional Reinsurance Contribution Will Affect You," (2013), http://www.aetna.com/health-reform-connection/documents/Aetna_HIP_RC_Brochure_FINAL.pdf.

101 NLM, "The Hippocratic Oath," National Library of Medicine, http://www.nlm.nih.gov/hmd/greek/greek_oath.html.

102 Clayton M. Christensen, Jerome H. Grossman, and Jason Hwang, *The Innovator's Prescription : A Disruptive Solution for Health Care* (New York: McGraw-Hill, 2009).

103 Daniel Scherr et al., "Effect of Home-Based Telemonitoring Using Mobile Phone Technology on the Outcome of Heart Failure Patients after an Episode of Acute Decompensation: Randomized Controlled Trial," *Journal of Medical Internet Research* 11, no. 3 (2009).

104 S. Dang, S. Dimmick, and G. Kelkar, "Evaluating the Evidence Base for the Use of Home Telehealth Remote Monitoring in Elderly with Heart Failure," *Telemed J E Health* 15, no. 8 (2009).

105   Ibid.

106   V. L. Roger, "The Heart Failure Epidemic," review of http://www.mdpi.com/journal/ijerph, *International Journal of Environmental Research and Public Health* 7, no. 4 (2010).

107   Karen Rowan, "Many Colonoscopies for Seniors Carry Unnecessary Risks," *Scientific American* (2013), http://www.scientificamerican.com/article/many-colonoscopies-for-seniors-carry-unnecessary-risks/.

108   "Screening for Prostate Cancer," U.S. Preventive Services Task Force, http://www.uspreventiveservicestaskforce.org/prostatecancerscreening/prostate-finalrs.htm.

109   G. V. Ramani, P. A. Uber, and M. R. Mehra, "Chronic Heart Failure: Contemporary Diagnosis and Management," *Mayo Clinic proceedings* 85, no. 2 (2010).

110   Helen Adamopoulos, "The Cost and Quality Conundrum of American End-of-Life Care," *The Medicare Newsgroup* (2013), http://www.medicarenewsgroup.com/context/understanding-medicare-blog/understanding-medicare-blog/2013/06/03/the-cost-and-quality-conundrum-of-american-end-of-life-care.

111   Eric J. Topol and Richard J. Ablin, "Psa Test Is Misused, Unreliable, Says the Antigen's Discoverer," *Medscape* (2014), http://www.medscape.com/viewarticle/828854.

112   Ibid.

113   Ibid.

114   Louise L. Liang, *Connected for Health : Transforming Care Delivery at Kaiser Permanente* (San Francisco, CA: Jossey-Bass, 2010).

115   John R. Patrick, *Net Attitude: What It Is, How to Get It, and Why Your Company Can't Survive Without It* (Cambridge MA: Perseus Publishing, 2001).

116 Amar Gupta and Deth Sao, "The Constitutionality of Current Legal Barriers to Telemedicine in the United States: Analysis and Future Directions of Its Relationship to National and International Health Care Reform," review of http://law.case.edu/journals/HealthMatrix/, *Health Matrix: Journal of Law-Medicine* 21, no. 2 (2011).

117 Sandeep Jauhar, "Why Doctors Are Sick of Their Profession," *The Wall Street Journal* (2014), http://online.wsj.com/articles/the-u-s-s-ailing-medical-system-a-doctors-perspective-1409325361.

118 Ibid.

119 Debra Cascardo, "Concierge Medicine: Is It Becoming Mainstream? Part I," *The Journal Of Medical Practice Management: MPM* 29, no. 6 (2014).

120 Ibid.

121 W. B. Weeks and E. B. Wadsworth, "Addressing Healthcare Complexity," *hfm (Healthcare Financial Management)* 67, no. 1 (2013).

122 Sunil Kripalani et al., "Clinical Research in Low-Literacy Populations: Using Teach-Back to Assess Comprehension of Informed Consent and Privacy Information," review of http://www.irbforum.org/, *IRB* 30, no. 2 (2008).

123 Clay Shirky, *Here Comes Everybody : The Power of Organizing without Organizations* (New York: Penguin Press, 2008).

124 "Healthcare.Gov and the Gulf between Planning and Reality," *Clay Shirky* (2013), http://www.shirky.com/weblog/2013/11/healthcare-gov-and-the-gulf-between-planning-and-reality/.

125 "Costs in the Coverage Gap," *Medicare.gov* (2013), http://www.medicare.gov/part-d/costs/coverage-gap/part-d-coverage-gap.html.

126 Reed Abelson and Julie Creswell, "In Second Look, Few Savings from Digital Health Records," *The New York Times* (2013), http://www.nytimes.com/2013/01/11/business/electronic-records-systems-have-not-reduced-health-costs-report-says.html.

127 Kevin Pho, "Electronic Medical Records No Cure-All Yet," (2014), http://www.usatoday.com/story/opinion/2014/01/19/kevin-pho-electronic-medical-records/4649043/.

128 Robert Lowes, "Ehr User Satisfaction Declines in Meaningful-Use Era," *Medscape* (2013), http://www.medscape.com/viewarticle/780336.

129 "The World Factbook," Central Intelligence Agency, http://cia.gov.

130 "World Health Education Initiative," world-prosperity.org, http://www.health-care-reform.net/causedeath.htm.

131 Barbara Starfield, "Is Us Health Really the Best in the World?," *JAMA* 284, no. 4 (2000).

132 Linda T. Kohn, Medicine Institute of, and America Committee on Quality of Health Care in, *To Err Is Human : Building a Safer Health System* (Washington: National Academy Press, 1999).

133 Robert M. Wachter, "The End of the Beginning: Patient Safety Five Years after 'to Err Is Human'," *Health Affairs* 23 (2004).

134 Ibid.

135 Marshall Allen, "How Many Die from Medical Mistakes in U.S. Hospitals?," *Shots Health News From NPR* (2013), http://www.npr.org/blogs/health/2013/09/20/224507654/how-many-die-from-medical-mistakes-in-u-s-hospitals.

136 John T. James, "A New, Evidence-Based Estimate of Patient Harms Associated with Hospital Care," *Journal of Patient Safety* 9, no. 3 (2013).

137 Allen, "How Many Die from Medical Mistakes in U.S. Hospitals?".

138 "FDA's Safe Use Initiative to Address Preventable Harm Due to Medication Misuse, Errors, and Other Related Problems," *Formulary* 45, no. 1 (2010).

139 "Inpatient Surgery," *Centers for Disease Control and Prevention* (2014), http://www.cdc.gov/nchs/fastats/inpatient-surgery.htm.

140 Card R et al., "Health Care Protocol: Perioperative," *Institute for Clinical Systems Improvement. Perioperative Protocol* (2014), https://www.icsi.org/_asset/0c2xkr/Periop.pdf.

141 Susan J. Collins et al., "Effectiveness of the Surgical Safety Checklist in Correcting Errors:Aliterature Review Applying Reason's Swiss Cheese Model," *AORN Journal* 100, no. 1 (2014).

142 "The Medical Device Industry in the United States," *SelectUSA* (2014), http://selectusa.commerce.gov/industry-snapshots/medical-device-industry-united-states.

143 Elizabeth Mattox, "Patient Safety. Medical Devices and Patient Safety," *Critical Care Nurse* 32, no. 4 (2012).

144 Sanket S. Dhruva and Rita F. Redberg, "Medical Device Regulation: Time to Improve Performance," *AORN* 9, no. 7 (2012).

145 Ibid.

146 "Hospital-Acquired Conditions," *CMS.gov* (2014), http://www.cms.gov/Medicare/Medicare-Fee-for-Service-Payment/HospitalAcqCond/Hospital-Acquired_Conditions.html.

147 Grace M Lee et al., "Effect of Nonpayment for Preventable Infections in U.S. Hospitals," *The New England Journal of Medicine* 367, no. 15 (2012).

148 Brenda Goodman, "Hospital-Acquired Infections Cost $10 Billion a Year: Study," *HealthDay* (2013), http://health.usnews.com/health-news/news/articles/2013/09/03/hospital-acquired-infections-cost-10-billion-a-year-study.

149 "Accident Database & Synopses," *NTSB Aviation* (2014), http://www.ntsb.gov/aviationquery/index.aspx.

150 Jeff Munn, "Looking Beyond Health Reform: The Future of Consumer-Focused Health Care," *Benefits Quarterly* 26, no. 1 (2010).

151 John L. Fortenberry, *Health Care Marketing : Tools and Techniques* (Sudbury, Mass.: Jones and Bartlett Publishers, 2010).

152 "Joint Center for Cancer Precision Medicine Established," *Dana-Farber Cancer Institute* (2013), http://www.dana-farber.org/Newsroom/News-Releases/joint-center-for-cancer-precision-medicine-established.aspx.

153 Ibid.

154 G. N. Samuel, C. F. C. Jordens, and I. Kerridge, "Direct-to-Consumer Personal Genome Testing: Ethical and Regulatory Issues That Arise from Wanting to ‚Äòknow‚Äô Your DNA," *Internal Medicine Journal* 40, no. 3 (2010).

155 N.J. Giffin et al., "Premonitory Symptoms in Migraine," *Neurology* 6, no. 60 (2003).

156 Susannah Fox and Maeve Duggan, "Tracking for Health," *Pew Research Internet Project* (2013), http://www.pewinternet.org/2013/01/28/tracking-for-health/#fn-87-1.

157 "Exercise: 7 Benefits of Regular Physical Activity," *Mayo Clinic Healthy Lifestyle Fitness* (2014), http://www.mayoclinic.org/healthy-living/fitness/in-depth/exercise/art-20048389.

158 "Mobile Medical Applications," *U.S. Food and Drug Aministration* (2014), http://www.fda.gov/MedicalDevices/ProductsandMedicalProcedures/ConnectedHealth/MobileMedicalApplications/ucm255978.htm.

159 Brian Dolan, "23 Notable Fda Clearances for Digital Health Apps, Devices So Far This Year," *mobihealthnews* (2014), http://mobihealthnews.com/36795/23-notable-fda-clearances-for-digital-health-apps-devices-so-far-this-year/#more-36795.

160 Alivecor, "Ecg Screening Made Easy," AliveCor, http://www.alivecor.com/en.

161 Eric J. Topol, *The Creative Destruction of Medicine : How the Digital Revolution Will Create Better Health Care* (New York, NY: Basic Books, 2012).

162 G. Steven Burrill, "Digital Health Investment Opportunities Abound, but Standouts Deliver Disruptive Change," *Journal of Commercial Biotechnology* 18, no. 1 (2012).

163 "Cellscope Oto," *Atlantic Pediatric Device Consortium* (2014), http://pediatricdevicesatlanta.org/cellscope-oto-formerly-known-remotoscope.

164 "A Smartphone-Enabled Diagnostic Toolkit to Get Better Answers, Faster.," *cellscope.com* (2014), https://www.cellscope.com.

165 "Smartphone App Uses Camera Accessory to Check Cholesterol Level," *Cornell University - CornellCast* (2013), http://www.cornell.edu/video/smartphone-app-uses-camera-to-check-cholesterol-level.

166 Noelle Knell, "Spare the Air," review of http://www.govtech.com, *Government Technology* 26, no. 1 (2013).

167 "Cue," *cue.me* (2014), https://cue.me/product.

168 Nazem Bassil, Saad Alkaade, and John E Morley, "The Benefits and Risks of Testosterone Replacement Therapy: A Review," *Therapeutics and Clinical Risk Management* 5 (2009).

169 Brian Dolan, "Alere Connect's Newly Fda-Cleared Homelink Hub Has Fitlinxx, Too," (2014), http://mobihealthnews.com/28873/alere-connects-newly-fda-cleared-homelink-hub-has-fitlinxx-too/.

170 "Finally a Smart Blood Pressure Monitor That Fits Your Daily Life," *QardioArm* (2014), https://www.getqardio.com.

171 "Finding Your Personalized Sound Match," *Otoharmonics* (2014), http://oto-harmonics.com/public/levo.

172 "Blood Glucose Meter: How to Choose," *Mayo Clinic Diseases and Conditions - Diabetes* (2012), http://www.mayoclinic.org/diseases-conditions/diabetes/in-depth/blood-glucose-meter/art-20046335.

173 "Eko: Stethoscope Intelligence," *Eko Devices* (2014), http://ekodevices.com.

174 Ibid.

175 Erika Check Hayden, "Technology: The $1,000 Genome," *nature.com* (2014), http://www.nature.com/news/technology-the-1-000-genome-1.14901.

176 Rick Merritt, "DNA Chip Will Plug into Handsets," *EE Times* (2014), http://www.eetimes.com/.

177 Ibid.

178 Ibid.

179 Ibid.

180 Tracey Walker, "Medication Safety and Reliability. Fda Adverse Drug Events App for Public Health Crises Could Expand to More General Adverse Event Reporting," review of formularyjournal.com, *Formulary* 47, no. 2 (2012).

181 "Skin Cancer Self-Exam Mobile App," *M Health System - University of Michigan* (2014), http://www.uofmhealth.org/patient%20and%20visitor%20 guide/my-skin-check-app.

182 "About Isabel," *isabelhealthcare.com* (2014), http://www.isabelhealthcare. com/home/ourmission.

183 Ibid.

184 Mark L. Graber and Ashlei Mathew, "Performance of a Web-Based Clinical Diagnosis Support System for Internists," *JGIM: Journal of General Internal Medicine* 23, no. S1 (2008).

185 Ibid.

186 Alexander Gaffney, "How Many Drugs Has Fda Approved in Its Entire History? New Paper Explains," *Regulatory Affairs Professionals Society* (2014), http:// www.raps.org/Regulatory-Focus/News/2014/10/03/20488/How-Many-Drugs-has-FDA-Approved-in-its-Entire-History-New-Paper-Explains/.

187 "A Better Online Diagnosis before the Doctor Visit," *The Wall Street Journal* (2013), http://online.wsj.com/news/articles/SB10001424127887324328904578621743278445114.

188 "1965 - "Moore's Law" Predicts the Future of Integrated Circuits," *Computer History Museum* (2014), http://www.computerhistory.org/semiconductor/timeline/1965-Moore.html.

189 Hayden, "Technology: The $1,000 Genome".

190 Antonio Regalado, "For One Baby, Life Begins with Genome Revealed," *MIT Technology Review* (2014), http://www.technologyreview.com/news/527936/for-one-baby-life-begins-with-genome-revealed/.

191 Ibid.

192 Robert Pear, "U.S. To Collect Genetic Data to Hone Care," (2015), http://www.nytimes.com/2015/01/31/us/obama-to-unveil-research-initiative-aiming-to-develop-tailored-medical-treatments.html?_r=0.

193 Ibid.

194 P. J. Parmar, "Who Still Uses Faxes? The Medical Industry Does," *KevinMD.com* (2014), http://www.kevinmd.com/blog/2014/10/still-uses-faxes-medical-industry.html.

195 Ibid.

196 "Applying Clinical Experience and Advanced Analytics to Help Optimize Quality of Care, Population Health and Wellness.," *ActiveHealth Management* (2014), http://www.activehealth.com.

197 Ibid.

198 Mark Hagland, "The State of Hie: One Health System Clo's View... The University of Pennsylvania Health System's Cio, Michael Restuccia, Shares His Perspectives on Hie Evolution," *Healthcare Informatics* 30, no. 7 (2013).

199 Mark H. Siska, "E-Prescribing: One Giant Leap toward Pharmacy Practice Integration," *American Journal of Health-System Pharmacy* (2011).

200 Ibid.

201 "The Nation's Most Comprehensive Health Information Network," *surescripts* (2014), http://surescripts.com/about-us.

202 "Reducing and Preventing Adverse Drug Events to Decrease Hospital Costs," *Agency for Healthcare Research and Quality* (2014), http://www.ahrq.gov/research/findings/factsheets/errors-safety/aderia/index.html.

203 Newt Gingrich, *Health Care - the Cure for What Ails Us* (Framingham, Mass.: CIO Publishing, 2003).

204 "Process Improvement in the Military Health System and Va Hospitals," (2013), http://www.novaces.com/hc_military.php.

205 Ibid.

206 Deth Sao, Amar Gupta, and David A. Gantz, "Interoperable Electronic Health Care Record: A Case for Adoption of a National Standard to Stem the Ongoing Health Care Crisis," *Journal of Legal Medicine* 34, no. 1 (2013).

207 Kenneth J Terry and Marrecca Fiore, "Docs Willing to Share Medical Practice with Patients? Sort Of," *Medscape Multispecialty* (2014), http://www.medscape.com/features/slideshow/public/digital-medicine-report#19.

208 "HHS Strengthens Patients' Right to Access Lab Test Reports," *U.S. Department of Health & Human Services* (2014), http://www.hhs.gov/news/press/2014pres/02/20140203a.html.

209 Ibid.

210 Ibid.

211 Sumanth G. Reddy, Valerie K. York, and Laura A. Brannon, "Travel for Treatment: Students' Perspective on Medical Tourism," review of http://onlinelibrary.wiley.com/journal/10.1002/%28ISSN%291522-1970, *International Journal of Tourism Research* 12, no. 5 (2010).

212 "Medical Tourism - Getting Medical Care in Another Country," *Centers for Disease Control and Prevention* (2014), http://www.cdc.gov/Features/MedicalTourism/.

213 "Databases, Tables & Calculators by Subject," *Bureau of Labor Statistics* (2013), http://www.bls.gov/data/#employment.

214 "High Regard for Leading Health Care Professions, Especially for Physicians," *harris: A Nielsen Company* (2014).

215 "Advanced Practice Nursing: A New Age in Health Care," *American Nurses Association Backgrounder* (2011), http://www.nursingworld.org/functional-menucategories/mediaresources/mediabackgrounders/aprn-a-new-age-in-health-care.pdf.

216 Mary D Naylor and Ellen T. Kurtzman, "The Role of Nurse Practitioners in Reinventing Primary Care," *HealthAffairs* (2010), http://content.healthaffairs.org/content/29/5/893.abstract.

217 Ibid.

218 Andrew Weber, "Senior Care Industry Analysis 2015 - Cost & Trends," *Franchise Help* (2014), https://www.franchisehelp.com/industry-reports/senior-care-industry-report/.

219 "Aging in Place," *AARP Public Policy Institute* (2014), http://assets.aarp.org/rgcenter/ppi/liv-com/ib190.pdf.

220 Owner of Home Helpers & Direct Link Fernand Sarrat, Personal communication, January 26, 2015.

221 Aaron Smithj, "Older Adults and Technology Use," (2014), http://www.pewinternet.org/2014/04/03/older-adults-and-technology-use/.

222 "Accountable," *Merriam Webster Online* (2014), http:// www.merriam-web-ster.com/dictionary/citation.

223 Kip Sullivan, "The History and Definition of the "Accountable Care Organization," *Physicians for a National Health Program* (2010), http://pnhp-california.org/2010/10/the-history-and-definition-of-the-"accountable-care-organization"/.

224 Trent Haywood and Keith Kosel, "The ACO Model -- a Three-Year Financial Loss?," *The New England Journal Of Medicine* 364, no. 14 (2011).

225 J. M. Harris, D. M. Grauman, and R. Hemnani, "Solving the ACO Conundrum," review of http://www.hfma.org/hfm/, *hfm (Healthcare Financial Management)* 64, no. 11 (2010).

226 Vanessa Azzone et al., "Workplace Stress, Organizational Factors and Eap Utilization," *Journal of Workplace Behavioral Health* 24, no. 3 (2009).

227 "Supporting Better Primary Care".

228 Co-founder and CEO of RubiconMD Gil Addo, Personal communication, September 2 2014.

229 David Brown, "'Comparative Effectiveness Research' Tackles Medicine's Unanswered Questions," *The Washington Post Health & Science* (2011), http://www.washingtonpost.com/national/health-science/comparative-ef-fectiveness-research-tackles-medicines-unanswered-questions/2011/08/01/gIQA7RJSHJ_story.html.

230 Ibid.

231 Marianne Kolbasuk McGee, "11 Bi Tools to Analyze Healthcare Operations," *InformationWeek Healthcare* (2012), http://www.informationweek.com/administration-systems/11-bi-tools-to-analyze-healthcare-operations/d/d-id/1104532?

232 Topol, *The Creative Destruction of Medicine : How the Digital Revolution Will Create Better Health Care.*

233 John Byrnes, "The Drive for Value: Key Roles for the Ceo," *Healthcare Financial Management: Journal Of The Healthcare Financial Management Association* 68, no. 6 (2014).

234 Atul Gawande, "The Checklist Manifesto : How to Get Things Right," (2010).

235 "State Health Information Exchange," *US Dept of Health and Human Services, HITECH Programs and Advisory Committees* (2012), http://www.healthit.gov/policy-researchers-implementers/state-health- information-exchange.

236 K. Costas, R Knorr, and S. K. Condon, "A Case-Control Study of Childhood Leukemia in Woburn, Massachusetts: The Relationship between Leukemia Incidence and Exposure to Public Drinking Water," *The Science of the Total Environment* 300, no. 1 (2002).

237 Paul A. Nutting et al., "Journey to the Patient-Centered Medical Home: A Qualitative Analysis of the Experiences of Practices in the National Demonstration Project," review of http://www.annfammed.org/, *Annals of Family Medicine* 8, no. S1 (2010).

238 Basel Kayyali, David Knott, and Steve Van Kuiken, "The Big-Data Revolution in Us Health Care: Accelerating Value and Innovation," *McKinsey & Company Insights & Publications* (2013), http://www.mckinsey.com/insights/health_systems_and_services/the_big-data_revolution_in_us_health_care.

239 David Nash, *Population Health: The Secret Sauce* (YouTube, 2014).

240 Atul Gawande, *Being Mortal : Medicine and What Matters in the End* (2014).

241 John Wasik, "Understanding Medicare: Tackling End-of-Life Costs," *USC Annenberg Reporting on Health* (2012), http://www.reportingonhealth.org/2012/10/05/understanding-medicare-tackling-end-life-costs.

242 Susan Pasternak, "End-of-Life Care Constitutes Third Rail of U.S. Health Care Policy Debate," *The Medicare Newsgroup* (2013), http://www.medicarenewsgroup.com/context/understanding-medicare-blog/understanding-medicare-blog/2013/06/03/end-of-life-care-constitutes-third-rail-of-u.s.-health-care-policy-debate.

243 M.D. Dempsey Springfield, Personal communication, January 26 2015.

244 Elizabeth Puffenbarger, "When to Refer Patients for Hospice Care," *American Nurse Today* 9, no. 9 (2014).

245 "Research Shows Patients May Live Longer with Hospice and Palliative Care," *National Hospice and Palliative Care Organization* (2010), http://www.nhpco.org/press-room/research-shows-patients-may-live-longer-hospice-and-palliative-care.

246 "Center for Comfort Care & Healing," *Regional Hospice and Home Care* (2015), http://regionalhospicect.org.

247 Bertha Coombs, "Apple's Ipad Tops with Doctors," *TheStreet* (2011), http://www.thestreet.com/story/11057201/1/apples-ipad-tops-with-doctors.html?cm_ven=RSSFeed&utm_source=feedburner&utm_medium=feed&utm_campaign=Feed%3A+tsc%2Ffeeds%2Frss%2Flatest-stories+%28TheStreet.com+Latest+Headlines%29.

248 Ibid.

249 "Healthcare Data Spotlight," *ITG Market Research* (2014), http://www.itg.com/itg-market-research/.

250 Michael Grothaus, "Daily Mac App: Muscle System Pro II," *Tuaw: The Unofficial Apple Weblog* (2011), http://www.tuaw.com/2011/11/08/daily-mac-app-muscle-system-pro-ii/.

251 David Lee Scher and Neil Chesanow, "15 Game-Changing Wireless Devices to Improve Patient Care," *Medscape Multispecialty* (2014), http://www. medscape.com/features/slideshow/wireless-devices?src=wnl_edit_ specol&uac=165842DT#1.

252 John Halamka, "The Perfect Storm for Electronic Health Records," (2006), http://www.himss.org/files/HIMSSorg/content/files/08_column_ehr.pdf.

253 "Telehealth," *Health Resources and Services Administration Rural Health* (2012), http://www.hrsa.gov/ruralhealth/about/telehealth/.

254 Centers, "Telemedicine," Centers for Medicare & Medicaid Services, http:// cms.hhs.gov/Telehealth/.

255 Biljana Maric et al., "A Systematic Review of Telemonitoring Technologies in Heart Failure," *European Journal of Heart Failure* 11, no. 5 (2009).

256 John R. Patrick, "Cardiac Telemonitoring for the Reduction of Hospital Readmissions for Congestive Heart Failure Patients" (University of Phoenix, 2013).

257 B. Singh, Stuart D. Russell, and Alan Cheng, "Update on Device Technologies for Monitoring Heart Failure," *Current Treatment Options in Cardiovascular Medicine* 14, no. 5 (2012).

258 Sarwat I. Chaudhry et al., "Telemonitoring in Patients with Heart Failure," review of http://www.nejm.org/, *The New England Journal Of Medicine* 363, no. 24 (2010).

259 Ayla Ellison, "82% of Young Adults Would Prefer Telehealth to in-Person Visit," *Becker's Health IT & CIO Review* (2014), http://www.beckershospital-review.com/healthcare-information-technology/82-of-young-adults-would-prefer-telehealth-to-in-person-visit.html.

260 Amit Chowdhry, "Google Is Testing a 'Talk with a Doctor' Feature within Medical Search Results," *Forbes* (2014), http://www.forbes.com/sites/amitchowdhry/2014/10/15/google-is-testing-a-talk-with-a-doctor-feature-within-medical-search-results/.

261 Dan Verel, "Get Treated by Mayo Clinic without Ever Visiting (the Future of Healthcare?)," *Medcity News* (2014), http://medcitynews.com/2014/10/mayo-clinic-telehealth-kiosks/.

262 Ibid.

263 "Chairman Proposal to Spur Innovation in Medical Body Area Networks," Federal Communications Commision, http://www.fcc.gov/document/chairman-proposal-spur-innovation-medical-body-area-networks.

264 IBM, "Bringing Big Data to the Enterprise," IBM Corporation, http://www-01.ibm.com/software/data/bigdata/.

265 Mary Shacklett, "IBM Watson's Impressive Healthcare Analytics Capabilities Continue to Evolve," *TechRepublic* (2014), http://www.techrepublic.com/article/ibm-watsons-impressive-healthcare-analytics-capabilities-continue-to-evolve/.

266 Bertalan Meskó, "IBM Watson Is the Stethoscope of the 21st Century," *LinedIn* (2014), https://www.linkedin.com/pulse/article/20141128122034-12233085-ibm-watson-is-the-stethoscope-of-the-21st-century.

267 Ibid.

268 Ibid.

269 James Anderson, "Colorimetrix App Puts Medical Diagnostics on Your Smartphone," *Techfragments* (2015), http://www.techfragments.com/2412/colorimetrix-app-medical-diagnostic-smartphones/.

270 Eric J. Topol and Craig Venter, "Venter and Topol on the True Revolution in Medicine," review of http://www.medscape.com/viewarticle/780324, *Medscape Today* 2013.

271 Jane Seward, "Suspect Measles and Act Fast," *Centers for Disease Control and Prevention* (2014), http://www.medscape.com/partners/cdc/public/cdc-commentary.

272 Ibid.

273 Ibid.

274 "2015 Measles Cases in the U.S.," ibid. (2015), http://www.cdc.gov/measles/cases-outbreaks.html.

275 Nancy Shute, "Fifteen Years after a Vaccine Scare, a Measles Epidemic," *Shots Health NewsFromNPR* (2013), http://www.npr.org/blogs/health/2013/05/21/185801259/fifteen-years-after-a-vaccine-scare-a-measles-epidemic.

276 Amy Dockser Marcus, "Researchers Show Gains in Finding Reusable Drugs," *Wall Street Journal* (2011), http://online.wsj.com/articles/SB10001424053111903639404576514542144726276.

277 "Researchers Show Gains in Finding Reusable Drugs," (2011), http://online.wsj.com/news/articles/SB10001424053111903639404576514542144726276?mg=reno64-wsj.

278 Scott Peterson, "Your Microbiome and You: What Clinicians Need to Know," *Medscape Multispecialty* (2013), http://www.medscape.com/features/slideshow/microbiome.

279 Sweeney TE and Morton JM, "The Human Gut Microbiome: A Review of the Effect of Obesity and Surgically Induced Weight Loss," *JAMA Surgery* 148, no. 6 (2013).

280 Erica Ollmann Saphire, "Help Researchers Find an Ebola Cure," *World Community Grid* (2014), http://www.worldcommunitygrid.org/about_us/viewNewsArticle.do?articleId=401.

281 Ibid.

282 "A Short History of Robots," *Rover Ranch* (2003), http://prime.jsc.nasa.gov/ROV/history.html.

283 Aaron Smith and Janna Anderson, "Ai, Robotics, and the Future of Jobs," *PewResearch Internet Project* (2014), http://www.pewinternet.org/2014/08/06/future-of-jobs/.

284 MaryJo Webster, "Could a a Robot Do You Job?," (2014), http://www.usatoday.com/story/news/nation/2014/10/28/low-skill-workers-face-mechanization-challenge/16392981/.

285 Melinda Beck, "Robotic Surgery Brings Higher Costs, More Complications, Study Shows," *The Wall Street Journal* (2014), http://online.wsj.com/articles/robotic-surgery-brings-higher-costs-more-complications-study-shows-1412715786.

286 "The Concentration of Health Care Spending," *National Institute for Health Care Management* (2012), http://www.nihcm.org/pdf/DataBrief3%20Final.pdf.

287 Adam Waytz and Michael Norton, "How to Make Robots Seem Less Creepy," *The Wall Street Journal* (2014), http://www.wsj.com/articles/how-to-make-robots-seem-less-creepy-1401473812.

288 Ibid.

289 John R. Patrick to patrickWeb2014, http://patrickweb.com/2014/04/05/inside-3d-printing/.

290 "Medical Automation Newsletter," *Medical Automation: Health care for the future* (2014), http://www.medicalautomation.org.

291 Jennifer Hicks, "Peking University Implants First 3d Printed Vertebra," *Forbes* (2014), http://www.forbes.com/sites/jenniferhicks/2014/08/19/peking-university-implants-first-3d-printed-vertebra/.

292 "Facts About Upper and Lower Limb Reduction Defects," *Centers for Disease Control and Prevention* (2014), http://www.cdc.gov/ncbddd/birthdefects/UL-LimbReductionDefects.html.

293 Meredith Cohn, "Kids Outfitted with New Hands Made on 3-D Printers," *The Baltimore Sun* (2014), http://articles.baltimoresun.com/2014-09-28/health/bs-hs-printing-prosthetic-hands-20140923_1_prosthetics-printers-hand.

294 "E-Nabling the Future," *enablingthefuture.org* (2014).

295 Parth Shah, "Helping Hand — in 3d," *The University of North Carolina at Chapel Hill* (2014), http://www.unc.edu/spotlight/helping-hand-in-3d/.

296 Susan Young Rojahn, "Artificial Organs May Finally Get a Blood Supply," *MIT Technology Review* (2014), http://www.technologyreview.com/news/525161/artificial-organs-may-finally-get-a-blood-supply/.

297 Brian Krassenstein, "3-D Printed Model of a 2-Week-Old Baby's Heart May Have Saved Its Life," *3D Printer & 3D Printing News* (2014), http://3dprint.com/17443/3d-printed-heart-baby/.

298 "2020: A New Vision - a Future for Regenerative Medicine," *U.S. Department of Health & Human Services* (2014), http://singularity-2045.org/HHS-regenerative-medicine-2020-vision-archive-2014.html.

299 John R. Patrick, "Regenerative Medicine," *patrickWeb* (2014), http://patrick-web.com/2014/04/11/regenerative-medicine/.

300 "2020: A New Vision - a Future for Regenerative Medicine".

301 "Engineers Make Strides toward Artificial Cartilage," *ScienceDaily* (2013), http://www.sciencedaily.com/releases/2013/12/131213135518.htm.

302 Blaine Brownell, "Duke Researchers Develop Synthetic Cartilage," *Architect* (2014), http://www.architectmagazine.com/research/duke-researchers-de-velop-synthetic-cartilage_o.aspx.

303 "Engineers Make Strides toward Artificial Cartilage".

304 "Monash Vision Direct to Brain Bionic Eye," *Monash University* (2014), http://www.monash.edu.au/bioniceye/.

305 "Nanosponges Soak up Toxins Released by Bacterial Infections and Venom," *UC San Diego Jacobs School of Engineering* (2013), http://www.jacobsschool.ucsd.edu/news/news_releases/release.sfe?id=1350.

306 "Predicting the Spread of Emerging Infectious Diseases," *IBM Research* (2012), http://ibmresearchnews.blogspot.com/2012/02/predicting-spread-of-emerging.html.

307 Matt Ridley, *Genome : The Autobiography of a Species in 23 Chapters* (New York: HarperCollins, 1999).

308 Elizabeth Weise, "Woodland Strawberry Genome Sequenced," *USA Today ScienceFair* (2010), http://content.usatoday.com/communities/sciencefair/post/2010/12/woodland-strawberry-genome-sequenced/1#.VIsmnMYyfuc.

309 Laird Harrison, "Genomic Entrepreneurs Promise to Personalize Medicine," *Medscape Multispecialty* (2014), http://www.medscape.com/viewarticle/832435?src=wnl_edit_specol&uac=165842DT.

310 Z. Wang, "New Imaging Technology: Phase Contrast X-Ray," *ScienceDaily* (2014), http://www.sciencedaily.com/releases/2014/05/140515103834.htm.

311 "U.S. Life Expectancy," *National Institutes of Health* (2012), http://www.nih.gov/about/impact/life_expectancy_graph.htm.

312 Stacy Simon, "Facts and Figures Report: Declines in Cancer Deaths Reach Milestone," *American Cancer Society* (2014), http://www.cancer.org/cancer/news/facts-and-figures-report-declines-in-cancer-deaths-reach-milestone.

313 "NIH Funding Mechanism "Totally Broken," Says Stanford Researcher," *SCOPE - Stanford Medicine* (2012), http://scopeblog.stanford.edu/2012/12/05/nih-funding-mechanism-totally-broken-says-stanford-researcher/#sthash.OU7MZUbA.dpuf.

314 "NIH Common Fund Announces 2014 High-Risk, High-Reward Research Awardees," *National Institutes of Health* (2014), http://www.nih.gov/news/health/oct2014/od-06.htm.

315 Louis Goodman and Tim Norbeck, "Survey of 20,000 Physicians Reports Morale Still Low, but Slightly Improving," *Forbes* (2014), http://www.forbes.com/sites/physiciansfoundation/2014/10/03/survey-of-20000-physicians-reports-morale-still-low-but-slightly-improving/.

316 Sarah Mann, "Record Number of Students Apply, Enroll in Medical School in 2013," *Association of American Medical Colleges* (2013), https://www.aamc.org/newsroom/reporter/november2013/362058/enrollment.html.

317 Chair of Medical Education Dr. Ramin Ahmadi, Research, and Global Health for Western Connecticut Health Network, Personal communication, January 22 2015.

318 Shute, "Imagining a Future When the Doctor's Office Is in Your Home".

319 "2013 Health Care Cost and Utilization Report," *Health Care Cost Institute* (2014), http://www.healthcostinstitute.org.

320 "Spending Per Privately Insured Grew 3.9% in 2013, as Falling Utilization Offset Rising Prices," *Health Care Cost Institute* (2014), http://www.health-costinstitute.org/news-and-events/new-report-spending-privately-insured-grew-39-2013-falling-utilization-offset-rising.

321 Robert S. Kaplan and Michael E. Porter, "The Big Idea: How to Solve the Cost Crisis in Health Care," *Harvard Business Review* (2011), https://hbr.org/2011/09/how-to-solve-the-cost-crisis-in-health-care.

322 Ibid.

323 D. U. Himmelstein, M. Jun, and R. Busse, "A Comparison of Hospital Administrative Costs in Eight Nations: U.S. Costs Exceed All Others by Far," *Health Affairs* 33, no. 9 (2014).

324 "Occupational Employment and Wages: 43-3021 Billing and Posting Clerks," *U.S. Department of Labor Bureau of Labor Statistics* (2012), http:// www.bls.gov/oes/current/oes433021.htm.

325 Elizabeth Wikler, Peter Basch, and David Cutler, "Paper Cuts: Reducing Health Care Administrative Costs," *The Center for American Progress* (2012), http://cdn.americanprogress.org/wp-content/uploads/issues/2012/06/pdf/paper-cuts_final.pdf.

326 Ibid.

327 Ibid.

328 Ibid.

329 Nick Tate, "Obamacare Regs Have Doctors Drowning in Paperwork: Harvard," *Newsmax Health* (2014), http://www.newsmaxhealth.com/Health-News/obamacare-paperwork-doctors-medical/2014/10/23/id/602747/.

330 Wikler, Basch, and Cutler, "Paper Cuts: Reducing Health Care Administrative Costs".

331 Ibid.

332 Ibid.

333 Ralph Losey, "Plato's Cave: Why Most Lawyers Love Paper and Hate E-Discovery and What This Means to the Future of Legal Education," *e-Discovery Team* (2014), http://e-discoveryteam.com/school/plato's-cave-why-most-lawyers-love-paper-and-hate-e-discovery-and-what-this-means-to-the-future-of-legal-education/.

334 Bruce Japsen, "Less Than Two Percent of Hospitals Are Paperless as Medicare Penalties Loom," *Forbes* (2013), http://www.forbes.com/sites/bruce-japsen/2013/01/16/less-than-two-percent-of-hospitals-are-paperless-as-medicare-penalties-loom/.

335 Richard MacManus, "Health 2.0 Challenge #1: Getting Doctors Off Fax Machines," *readwrite* (2012), http://readwrite.com/2012/10/10/health-20-challenges-getting-doctors-off-fax-machines-onto-ipads.

336 Ibid.

337 Executive Director Doug Hayes, Blueprint Health, Personal communication, December 22.

338 "Blueprint Health Showcases Its Fifth Class of 7 Startups at Demo Day in Nyc," *HIT Consultant: Insightful coverage of healthcare technology* (2014), http://hitconsultant.net/2014/04/03/blueprint-health-showcases-its-fifth-class-of-7-startups-at-demo-day-in-nyc/.

339 "Health Insurance Marketplace 2015 Open Enrollment Period: January Enrollment Report," *U.S. Department of Health & Human Services* (2014), http://aspe.hhs.gov/health/reports/2015/MarketPlaceEnrollment/Jan2015/ib_2015jan_enrollment.pdf.

340 Cal Woodward, "Millions Flock to New Us Health Insurance Markets," *Canadian Medical Association. Journal* 186, no. 8 (2014).

341 Louise Radnofsky, "Tally of Uninsured Fell by 3.8 Million in Early 2014," *The Wall Street Journal* (2014), http://online.wsj.com/articles/tally-of-uninsured-fell-by-3-8-million-in-early-2014-1410840199#printMode.

342 Robin A. Cohen and Michael E. Martinez, "Health Insurance Coverage: Early Release of Estimates from the National Health Interview Survey, January–March 2014," *National Health Interview Survey* (2014), http://www.cdc.gov/nchs/data/nhis/earlyrelease/insur201409.pdf.

343 T. R. Reid, *The Healing of America : A Global Quest for Better, Cheaper, and Fairer Health Care* (New York: Penguin Press, 2009).

344 Morgan A. Muir, Stephanie A. Alessi, and Jaime S. King, "Clarifying Costs: Can Increased Price Transparency Reduce Healthcare Spending?," *UC Hastings College of the Law Legal Studies Research Paper Series* (2013).

345 Ibid.

346 Judy Mottl, "Mobile Apps Help Consumers Make Informed Healthcare, Provider Decisions," *InformationWeek Healthcare* (2014), http://www.informationweek.com/healthcare/mobile-and-wireless/mobile-healthcare-tools-empower-consumers/a/d-id/1316018?_mc=RSS_IWK_EDT.

347 Jose Pagliery, "Starbucks Ceo: We Won't Cut Benefits Because of Obamacare," *CNN Money* (2013).

348 Ibid.

349 "Reforming the Ed: A New Vision for Emergency Medicine," *Physician Executive* 36, no. 6 (2010).

350 "Care without Coverage: Too Little, Too Late," *Institute of Medicine* (2002), http://www.iom.edu/Reports/2002/Care-Without-Coverage-Too-Little-Too-Late.aspx.

351 "Dying from Lack of Insurance," FactCheck.org, http://www.factcheck.org/2009/09/dying-from-lack-of-insurance/.

352 "Care without Coverage: Too Little, Too Late".

353 David Dranove and Michael L. Millenson, "Medical Bankruptcy: Myth Versus Fact," (2006), http://content.healthaffairs.org/content/25/2/w74.full.

354 David Himmelstein, "Marketwatch: Illness and Injury as Contributors to Bankruptcy," *Health Affairs* (2005).

355 Joseph R. Betancourt, Sarah Beiter, and Alden Landry, "Improving Quality, Achieving Equity, and Increasing Diversity in Healthcare: The Future Is Now," *Journal of Best Practices in Health Professions Diversity: Education, Research & Policy* 6, no. 1 (2013).

356 Ibid.

357 Thomas J Papadimos, "Healthcare Access as a Right, Not a Privilege: A Construct of Western Thought," *Philosophy, Ethics, and Humanities in Medicine* 2, no. 2 (2007).

358 Ibid.

359 Ibid.

360 "Jimmy Carter on Health Care," *OnTheIssues: Every Political Leader on Every Issue* (2014), http://www.ontheissues.org/Celeb/Jimmy_Carter_Health_Care.htm.

361 Ibid.

362 "Bill Clinton on Health Care," *OnTheIssues: Every Political Leader on Every Issue* (2014), http://www.ontheissues.org/Celeb/Bill_Clinton_Health_Care.htm.

363 "George W. Bush on Health Care," *OnTheIssues: Every Political Leader on Every Issue* (2014), http://www.ontheissues.org/Celeb/George_W__Bush_Health_Care.htm.

364 Suevon Lee, "Everything You've Ever Wanted to Know About Voter Id Laws," (2012), http://www.propublica.org/article/everything-youve-ever-wanted-to-know-about-voter-id-laws.

365 "Nhe Fact Sheet," *Centers for Medicare & Medicaid Services* (2014), http://www.cms.gov/Research-Statistics-Data-and-Systems/Statistics-Trends-and-Reports/NationalHealthExpendData/NHE-Fact-Sheet.html.

366 Ibid.

367 "Jimmy Carter on Health Care".

368 R. Preston McAfee and John McMillan, "Organizational Diseconomies of Scale," *Journal of Economics & Management Strategy* 4, no. 3 (2005).

369 John E. McDonough, "ACA Implementation: How's It Going?," review of http://www.medscape.com/viewarticle/811334, *Medscape Family Medicine* 2013.

370 Victor R. Fuchs, "Health Reform: Getting the Essentials Right," *Health Affairs* 28, no. 2 (2009).

371 "What Would Happen If Health Care in Your State Improved?," *The Commonwealth Fund* (2014), http://www.commonwealthfund.org/interactives-and-data/estimated-impact-interactive#?ind=a_Adults_ages_1964_insured_2014&loc=AL.

372 Ibid.

373 Patrick, *Net Attitude: What It Is, How to Get It, and Why Your Company Can't Survive Without It.*

374 Ibid.

375 Shirky, "Healthcare.Gov and the Gulf between Planning and Reality".

376 "Skunk Works Origin Story," *Lockheed Martin* (2014), http://www.lockheed-martin.com/us/aeronautics/skunkworks/origin.html.

377 Ibid.

Made in the USA
Lexington, KY
22 July 2018